A DISH OF ORTS

Chiefly Papers on the Imagination, and on Shakespeare

Annotated Edition

George MacDonald

Edited by C.M. Alvarez

CRANBERRY
CLASSICS

Cranberry Classics
Houston, TX

An imprint of Efusion Media Group
www.efusionmg.com

LIBRARY OF CONGRESS CATALOGING IN PUBLICATION DATA
MacDonald, George, 1824-1905.
Print edition: 978-1-953279-00-2
Ebook: 978-1-953279-01-9
Hardback: 978-1-953279-02-6
Audiobook: 978-1-953279-03-3
A Dish of Orts Annotated Edition: Chiefly Papers on the Imagination, and on Shakespeare /
George MacDonald : annotated, with an introduction by C.M. Alvarez (Cranberry Classics)
1. Philosophy--Nonfiction 2. Literary criticism--Nonfiction 3. Theology--Nonfiction 4.
Religious studies--Nonfiction 5. England--Social life and customs--19th century--Nonfiction
I. Alvarez, C.M. 1969-.

TABLE OF CONTENTS

EDITOR'S NOTE

It was a library in a small Baptist church where I first encountered George MacDonald. The illustrated cover of a princess and a forest caught my attention, but it was the quote on the cover, "I have never concealed the fact that I regard him as my master" by C.S. Lewis that made the book my next library selection.

MacDonald inhabited quite a bit of my reading time in my preteen and teenage years. After I read through the fairy tales available to me (in the days before eBooks and online libraries), I moved on to his adult fiction which was republished in abridgements by Michael Phillips. A pastor with a theology that was often unpalatable to the staunchly Calvinistic congregations of his day, MacDonald put food on the table for his eleven children by what we would call today "writing to market." The adult novels, set in his native Scotland, were often written in the gothic genre that was so popular in the Victorian age. But however much he catered to cultural tastes, the novels never failed to deliver profound moral truths.

It was not until I rediscovered Lewis and MacDonald decades later as an adult that I realized how much of an impact MacDonald had on shaping my ideas about morality, true virtue, our relation to God, and the belief that the internal should match the external. As a teen, I was just reading a story, but the truth packed within the stories have stayed with me throughout my life.

A Dish of Orts is not a story, but it illuminates the thoughts of the mind behind the stories. "A dish of orts" refers to a collection of odds and ends, not related at all except that each piece in the random collection of items holds meaning for the keeper. In this collection of essays, MacDonald shares his thoughts on imagination and the importance of fairy tales. In essays like "On Polish," we see the thoughts on virtue and the trueness of character that are illustrated by Princess Irene's fire in *The Princess and the Goblin*. We see in his repeated references to the birds of the air and the lilies of the field in Matthew 6 how often he must have reflected on that passage.

This is a book for both writers and readers; however, one of the challenges to reading *A Dish of Orts* is its unfamiliarity. Sentences are longer requiring the reader to hold a thought longer than we are used to in our truncated digital world with a steady diet of TikTok and memes. Also, MacDonald makes references throughout his essays with which most modern readers, even those who are fairly well-read, are not familiar.

The goal of this annotated edition is to help bridge that gap of unfamiliarity. Any reference to a source not clearly cited and easily identifiable within the text, I have provided a footnote with identification. References to Bible passages are cited. If MacDonald refers to a historical event, an explanation is provided. There are several places throughout the book where there is either more than one source he could be referring to or I simply could not determine the reference, I have made a note of those passages as well.

Some of the essays in *A Dish of Orts* were originally published in various journals of MacDonald's time. Comparing some of those original publications with later publications of the collection in *A Dish of Orts*, often MacDonald's original footnotes were left out. I have restored MacDonald's original footnotes where possible. Those footnotes are denoted by an asterisk. It is my hope that this edition of *A Dish of Orts* will make the work more accessible and that you enjoy exploring MacDonald's thoughts as much as I did while editing.

C.M. Alvarez

$\mathcal{P}$REFACE

Since printing throughout the title *Orts*, a doubt has arisen in my mind as to its fitting the nature of the volume. It could hardly, however, be imagined that I associate the idea of *worthlessness* with the work contained in it. No one would insult his readers by offering them what he counted valueless scraps, and telling them they were such. These papers, those two even which were caught in the net of the ready -- writer from extempore utterance, whatever their merits in themselves; are the results of by no means trifling labour. So much a man *ought* to be able to say for his work. And hence I might defend, if not quite justify my title—for they are but fragmentary presentments of larger meditation. My friends at least will accept them as such, whether they like their collective title or not.

The title of the last is not quite suitable. It is that of the religious newspaper which reported the sermon. I noted the fact too late for correction. It ought to be *True Greatness*.

The paper on *The Fantastic Imagination* had its origin in the repeated request of readers for an explanation of things in certain shorter stories I had written. It forms the preface to an American edition of my so -- called Fairy Tales.

GEORGE MACDONALD.
EDENBRIDGE, KENT. *August 5, 1893.*

The Imagination:
Its Function and its Culture

There are in whose notion education would seem to consist in the production of a certain repose through the development of this and that faculty, and the depression, if not eradication, of this and that other faculty. But if mere repose were the end in view, an unsparing depression of all the faculties would be the surest means of approaching it, provided always the animal instincts could be depressed likewise, or, better still, kept in a state of constant repletion. Happily, however, for the human race, it possesses in the passion of hunger even, a more immediate saviour than in the wisest selection and treatment of its faculties. For repose is not the end of education; its end is a noble unrest, an ever-renewed awaking from the dead, a ceaseless questioning of the past for the interpretation of the future, an urging on of the motions of life, which had better far be accelerated into fever, than retarded into lethargy.

By those who consider a balanced repose the end of culture, the imagination must necessarily be regarded as the one faculty before all others to be suppressed. "Are there not facts?" say they. "Why forsake them for fancies? Is there not that which may be known? Why forsake it for inventions? What God hath made, into that let man inquire."

We answer: To inquire into what God has made is the main function of the imagination. It is aroused by facts, is nourished by facts, seeks for higher and yet higher laws in those facts; but refuses to regard science as the sole interpreter of nature, or the laws of science as the only region of discovery.

We must begin with a definition of the word imagination, or rather some description of the faculty to which we give the name.

The word itself means an imaging or a making of likenesses. The imagination is that faculty which gives form to thought -- not necessarily uttered form, but form capable of being uttered in shape or in sound, or in any mode upon which the senses can lay hold. It is, therefore, that faculty in man which is likest to the prime operation of the power of God, and has, therefore, been called the creative faculty, and its exercise creation. Poet means maker. We must not forget, however, that between creator and poet lies the one unpassable gulf which distinguishes -- far be it from us to say divides -- all that is God's from all that is man's; a gulf teeming with infinite revelations, but a gulf over which no man can pass to find out God, although God needs not to pass over it to find man; the gulf between that which calls, and that which is thus called into being; between that which makes in its own image and that which is made in that image. It is better to keep the word creation for that calling out of nothing which is the imagination of God; except it be as an occasional symbolic expression, whose daring is fully recognized, of the likeness of man's work to the work of his maker. The necessary unlikeness between the creator and the created holds within it the equally necessary likeness of the thing made to him who makes it, and so of the work of the made to the work of the maker. When therefore, refusing to employ the word creation of the work of man, we yet use the word imagination of the work of God, we cannot be said to dare at all. It is only to give the name of man's faculty to that power after which and by which it was fashioned. The imagination of man is made in the image of the imagination of God. Everything of man must have been of God first; and it will help much towards our understanding of the imagination and its functions in man if we first succeed in regarding aright the imagination of God, in which the imagination of man lives and moves and has its being.

As to what thought is in the mind of God ere it takes form, or what the form is to him ere he utters it; in a word, what the consciousness of God is in either case, all we can say is, that our consciousness in the resembling conditions must, afar off, resemble his. But when we come to consider the acts embodying the Divine thought (if indeed thought and act be not with him one and the same), then we enter a region of large difference. We discover at once, for instance, that where a man would make a machine, or a picture, or a book, God makes the man that makes the book, or the picture, or the machine. Would God give us a drama? He makes a Shakespeare. Or would he construct a drama more immediately his own? He begins with the building of the stage itself, and that stage is a world -- a universe of worlds. He makes the actors, and they do not act, they are their part. He utters them into the visible to work out their life -- his drama. When he would have an epic, he sends a thinking hero into his drama, and the epic is the soliloquy of his Hamlet. Instead of writing his lyrics, he sets his birds and his maidens a-singing. All the processes of the ages are God's science; all the flow of history is his poetry. His sculpture is not in marble, but in living and speech-giving forms, which pass away, not to yield place to those that come after, but to be perfected in a nobler studio. What he has done remains, although it vanishes; and he never either forgets what he has once done, or does it even once again. As the thoughts move in the mind of a man, so move the worlds of men and women in the mind of God, and make no confusion there, for there they had their birth, the offspring of his imagination. Man is but a thought of God.

If we now consider the so-called creative faculty in man, we shall find that in no primary sense is this faculty creative. Indeed, a man is rather being thought than thinking, when a new thought arises in his mind. He knew it not till he found it there, therefore he could not even have sent for it. He did not create it, else how could it be the surprise that it was when it arose? He may, indeed, in rare instances foresee that something is coming, and make ready the place for its birth; but that is the utmost relation of consciousness and will he can bear to the dawning idea. Leaving this aside, however, and turning to the embodiment or revelation of thought, we shall find that a man no more creates the forms by which he would reveal his thoughts, than he creates those thoughts themselves.

For what are the forms by means of which a man may reveal his thoughts? Are they not those of nature? But although he is created in the closest sympathy with these forms, yet even these forms are not born in his mind. What springs there is the perception that this or that form is already an expression of this or that phase of thought or of feeling. For the world around him is an outward figuration of the condition of his mind; an inexhaustible storehouse of forms whence he may choose exponents -- the crystal pitchers that shall protect his thought and not need to be broken that the light may break forth. The meanings are in those forms already, else they could be no garment of unveiling. God has made the world that it should thus serve his creature, developing in the service that imagination whose necessity it meets. The man has but to light the lamp within the form: his imagination is the light, it is not the form. Straightway the shining thought makes the form visible, and becomes itself visible through the form.[1] [2] In illustration of what we mean, take a passage from the poet Shelley.

In his poem *Adonais,* written upon the death of Keats, representing death as the revealer of secrets, he says:

> The one remains; the many change and pass; Heaven's light
> for ever shines; earth's shadows fly; Life, like a dome of
> many coloured glass, Stains the white radiance of eternity,
> Until death tramples it to fragments.[3]

This is a new embodiment, certainly, whence he who gains not, for the moment at least, a loftier feeling of death, must be dull either of heart or of understanding. But has Shelley created this figure, or only put together its parts according to the harmony of truths already embodied in each of the parts? For first he takes the inventions of his fellow-men, in glass, in colour, in dome: with these he represents life as finite though elevated, and as an analysis although a lovely one. Next he presents eternity as the dome of the sky above this dome of coloured glass -- the sky having ever been regarded as the true symbol of eternity. This portion of the figure he enriches by the attribution of whiteness, or unity and radiance. And last, he shows us Death as the destroying revealer, walking aloft through the upper region, treading out this life -- bubble of colours, that the man may look beyond it and behold the true, the uncoloured, the all-coloured.

But although the human imagination has no choice but to make use of the forms already prepared for it, its operation is the same as that of the divine inasmuch as it does put thought into form. And if it be to man what creation is to God, we must expect to find it operative in every sphere of human activity. Such is, indeed, the fact, and that to a far greater extent than is commonly supposed.

---

[1] Editor's note: some of MacDonald's original footnotes were not included in the republication of 1893. MacDonald also did not cite many references that were well known in his day but that are not as familiar to modern readers. We have included the footnotes as they were in the original publication in the *British Quarterly Review* in 1867. We have also cited references that were originally unsourced when we could find them. MacDonald's original footnotes are denoted by a * as they were in the first publication.

[2] * We would not be understood to say that the man works consciously even in this. Oftentimes, if not always, the vision arises in the mind, thought and form together.

[3] Percy Bysshe Shelley, "Adonais," Lines 460-64.

The sovereignty of the imagination, for instance, over the region of poetry will hardly, in the present day at least, be questioned; but not every one is prepared to be told that the imagination has had nearly as much to do with the making of our language as with "Macbeth" or the "Paradise Lost." The half of our language is the work of the imagination.

For how shall two agree together what name they shall give to a thought or a feeling? How shall the one show the other that which is invisible? True, he can unveil the mind's construction in the face -- that living eternally changeful symbol which God has hung in front of the unseen spirit -- but that without words reaches only to the expression of present feeling. To attempt to employ it alone for the conveyance of the intellectual or the historical would constantly mislead; while the expression of feeling itself would be misinterpreted, especially with regard to cause and object: the dumb show would be worse than dumb.

But let a man become aware of some new movement within him. Loneliness comes with it, for he would share his mind with his friend, and he cannot; he is shut up in speechlessness. Thus

He may live a man forbid
Weary seven nights nine times nine, [4]

or the first moment of his perplexity may be that of his release. Gazing about him in pain, he suddenly beholds the material form of his immaterial condition. There stands his thought! God thought it before him, and put its picture there ready for him when he wanted it. Or, to express the thing more prosaically, the man cannot look around him long without perceiving some form, aspect, or movement of nature, some relation between its forms, or between such and himself which resembles the state or motion within him. This he seizes as the symbol, as the garment or body of his invisible thought, presents it to his friend, and his friend understands him. Every word so employed with a new meaning is henceforth, in its new character, born of the spirit and not of the flesh, born of the imagination and not of the understanding, and is henceforth submitted to new laws of growth and modification.

"Thinkest thou," says Carlyle in "Past and Present,"

there were no poets till Dan Chaucer? No heart burning with a thought which it could not hold, and had no word

---

[4] Shakespeare, *Macbeth*, I.iii, 21-22.

for; and needed to shape and coin a word for -- what thou callest a metaphor, trope, or the like? For every word we have there was such a man and poet. The coldest word was once a glowing new metaphor and bold questionable originality. Thy very ATTENTION, does it not mean an attention, a STRETCHING -- TO? Fancy that act of the mind, which all were conscious of, which none had yet named, -- when this new poet first felt bound and driven to name it. His questionable originality and new glowing metaphor was found adoptable, intelligible, and remains our name for it to this day.[5]

All words, then, belonging to the inner world of the mind, are of the imagination, are originally poetic words. The better, however, any such word is fitted for the needs of humanity, the sooner it loses its poetic aspect by commonness of use. It ceases to be heard as a symbol, and appears only as a sign. Thus thousands of words which were originally poetic words owing their existence to the imagination, lose their vitality, and harden into mummies of prose. Not merely in literature does poetry come first, and prose afterwards, but poetry is the source of all the language that belongs to the inner world, whether it be of passion or of metaphysics, of psychology or of aspiration. No poetry comes by the elevation of prose; but the half of prose comes by the "massing into the common clay" of thousands of winged words, whence, like the lovely shells of by -- gone ages, one is occasionally disinterred by some lover of speech, and held up to the light to show the play of colour in its manifold laminations.

For the world is -- allow us the homely figure -- the human being turned inside out. All that moves in the mind is symbolized in Nature. Or, to use another more philosophical, and certainly not less poetic figure, the world is a sensuous analysis of humanity, and hence an inexhaustible wardrobe for the clothing of human thought. Take any word expressive of emotion -- take the word *emotion* itself -- and you will find that its primary meaning is of the outer world. In the swaying of the woods, in the unrest of the "wavy plain," the imagination saw the picture of a well-known condition of the human mind; and hence the word *emotion.*[6]

---

[5] Thomas Carlyle, *Past and Present* (1843) Book II, chap. XVII.

[6] * This passage contains only a repetition of what is far better said in the preceding extract from Carlyle, but it was written before we had read (if reviewers

But while the imagination of man has thus the divine function of putting thought into form, it has a duty altogether human, which is paramount to that function -- the duty, namely, which springs from his immediate relation to the Father, that of following and finding out the divine imagination in whose image it was made. To do this, the man must watch its signs, its manifestations. He must contemplate what the Hebrew poets call the works of His hands.

"But to follow those is the province of the intellect, not of the imagination." -- We will leave out of the question at present that poetic interpretation of the works of Nature with which the intellect has almost nothing, and the imagination almost everything, to do. It is unnecessary to insist that the higher being of a flower even is dependent for its reception upon the human imagination; that science may pull the snowdrop to shreds, but cannot find out the idea of suffering hope and pale confident submission, for the sake of which that darling of the spring looks out of heaven, namely, God's heart, upon us his wiser and more sinful children; for if there be any truth in this region of things acknowledged at all, it will be at the same time acknowledged that that region belongs to the imagination. We confine ourselves to that questioning of the works of God which is called the province of science.

"Shall, then, the human intellect," we ask, "come into readier contact with the divine imagination than that human imagination?" The work of the Higher must be discovered by the search of the Lower in degree which is yet similar in kind. Let us not be supposed to exclude the intellect from a share in every highest office. Man is not divided when the manifestations of his life are distinguished. The intellect "is all in every part."[7] There were no imagination without intellect, however much it may appear that intellect can exist without imagination. What we mean to insist upon is, that in finding out the works of God, the Intellect must labour, workman -- like, under the

---

may be allowed to confess such ignorance) the book from which that extract is taken. From Percy Bysshe Shelley, "The Sensitive Plant," lines 30-33.

[7] Samuel Taylor Coleridge, *The Complete Works of Samuel Taylor Coleridge: With an Introductory Essay Upon His Philosophical and Theological Opinions*, vol. 2 (New York, NY: Harper & brothers, 1853), 465. Here MacDonald references Coleridge's explanation of the mind as man's connection to his Creator. Please see the appendix for the referenced passage.

direction of the architect, Imagination. Herein, too, we proceed in the hope to show how much more than is commonly supposed the imagination has to do with human endeavour; how large a share it has in the work that is done under the sun.

"But how can the imagination have anything to do with science? That region, at least, is governed by fixed laws."

"True," we answer. "But how much do we know of these laws? How much of science already belongs to the region of the ascertained -- in other words, has been conquered by the intellect? We will not now dispute your vindication of the ascertained from the intrusion of the imagination; but we do claim for it all the undiscovered, all the unexplored." "Ah, well! There it can do little harm. There let it run riot if you will." "No," we reply. "Licence is not what we claim when we assert the duty of the imagination to be that of following and finding out the work that God maketh. Her part is to understand God ere she attempts to utter man. Where is the room for being fanciful or riotous here? It is only the ill-bred, that is, the uncultivated imagination that will amuse itself where it ought to worship and work."

"But the facts of Nature are to be discovered only by observation and experiment." True. But how does the man of science come to think of his experiments? Does observation reach to the non-present, the possible, the yet unconceived? Even if it showed you the experiments which ought to be made, will observation reveal to you the experiments which might be made? And who can tell of which kind is the one that carries in its bosom the secret of the law you seek? We yield you your facts. The laws we claim for the prophetic imagination. "He hath set the world in man's heart," not in his understanding.[8] And the heart must open the door to the understanding. It is the far -- seeing imagination which beholds what might be a form of things, and says to the intellect: "Try whether that may not be the form of these things;" which beholds or invents a harmonious relation of parts and operations, and sends the intellect to find out whether that be not the harmonious relation of them -- that is, the law of the phenomenon it contemplates. Nay, the poetic relations themselves in the phenomenon may suggest to the imagination the law that rules its scientific life. Yea, more than this: we dare to claim for the true, childlike, humble imagination, such an inward oneness with the laws of

---

[8] Ecclesiastes 3:11.

the universe that it possesses in itself an insight into the very nature of things.

Lord Bacon tells us that a prudent question is the half of knowledge. Whence comes this prudent question? we repeat. And we answer, From the imagination. It is the imagination that suggests in what direction to make the new inquiry -- which, should it cast no immediate light on the answer sought, can yet hardly fail to be a step towards final discovery. Every experiment has its origin in hypothesis; without the scaffolding of hypothesis, the house of science could never arise. And the construction of any hypothesis whatever is the work of the imagination. The man who cannot invent will never discover. The imagination often gets a glimpse of the law itself long before it is or can be ascertained to be a law.[9]

The region belonging to the pure intellect is straitened: the imagination labours to extend its territories, to give it room. She sweeps across the borders, searching out new lands into which she may guide her plodding brother. The imagination is the light which redeems from the darkness for the eyes of the understanding. Novalis says, "The imagination is the stuff of the intellect" -- affords, that is, the material upon which the intellect works.[10] And Bacon, in his "Advancement of

---

[9] * This paper was already written when, happening to mention the present subject to a mathematical friend, a lecturer at one of the Universities, he gave us a corroborative instance. He had lately guessed that a certain algebraic process could be shortened exceedingly if the method which his imagination suggested should prove to be a true one -- that is, an algebraic law. He put it to the test of experiment -- committed the verification, that is, into the hands of his intellect--and found the method true. It has since been accepted by the Royal Society.

Noteworthy illustration we have lately found in the record of the experiences of an Edinburgh detective, an Irishman of the name of McLevy. That the service of the imagination in the solution of the problems peculiar to his calling is well known to hi, we could adduce many proofs. He recognizes its function in the construction of the theory which shall unite this and that hint into an organic whole, and he expressly acts forth the need of a theory before facts can be serviceable;-- 'I would wait for my "idea." . . . I never did any good without mine . . . Chance never smiled on me unless I poked her some way; so that my "notion," after all, has been in the getting of it my own work only perfected by a higher hand.'

'On leaving the shop I went direct to Prince's Street,--of course with an idea in my mind; and somehow I have always been contented with one idea when I could not get another; and the advantage of sticking by one is, that the other don't jostle it and turn you about in a circle when you should go in a straight line.'

[10] George MacDonald was greatly influenced by the German writer Georg Philipp Friedrich Freiherr von Hardenberg, who wrote under the pen name "Novalis." MacDonald translated Novalis's *Hymns of the Night* and mentioned the

Learning," fully recognizes this its office, corresponding to the foresight of God in this, that it beholds afar off. And he says: "Imagination is much akin to miracle-working faith."[11]

In the scientific region of her duty of which we speak, the Imagination cannot have her perfect work; this belongs to another and higher sphere than that of intellectual truth -- that, namely, of full-globed humanity, operating in which she gives birth to poetry -- truth in beauty. But her function in the complete sphere of our nature, will, at the same time, influence her more limited operation in the sections that belong to science. Coleridge says that no one but a poet will make any further great discoveries in mathematics; and Bacon says that "wonder," that faculty of the mind especially attendant on the child -- like imagination, "is the seed of knowledge."[12] The influence of the poetic upon the scientific imagination is, for instance, especially present in the construction of an invisible whole from the hints afforded by a visible part; where the needs of the part, its uselessness, its broken relations, are the only guides to a multiplex harmony, completeness, and end, which is the whole. From a little bone, worn with ages of death, older than the man can think, his scientific imagination dashed with the poetic, calls up the form, size, habits, periods, belonging to an animal never beheld by human eyes, even to the mingling contrasts of scales and wings, of feathers and hair. Through the combined lenses of science and imagination, we look back into ancient times, so dreadful in their incompleteness, that it may well have been the task of seraphic faith, as well as of cherubic imagination, to behold in the wallowing

---

novel *Heinrich von Ofterdingen*. While this idea is found in both *Hymns* and *HvO*, it is not a direct quotation from either. MacDonald could be paraphrasing this idea presented by Novalis or he may be quoting directly from one of Novalis's many philosophical writings that were published in a variety of formats after his death in 1801.

[11] * We are sorry we cannot verify this quotation, for which we are indebted to Mr. Oldbuck the Antiquary, in the novel of that ilk. There is, however, little room for doubt that it is sufficiently correct.

Editor's Note: The quote is found in Francis Bacon's *Advancement of Learning*. VI.xi.3.

"Fascination is the power and act of imagination intensive upon other bodies than the body of the imaginant, for of that we spake in the proper place. Wherein the school of Paracelsus, and the disciples of pretended natural magic, have been so intemperate, as they have exalted the power of the imagination to be much one with the power of miracle-working faith"

[12] Bacon, *Advancement of Learning*, V1.i.3.

monstrosities of the terror -- teeming earth, the prospective, quiet, age -- long labour of God preparing the world with all its humble, graceful service for his unborn Man. The imagination of the poet, on the other hand, dashed with the imagination of the man of science, revealed to Goethe the prophecy of the flower in the leaf. No other than an artistic imagination, however, fulfilled of science, could have attained to the discovery of the fact that the leaf is the imperfect flower.

When we turn to history, however, we find probably the greatest operative sphere of the intellectuo-constructive imagination. To discover its laws; the cycles in which events return, with the reasons of their return, recognizing them notwithstanding metamorphosis; to perceive the vital motions of this spiritual body of mankind; to learn from its facts the rule of God; to construct from a succession of broken indications a whole accordant with human nature; to approach a scheme of the forces at work, the passions overwhelming or upheaving, the aspirations securely upraising, the selfishnesses debasing and crumbling, with the vital interworking of the whole; to illuminate all from the analogy with individual life, and from the predominant phases of individual character which are taken as the mind of the people -- this is the province of the imagination. Without her influence no process of recording events can develop into a history. As truly might that be called the description of a volcano which occupied itself with a delineation of the shapes assumed by the smoke expelled from the mountain's burning bosom. What history becomes under the full sway of the imagination may be seen in the "History of the French Revolution," by Thomas Carlyle, at once a true picture, a philosophical revelation, a noble poem.[13]

There is a wonderful passage about *Time* in Shakespeare's "Rape of Lucrece," which shows how he understood history. The passage is really about history, and not about time; for time itself does nothing -- not even "blot old books and alter their contents." It is the forces at work in time that produce all the changes; and they are history. We quote for the sake of one line chiefly but the whole stanza is pertinent.

> Time's glory is to calm contending kings, To unmask
> falsehood, and bring truth to light,
> To stamp the seal of time in aged things, To wake the morn
> and sentinel the night,

---

[13] 1837.

To wrong the wronger till he render right;
To ruinate proud buildings with thy hours,
And smear with dust their glittering golden towers.[14]

To wrong the wronger till he render right. Here is a historical cycle worthy of the imagination of Shakespeare, yea, worthy of the creative imagination of our God -- the God who made the Shakespeare with the imagination, as well as evolved the history from the laws which that imagination followed and found out.

In full instance we would refer our readers to Shakespeare's historical plays; and, as a side-illustration, to the fact that he repeatedly represents his greatest characters, when at the point of death, as relieving their overcharged minds by prophecy. Such prophecy is the result of the light of imagination, cleared of all distorting dimness by the vanishing of earthly hopes and desires, cast upon the facts of experience. Such prophecy is the perfect working of the historical imagination.

In the interpretation of individual life, the same principles hold; and nowhere can the imagination be more healthily and rewardingly occupied than in endeavouring to construct the life of an individual out of the fragments which are all that can reach us of the history of even the noblest of our race. How this will apply to the reading of the gospel story we leave to the earnest thought of our readers.

We now pass to one more sphere in which the student imagination works in glad freedom -- the sphere which is understood to belong more immediately to the poet.

We have already said that the forms of Nature (by which word *forms* we mean any of those conditions of Nature which affect the senses of man) are so many approximate representations of the mental conditions of humanity. The outward, commonly called the material, is *informed* by, or has form in virtue of, the inward or immaterial -- in a word, the thought. The forms of Nature are the representations of human thought in virtue of their being the embodiment of God's thought. As such, therefore, they can be read and used to any depth, shallow or profound. Men of all ages and all developments have discovered in them the means of expression; and the men of ages to come, before us in every path along which we are now striving, must likewise find such means in those forms, unfolding with their unfolding

---

[14] William Shakespeare, "Time's Glory" from "The Rape of Lucrece," lines 1-7.

necessities. The man, then, who, in harmony with nature, attempts the discovery of more of her meanings, is just searching out the things of God. The deepest of these are far too simple for us to understand as yet. But let our imagination interpretive reveal to us one severed significance of one of her parts, and such is the harmony of the whole, that all the realm of Nature is open to us henceforth -- not without labour -- and in time. Upon the man who can understand the human meaning of the snowdrop, of the primrose, or of the daisy, the life of the earth blossoming into the cosmical flower of a perfect moment will one day seize, possessing him with its prophetic hope, arousing his conscience with the vision of the "rest that remaineth," and stirring up the aspiration to enter into that rest:[15]

> Thine is the tranquil hour, purpureal Eve! But long as
> godlike wish, or hope divine,
> Informs my spirit, ne'er can I believe, That this
>   magnificence is wholly thine! -- From worlds not
> aquickened by the sun
> A portion of the gift is won;
> An intermingling of Heaven's pomp is spread
> On ground which British shepherds tread![16]

Even the careless curve of a frozen cloud across the blue will calm some troubled thoughts, may slay some selfish thoughts. And what shall be said of such gorgeous shows as the scarlet poppies in the green corn, the likest we have to those lilies of the field which spoke to the Saviour himself of the care of God, and rejoiced His eyes with the glory of their God -- devised array?[17] From such visions as these the imagination reaps the best fruits of the earth, for the sake of which all the science involved in its construction, is the inferior, yet willing and beautiful support.

---

[15] In this essay on imagination, there are repeatedly implicit references to the Book of Hebrews and the forms of things unseen. The quotation, the "rest that remaineth" seems to be another reference to Hebrews, specifically chapter 4, verse 9, where Christ is identified as that Sabbath rest. "The rest that remaineth" is found as a common topic in sermons, essays, hymns and poetry of the time. MacDonald seems to be referencing the common cultural identification with the phrase rather than a specific work.

[16] William Wordsworth, "Evening Ode," lines 13-20.

[17] Matthew 6:25-34, Luke 12:22-32

From what we have now advanced, will it not then appear that, on the whole, the name given by our Norman ancestors is more fitting for the man who moves in these regions than the name given by the Greeks? Is not the *Poet*, the *Maker*, a less suitable name for him than the *TrouvÁ're*, the *Finder?* At least, must not the faculty that finds precede the faculty that utters?

But is there nothing to be said of the function of the imagination from the Greek side of the question? Does it possess no creative faculty? Has it no originating power?

Certainly it would be a poor description of the Imagination which omitted the one element especially present to the mind that invented the word *Poet.* -- It can present us with new thought-forms -- new, that is, as revelations of thought. It has created none of the material that goes to make these forms. Nor does it work upon raw material. But it takes forms already existing, and gathers them about a thought so much higher than they, that it can group and subordinate and harmonize them into a whole which shall represent, unveil that thought.[18] The nature of this process we will illustrate by an examination of the well-known *Bugle Song* in Tennyson's "Princess."

First of all, there is the new music of the song, which does not even remind one of the music of any other. The rhythm, rhyme, melody, harmony are all an embodiment in sound, as distinguished from word, of what can be so embodied --the *feeling* of the poem, which goes before, and prepares the way for the following thought -- tunes the heart into a receptive harmony. Then comes the new arrangement of thought and figure whereby the meaning contained is presented as it never was before. We give a sort of paraphrastical synopsis of the poem, which, partly in virtue of its disagreeableness, will enable the lovers of the song to return to it with an increase of pleasure.

The glory of midsummer mid-day upon mountain, lake, and ruin. Give nature a voice for her gladness. Blow, bugle.

---

[18] * Just so Spenser describes the process of the embodiment of a human soul in his Platonic "Hymn in Honour of Beauty."

> She frames her house in which she will be placed
> Fit for herself
> And the gross matter by a sovereign might
> Tempers so trim
> For of the soul the body form doth take;
> For soul is form, and doth the body make.

Nature answers with dying echoes, sinking in the midst of her splendour into a sad silence.

Not so with human nature. The echoes of the word of truth gather volume and richness from every soul that re-echoes it to brother and sister souls.

With poets the *fashion* has been to contrast the stability and rejuvenescence of nature with the evanescence and unreturning decay of humanity:

> Yet soon reviving plants and flowers,
>   anew shall deck the plain;
> The woods shall hear the voice of Spring,
>   and flourish green again.
>
> But man forsakes this earthly scene, ah!
>   never to return:
> Shall any following Spring revive the
>   ashes of the urn?[19]

But our poet vindicates the eternal in humanity:

> O Love, they die in yon rich sky,
> They faint on hill or field or river:
> Our echoes roll from soul to soul,
> And grow for ever and for ever.
> Blow, bugle, blow, set the wild echoes
>   flying;
> And answer echoes, answer, Dying,
>   dying, dying.[20]

Is not this a new form to the thought -- a form which makes us feel the truth of it afresh? And every new embodiment of a known truth must be a new and wider revelation. No man is capable of seeing for himself the whole of any truth: he needs it echoed back to him from every soul in the universe; and still its centre is hid in the Father of Lights. In so far, then, as either form or thought is new, we may grant the use of the word Creation, modified according to our previous definitions.

---

[19] This is a stanza from a Scottish hymn. Michael Bruce, "Few are thy Days, and Full of Woe." (1764) lines 29-36.

[20] Lord Alfred Tennyson, "The Splendor Falls" from *The Princess*. lines 13-18.

This operation of the imagination in choosing, gathering, and vitally combining the material of a new revelation, may be well illustrated from a certain employment of the poetic faculty in which our greatest poets have delighted. Perceiving truth half hidden and half revealed in the slow speech and stammering tongue of men who have gone before them, they have taken up the unfinished form and completed it; they have, as it were, rescued the soul of meaning from its prison of uninformed crudity, where it sat like the Prince in the "Arabian Nights," half man, half marble; they have set it free in its own form, in a shape, namely, which it could "through every part impress." Shakespeare's keen eye suggested many such a rescue from the tomb -- of a tale drearily told -- a tale which no one now would read save for the glorified form in which he has re-embodied its true contents. And from Tennyson we can produce one specimen small enough for our use, which, a mere chip from the great marble re-embodying the old legend of Arthur's death, may, like the hand of Achilles holding his spear in the crowded picture,

'Stand for the whole to be imagined.'

In the "History of Prince Arthur," when Sir Bedivere returns after hiding Excalibur the first time, the king asks him what he has seen, and he answers --

'Sir, I saw nothing but waves and wind.'[21]

The second time, to the same question, he answers --

'Sir, I saw nothing but the water wap, and the waves wan.'[22]

This answer Tennyson has expanded into the well-known lines --

---

[21] Thomas Malory, *Le Morte D'Arthur*, II.XXI.V.

[22] Ibid., II.XXI.V.

* The word *wap* is plain enough; the word *wan* we cannot satisfy ourselves about. Had it been used with regard to the water, it might have been worth remarking that *wan*, meaning dark, gloomy, turbid, is a common adjective to a river in the old Scotch ballad. And it might be an adjective here; but that is not likely, seeing it is conjoined with the verb *wap*. The Anglo-Saxon *wanian*, to decrease, might be the root-word, perhaps, (in the sense of *to ebb*,) if this water had been the sea and not a lake. But possibly the meaning is, 'I heard the water *whoop* or *wail aloud*' from (*Wopan*); and 'the waves whine or bewail" (from *Wduian* to lament). But even then the two verbs would seem to predicate of transposed subjects.

'I heard the ripple washing in the reeds, And the wild water lapping on the crag;'[23]

slightly varied, for the other occasion, into --

'I heard the water lapping on the crag, And the long ripple washing in the reeds.'[24]

But, as to this matter of creation, is there, after all, I ask yet, any genuine sense in which a man may be said to create his own thought-forms? Allowing that a new combination of forms already existing might be called creation, is the man, after all, the author of this new combination? Did he, with his will and his knowledge, proceed wittingly, consciously, to construct a form which should embody his thought? Or did this form arise within him without will or effort of his -- vivid if not clear -- certain if not outlined? Ruskin (and better authority we do not know) will assert the latter, and we think he is right: though perhaps he would insist more upon the absolute perfection of the vision than we are quite prepared to do. Such embodiments are not the result of the man's intention, or of the operation of his conscious nature. His feeling is that they are given to him; that from the vast unknown, where time and space are not, they suddenly appear in luminous writing upon the wall of his consciousness. Can it be correct, then, to say that he created them? Nothing less so, as it seems to us. But can we not say that they are the creation of the unconscious portion of his nature? Yes, provided we can understand that that which is the individual, the man, can know, and not know that it knows, can create and yet be ignorant that virtue has gone out of it. From that unknown region we grant they come, but not by its own blind working. Nor, even were it so, could any amount of such production, where no will was concerned, be dignified with the name of creation. But God sits in that chamber of our being in which the candle of our consciousness goes out in darkness, and sends forth from thence wonderful gifts into the light of that understanding which is His candle. Our hope lies in no most perfect mechanism even of the spirit, but in the wisdom wherein we live and move and have our being. Thence we hope for endless forms of beauty informed of truth. If the dark portion of our own being were the origin of our imaginations, we might well

---

[23] Lord Alfred Tennyson, "Morte d'Arthur," lines 70-71.

[24] Ibid., lines 116-117.

fear the apparition of such monsters as would be generated in the sickness of a decay which could never feel -- only declare -- a slow return towards primeval chaos. But the Maker is our Light.

One word more, ere we turn to consider the culture of this noblest faculty, which we might well call the creative, did we not see a something in God for which we would humbly keep our mighty word: -- the fact that there is always more in a work of art -- which is the highest human result of the embodying imagination -- than the producer himself perceived while he produced it, seems to us a strong reason for attributing to it a larger origin than the man alone -- for saying at the last, that the inspiration of the Almighty shaped its ends.

We return now to the class which, from the first, we supposed hostile to the imagination and its functions generally. Those belonging to it will now say: "It was to no imagination such as you have been setting forth that we were opposed, but to those wild fancies and vague reveries in which young people indulge, to the damage and loss of the real in the world around them."

"And," we insist, "you would rectify the matter by smothering the young monster at once -- because he has wings, and, young to their use, flutters them about in a way discomposing to your nerves, and destructive to those notions of propriety of which this creature -- you stop not to inquire whether angel or pterodactyle -- has not yet learned even the existence. Or, if it is only the creature's vagaries of which you disapprove, why speak of them as the exercise of the imagination? As well speak of religion as the mother of cruelty because religion has given more occasion of cruelty, as of all dishonesty and devilry, than any other object of human interest. Are we not to worship, because our forefathers burned and stabbed for religion? It is more religion we want. It is more imagination we need. Be assured that these are but the first vital motions of that whose results, at least in the region of science, you are more than willing to accept." That evil may spring from the imagination, as from everything except the perfect love of God, cannot be denied. But infinitely worse evils would be the result of its absence. Selfishness, avarice, sensuality, cruelty, would flourish tenfold; and the power of Satan would be well established ere some children had begun to choose. Those who would quell the apparently lawless tossing of the spirit, called the youthful imagination, would suppress all that is to grow out of it. They fear the enthusiasm they never felt; and instead of cherishing this divine thing, instead of giving it room and air for healthful growth, they would crush and confine it -- with but one result of their victorious endeavours -- imposthume, fever, and corruption. And the disastrous consequences would soon appear in the intellect likewise which they worship. Kill that whence spring the crude fancies and wild day-dreams of the young, and you will never lead them beyond dull facts -- dull because their relations to each other, and the one life that works in them all, must remain undiscovered. Whoever would have his children avoid this arid region will do well to allow no teacher to approach them -- not even of mathematics -- who has no imagination.

"But although good results may appear in a few from the indulgence of the imagination, how will it be with the many?"

We answer that the antidote to indulgence is development, not restraint, and that such is the duty of the wise servant of Him who made the imagination.

"But will most girls, for instance, rise to those useful uses of the imagination? Are they not more likely to exercise it in building castles in the air to the neglect of houses on the earth? And as the world affords such poor scope for the ideal, will not this habit breed vain desires and vain regrets? Is it not better, therefore, to keep to that which is known, and leave the rest?"

"Is the world so poor?" we ask in return. The less reason, then, to be satisfied with it; the more reason to rise above it, into the region of the true, of the eternal, of things as God thinks them.[25] This outward world is but a passing vision of the persistent true.[26] We shall not live in it always.[27] We are dwellers in a divine universe where no desires are in vain, if only they be large enough. Not even in this world do all disappointments breed only vain regrets.[28]

And as to keeping to that which is known and leaving the rest -- how many affairs of this world are so well-defined, so capable of being

---

[25] 2 Corinthians 4:18

[26] 1 Corinthians 7:31, 1 John 2:17

[27] Philippians 3:20, Hebrews 13:14, 1 Peter 1:4

[28] "We will grieve not, rather find
Strength in what remains behind;
In the primal sympathy
Which, having been, must ever be;
In the soothing thoughts that spring
Out of human suffering;
In the faith that looks through death,
In years that bring the philosophic mind."

clearly understood, as not to leave large spaces of uncertainty, whose very correlate faculty is the imagination? Indeed it must, in most things, work after some fashion, filling the gaps after some possible plan, before action can even begin. In very truth, a wise imagination, which is the presence of the spirit of God, is the best guide that man or woman can have; for it is not the things we see the most clearly that influence us the most powerfully; undefined, yet vivid visions of something beyond, something which eye has not seen nor ear heard, have far more influence than any logical sequences whereby the same things may be demonstrated to the intellect.[29] It is the nature of the thing, not the clearness of its outline, that determines its operation. We live by faith, and not by sight. Put the question to our mathematicians -- only be sure the question reaches them -- whether they would part with the well-defined perfection of their diagrams, or the dim, strange, possibly half-obliterated characters woven in the web of their being; their science, in short, or their poetry; their certainties, or their hopes; their consciousness of knowledge, or their vague sense of that which cannot be known absolutely: will they hold by their craft or by their inspirations, by their intellects or their imaginations? If they say the former in each alternative, I shall yet doubt whether the objects of the choice are actually before them, and with equal presentation.

What can be known must be known severely; but is there, therefore, no faculty for those infinite lands of uncertainty lying all about the sphere hollowed out of the dark by the glimmering lamp of our knowledge? Are they not the natural property of the imagination? there, *for* it, that it may have room to grow? there, that the man may learn to imagine greatly like God who made him, himself discovering their mysteries, in virtue of his following and worshipping imagination?

All that has been said, then, tends to enforce the culture of the imagination. But the strongest argument of all remains behind. For, if the whole power of pedantry should rise against her, the imagination will yet work; and if not for good, then for evil; if not for truth, then for falsehood; if not for life, then for death; the evil alternative becoming the more likely from the unnatural treatment she has experienced from those who ought to have fostered her. The power that might have gone forth in conceiving the noblest forms of action, in realizing the lives of the true-hearted, the self-forgetting, will go

---

[29] 1 Corinthians 2:9

forth in building airy castles of vain ambition, of boundless riches, of unearned admiration. The imagination that might be devising how to make home blessed or to help the poor neighbour, will be absorbed in the invention of the new dress, or worse, in devising the means of procuring it. For, if she be not occupied with the beautiful, she will be occupied by the pleasant; that which goes not out to worship, will remain at home to be sensual. Cultivate the mere intellect as you may, it will never reduce the passions: the imagination, seeking the ideal in everything, will elevate them to their true and noble service. Seek not that your sons and your daughters should not see visions, should not dream dreams; seek that they should see true visions, that they should dream noble dreams.[30] Such out-going of the imagination is one with aspiration, and will do more to elevate above what is low and vile than all possible inculcations of morality. Nor can religion herself ever rise up into her own calm home, her crystal shrine, when one of her wings, one of the twain with which she flies, is thus broken or paralyzed.

> The universe is infinitely wide,
> And conquering Reason, if self-glorified, Can nowhere
> move uncrossed by some new wall,
> Or gulf of mystery, which thou alone, Imaginative Faith!
> Canst overleap,
> In progress towards the fount of love.[31]

The danger that lies in the repression of the imagination may be well illustrated from the play of "Macbeth." The imagination of the hero (in him a powerful faculty), representing how the deed would appear to others, and so representing its true nature to himself, was his great impediment on the path to crime. Nor would he have succeeded in reaching it, had he not gone to his wife for help -- sought refuge from his troublesome imagination with her. She, possessing far less of the faculty, and having dealt more destructively with what she had, took his hand, and led him to the deed. From her imagination, again, she for her part takes refuge in unbelief and denial, declaring to herself and her

---

[30] This is an integration of the prophecy in Joel 2:28, identified as fulfilled in Acts 2:17. A fully developed and reclaimed imagination is a fulfillment of the promise of God. From Acts, "And it shall come to pass in the last days, saith God, I will pour out my Spirit upon all flesh: and your sons and your daughters shall prophesy, an dyour young men shall see visions, and your old men shall dream dreams"

[31] Williams Wordsworth, "Desire We Past Illusions to Recall," (1833) lines 6-11.

husband that there is no reality in its representations; that there is no reality in anything beyond the present effect it produces on the mind upon which it operates; that intellect and courage are equal to any, even an evil emergency; and that no harm will come to those who can rule themselves according to their own will. Still, however, finding her imagination, and yet more that of her husband, troublesome, she effects a marvellous combination of materialism and idealism, and asserts that things are not, cannot be, and shall not be more or other than people choose to think them. She says, --

> These deeds must not be thought
>   After these ways; so, it will make us
>   mad.
> The sleeping and the dead
>   Are but as pictures.[32]

But she had over-estimated the power of her will, and under-estimated that of her imagination. Her will was the one thing in her that was bad, without root or support in the universe, while her imagination was the voice of God himself out of her own unknown being. The choice of no man or woman can long determine how or what he or she shall think of things. Lady Macbeth's imagination would not be repressed beyond its appointed period -- a time determined by laws of her being over which she had no control. It arose, at length, as from the dead, overshadowing her with all the blackness of her crime. The woman who drank strong drink that she might murder, dared not sleep without a light by her bed; rose and walked in the night, a sleepless spirit in a sleeping body, rubbing the spotted hand of her dreams, which, often as water had cleared it of the deed, yet smelt so in her sleeping nostrils, that all the perfumes of Arabia would not sweeten it. Thus her long down-trodden imagination rose and took vengeance, even through those senses which she had thought to subordinate to her wicked will.

But all this is of the imagination itself, and fitter, therefore, for illustration than for argument. Let us come to facts. -- Dr. Pritchard, lately executed for murder, had no lack of that invention, which is, as it were, the intellect of the imagination -- its lowest form. One of the clergymen who, at his own request, attended the prisoner, went

---

[32] William Shakespeare, *Macbeth*, 2.2.44-45, 67-68.

through indescribable horrors in the vain endeavour to induce the man simply to cease from lying: one invention after another followed the most earnest asseverations of truth. The effect produced upon us by this clergyman's report of his experience was a moral dismay, such as we had never felt with regard to human being, and drew from us the exclamation, "The man could have had no imagination." The reply was, "None whatever." Never seeking true or high things, caring only for appearances, and, therefore, for inventions, he had left his imagination all undeveloped, and when it represented his own inner condition to him, had repressed it until it was nearly destroyed, and what remained of it was set on fire of hell.[33]

Man is "the roof and crown of things."[34] He is the world, and more. Therefore the chief scope of his imagination, next to God who made him, will be the world in relation to his own life therein. Will he do better or worse in it if this imagination, touched to fine issues and having free scope, present him with noble pictures of relationship and duty, of possible elevation of character and attainable justice of behaviour, of friendship and of love; and, above all, of all these in that life to understand which as a whole, must ever be the loftiest aspiration of this noblest power of humanity? Will a woman lead a more or a less troubled life that the sights and sounds of nature break through the crust of gathering anxiety, and remind her of the peace of the lilies and the well-being of the birds of the air? Or will life be less interesting to her, that the lives of her neighbours, instead of passing like shadows upon a wall, assume a consistent wholeness, forming themselves into stories and phases of life? Will she not hereby love more and talk less? Or will she be more unlikely to make a good match -- ? But here we arrest ourselves in bewilderment over the word *good*, and seek to re-arrange our thoughts. If what mothers mean by a *good* match, is the alliance of a man of position and means -- or let them throw intellect, manners, and personal advantages into the same scale -- if this be all, then we grant the daughter of cultivated imagination may not be manageable, will probably be obstinate. We hope she will be obstinate

---

[33] * One of the best weekly papers in London, evidently as much in ignorance of the man as of the facts of the case, spoke of Dr. MacLeod as having been engaged in "whitewashing the murderer for heaven." So far is this from a true representation, that Dr. MacLeod actually refused to pray with him, telling hi that if there was a hell to go to, he must go to it.

[34] Alfred Tennyson, "The Lotos-eaters," line 69.

enough.[35] But will the girl be less likely to marry a gentleman, in the grand old meaning of the sixteenth century? when it was no irreverence to call our Lord

> The first true gentleman that ever breathed;[36]
> or in that of the fourteenth? -- when Chaucer teaching
> "whom is worthy to be called gentill," writes thus: --

> The first stocke was full of rightwisnes, Trewe of his
>   worde, sober, pitous and free,
> Clene of his goste, and loved besinesse, Against the vice of
>   slouth in honeste;
> And but his heire love vertue as did he, He is not gentill
>   though he rich seme,
> All weare he miter, crowne, or diademe.[37]

Will she be less likely to marry one who honours women, and for their sakes, as well as his own, honours himself? Or to speak from what many would regard as the mother's side of the question -- will the girl be more likely, because of such a culture of her imagination, to refuse the wise, true-hearted, generous rich man, and fall in love with the talking, verse-making fool, because he is poor, as if that were a virtue for which he had striven? The highest imagination and the lowliest common sense are always on one side.

For the end of imagination is harmony. A right imagination, being the reflex of the creation, will fall in with the divine order of things as the highest form of its own operation; "will tune its instrument here at the door" to the divine harmonies within; will be content alone with growth towards the divine idea, which includes all that is beautiful in the imperfect imaginations of men; will know that every deviation from that growth is downward; and will therefore send the man forth from its loftiest representations to do the commonest duty of the most

---

[35] * Let women who feel the wrongs of their kind teach women to be high-minded in their relation to men, and they will do more for the social elevation of women, and the establishment of their rights, whatever those rights may be, than by any amount of intellectual development or noisy assertion of equality. Nor if they are other than mere partisans will they refuse the attempt, because in its success men will, after all, be equal, if not greater gainers, if only thereby they should be feelingly persuaded what they are.

[36] Thomas Dekker, "An Honest Whore," (1604) *Candido* in I.IV.ii.

[37] Geoffrey Chaucer, "A Ballad" in *Chaucer's Romaunt of the Rose and Other Poems*, (1360) Vol 3, lines 1-7.

wearisome calling in a hearty and hopeful spirit. This is the work of the right imagination; and towards this work every imagination, in proportion to the rightness that is in it, will tend. The reveries even of the wise man will make him stronger for his work; his dreaming as well as his thinking will render him sorry for past failure, and hopeful of future success.

To come now to the culture of the imagination. Its development is one of the main ends of the divine education of life with all its efforts and experiences. Therefore the first and essential means for its culture must be an ordering of our life towards harmony with its ideal in the mind of God. As he that is willing to do the will of the Father, shall know of the doctrine, so, we doubt not, he that will do the will of The Poet, shall behold the Beautiful. For all is God's; and the man who is growing into harmony with His will, is growing into harmony with himself; all the hidden glories of his being are coming out into the light of humble consciousness; so that at the last he shall be a pure microcosm, faithfully reflecting, after his manner, the mighty macrocosm. We believe, therefore, that nothing will do so much for the intellect or the imagination as *being good* -- we do not mean after any formula or any creed, but simply after the faith of Him who did the will of his Father in heaven.

But if we speak of direct means for the culture of the imagination, the whole is comprised in two words -- food and exercise. If you want strong arms, take animal food, and row. Feed your imagination with food convenient for it, and exercise it, not in the contortions of the acrobat, but in the movements of the gymnast. And first for the food.

Goethe has told us that the way to develop the aesthetic faculty is to have constantly before our eyes, that is, in the room we most frequent, some work of the best attainable art. This will teach us to refuse the evil and choose the good. It will plant itself in our minds and become our counsellor. Involuntarily, unconsciously, we shall compare with its perfection everything that comes before us for judgment. Now, although no better advice could be given, it involves one danger, that of narrowness. And not easily, in dread of this danger, would one change his tutor, and so procure variety of instruction. But in the culture of the imagination, books, although not the only, are the readiest means of supplying the food convenient for it, and a hundred books may be had where even one work of art of the right sort is unattainable, seeing such must be of some size as well as of thorough excellence. And in variety alone is safety from the danger of the convenient food becoming the inconvenient model.

Let us suppose, then, that one who himself justly estimates the imagination is anxious to develop its operation in his child. No doubt the best beginning, especially if the child be young, is an acquaintance with nature, in which let him be encouraged to observe vital phenomena, to put things together, to speculate from what he sees to what he does not see. But let earnest care be taken that upon no matter shall he go on talking foolishly. Let him be as fanciful as he may, but let him not, even in his fancy, sin against fancy's sense; for fancy has its laws as certainly as the most ordinary business of life. When he is silly, let him know it and be ashamed.

But where this association with nature is but occasionally possible, recourse must be had to literature. In books, we not only have store of all results of the imagination, but in them, as in her workshop, we may behold her embodying before our very eyes, in music of speech, in wonder of words, till her work, like a golden dish set with shining jewels, and adorned by the hands of the cunning workmen, stands finished before us. In this kind, then, the best must be set before the learner, that he may eat and not be satisfied; for the finest products of the imagination are of the best nourishment for the beginnings of that imagination. And the mind of the teacher must mediate between the work of art and the mind of the pupil, bringing them together in the vital contact of intelligence; directing the observation to the lines of expression, the points of force; and helping the mind to repose upon the whole, so that no separable beauties shall lead to a neglect of the scope -- that is the shape or form complete. And ever he must seek to *show* excellence rather than talk about it, giving the thing itself, that it may grow into the mind, and not a eulogy of his own upon the thing; isolating the point worthy of remark rather than making many remarks upon the point.

Especially must he endeavour to show the spiritual scaffolding or skeleton of any work of art; those main ideas upon which the shape is constructed, and around which the rest group as ministering dependencies.

But he will not, therefore, pass over that intellectual structure without which the other could not be manifested. He will not forget the builder while he admires the architect. While he dwells with delight on the relation of the peculiar arch to the meaning of the whole cathedral, he will not think it needless to explain the principles on which it is constructed, or even how those principles are carried out in actual process. Neither yet will the tracery of its windows, the foliage of its crockets, or the fretting of its mouldings be forgotten. Every beauty will have its word, only all beauties will be subordinated to the final beauty -- that is, the unity of the whole.

Thus doing, he shall perform the true office of friendship. He will introduce his pupil into the society which he himself prizes most, surrounding him with the genial presence of the high-minded, that this good company may work its own kind in him who frequents it.

But he will likewise seek to turn him aside from such company, whether of books or of men, as might tend to lower his reverence, his choice, or his standard. He will, therefore, discourage indiscriminate reading, and that worse than waste which consists in skimming the books of a circulating library. He knows that if a book is worth reading at all, it is worth reading well; and that, if it is not worth reading, it is only to the most accomplished reader that it *can* be worth skimming. He will seek to make him discern, not merely between the good and the evil, but between the good and the not so good. And this not for the sake of sharpening the intellect, still less of generating that self-satisfaction which is the closest attendant upon criticism, but for the sake of choosing the best path and the best companions upon it. A spirit of criticism for the sake of distinguishing only, or, far worse, for the sake of having one's opinion ready upon demand, is not merely repulsive to all true thinkers, but is, in itself, destructive of all thinking. A spirit of criticism for the sake of the truth -- a spirit that does not start from its chamber at every noise, but waits till its presence is desired -- cannot, indeed, garnish the house, but can sweep it clean. Were there enough of such wise criticism, there would be ten times the study of the best writers of the past, and perhaps one-tenth of the admiration for the ephemeral productions of the day. A gathered mountain of misplaced worships would be swept into the sea by the study of one good book; and while what was good in an inferior book would still be admired, the relative position of the book would be altered and its influence lessened.

Speaking of true learning, Lord Bacon says: "It taketh away vain admiration of anything, which is the root of all weakness."[38]

---

[38] Bacon, *The Advancement of Learning*, V1.viii.1

The right teacher would have his pupil easy to please, but ill to satisfy; ready to enjoy, unready to embrace; keen to discover beauty, slow to say, "Here I will dwell."

But he will not confine his instructions to the region of art. He will encourage him to read history with an eye eager for the dawning figure of the past. He will especially show him that a great part of the Bible is only thus to be understood; and that the constant and consistent way of God, to be discovered in it, is in fact the key to all history.

In the history of individuals, as well, he will try to show him how to put sign and token together, constructing not indeed a whole, but a probable suggestion of the whole.

And, again, while showing him the reflex of nature in the poets, he will not be satisfied without sending him to Nature herself; urging him in country rambles to keep open eyes for the sweet fashionings and blendings of her operation around him; and in city walks to watch the "human face divine."[39]

Once more: he will point out to him the essential difference between reverie and thought; between dreaming and imagining. He will teach him not to mistake fancy, either in himself or in others, for imagination, and to beware of hunting after resemblances that carry with them no interpretation.

Such training is not solely fitted for the possible development of artistic faculty. Few, in this world, will ever be able to utter what they feel. Fewer still will be able to utter it in forms of their own. Nor is it necessary that there should be many such. But it is necessary that all should feel. It is necessary that all should understand and imagine the good; that all should begin, at least, to follow and find out God.

"The glory of God is to conceal a thing, but the glory of the king is to find it out," says Solomon.[40] "As if," remarks Bacon on the passage,

> according to the innocent play of children, the Divine
> Majesty took delight to hide his works, to the end to have

---

[39] John Milton, *Paradise Lost*, Book 3, Line 44.

[40] Proverbs 25:2

them found out; and as if kings could not obtain a greater honour than to be God's playfellows in that game.[41]

One more quotation from the book of Ecclesiastes, setting forth both the necessity we are under to imagine, and the comfort that our imagining cannot outstrip God's making.

> I have seen the travail which God hath given to the sons of men to be exercised in it. He hath made everything beautiful in his time; also he hath set the world in their heart, so that no man can find out the work that God maketh from the beginning to the end.[42]

Thus to be playfellows with God in this game, the little ones may gather their daisies and follow their painted moths; the child of the kingdom may pore upon the lilies of the field, and gather faith as the birds of the air their food from the leafless hawthorn, ruddy with the stores God has laid up for them; and the man of science[43]

> May sit and rightly spell
> Of every star that heaven doth shew,
> And every herb that sips the dew;
> Till old experience do attain To something like prophetic strain.[44]

---

[41] Francis Bacon, "Advancement of Learning" in *The Works of Francis Bacon* (1884) Vol 1, Book 1, 176.

[42] Ecclesiastes 3:9-10.

[43] Matthew 6:25-34, Luke 12:22-32

[44] John Milton, "Penseroso," lines 170-174.

The Imagination: Its Function and Its Culture

A Sketch of Individual Development

"I wish I had thought to watch when God was making me!" said a child once to his mother. "Only," he added, "I was not made till I was finished, so I couldn't." We cannot recall whence we came, nor tell how we began to be. We know approximately how far back we can remember, but have no idea how far back we may not have forgotten. Certainly we knew once much that we have forgotten now. My own earliest definable memory is of a great funeral of one of the Dukes of Gordon, when I was between two and three years of age.[1] Surely my first knowledge was not of death. I must have known much and many things before, although that seems my earliest memory. As in what we foolishly call maturity, so in the dawn of consciousness, both before and after it has begun to be buttressed with *self*-consciousness, each succeeding consciousness dims -- often obliterates -- that which went before, and with regard to our past as well as our future, imagination and faith must step into the place vacated of knowledge. We are aware, and we know that we are aware, but when or how we began to be aware, is wrapt in a mist that deepens on the one side into deepest night, and on the other brightens into the full assurance of existence. Looking back we can but dream, looking forward we lose ourselves in speculation; but we may both speculate and dream, for all speculation is not false, and all dreaming is not of the unreal. What may we fairly imagine as to the inward condition of the child before the first moment of which his memory affords him testimony?

It is one, I venture to say, of absolute, though, no doubt, largely negative faith. Neither memory of pain that is past, nor apprehension of pain to come, once arises to give him the smallest concern. In some way, doubtless very vague, for his being itself is a border -- land of awful mystery, he is aware of being surrounded, enfolded with an

---

[1] The Duke of Gordon MacDonald is referring to is likely Alexander Gordon, 4th Duke of Gordon (1743-1827).

atmosphere of love; the sky over him is his mother's face; the earth that nourishes him is his mother's bosom. The source, the sustentation, the defence of his being, the endless mediation betwixt his needs and the things that supply them, are all one. There is no type so near the highest idea of relation to a God, as that of the child to his mother. Her face is God, her bosom Nature, her arms are Providence -- all love -- one love -- to him an undivided bliss.

The region beyond him he regards from this vantage -- ground of unquestioned security. There things may come and go, rise and vanish -- he neither desires nor bemoans them. Change may grow swift, its swiftness grow fierce, and pass into storm: to him storm is calm; his haven is secure; his rest cannot be broken: he is accountable for nothing, knows no responsibility. Conscience is not yet awake, and there is no conflict. His waking is full of sleep, yet his very being is enough for him.

But all the time his mother lives in the hope of his growth. In the present babe, her heart broods over the coming boy -- the unknown marvel closed in the visible germ. Let mothers lament as they will over the change from childhood to maturity, which of them would not grow weary of nursing for ever a child in whom no live law of growth kept unfolding an infinite change! The child knows nothing of growth -- desires none -- but grows. Within him is the force of a power he can no more resist than the peach can refuse to swell and grow ruddy in the sun. By slow, inappreciable, indivisible accretion and outfolding, he is lifted, floated, drifted on towards the face of the awful mirror in which he must encounter his first foe -- must front himself.

By degrees he has learned that the world is around, and not within him -- that he is apart, and that is apart; from consciousness he passes to self-consciousness. This is a second birth, for now a higher life begins. When a man not only lives, but knows that he lives, then first the possibility of a real life commences. By *real life*, I mean life which has a share in its own existence.

For now, towards the world around him -- the world that is not his mother, and, actively at least, neither loves him nor ministers to him, reveal themselves certain relations, initiated by fancies, desires, preferences, that arise within himself -- reasonable or not matters little: -- founded in reason, they can in no case be *devoid* of reason. Every object concerned in these relations presents itself to the man as lovely, desirable, good, or ugly, hateful, bad; and through these relations, obscure and imperfect, and to a being weighted with a strong faculty for mistake, begins to be revealed the existence and force of Being other and higher than his own, recognized as *Will*, and first of all in its opposition to his desires. Thereupon begins the strife without which there never was, and, I presume, never can be, any growth, any progress; and the first result is what I may call the third birth of the human being.

The first opposing glance of the mother wakes in the child not only answering opposition, which is as the rudimentary sac of his own coming will, but a new something, to which for long he needs no name, so natural does it seem, so entirely a portion of his being, even when most he refuses to listen to and obey it. This new something -- we call it *Conscience* -- sides with his mother, and causes its presence and judgment to be felt not only before but after the event, so that he soon comes to know that it is well with him or ill with him as he obeys or disobeys it. And now he not only knows, not only knows that he knows, but knows he knows that he knows -- knows that he is self-conscious -- that he has a conscience. With the first sense of resistance to it, the power above him has drawn nearer, and the deepest within him has declared itself on the side of the highest without him. At one and the same moment, the heaven of his childhood has, as it were, receded and come nigher. He has run from under it, but it claims him. It is farther, yet closer -- immeasurably closer: he feels on his being the grasp and hold of his mother's. Through the higher individuality he becomes aware of his own. Through the assertion of his mother's will, his own begins to awake. He becomes conscious of himself as capable of action -- of doing or of not doing; his responsibility has begun.

He slips from her lap; he travels from chair to chair; he puts his circle round the room; he dares to cross the threshold; he braves the precipice of the stair; he takes the greatest step that, according to George Herbert, is possible to man -- that out of doors, changing the house for the universe; he runs from flower to flower in the garden; crosses the road; wanders, is lost, is found again.[2] His powers expand, his activity increases; he goes to school, and meets other boys like himself; new objects of strife are discovered, new elements of strife developed; new desires are born, fresh impulses urge. The old heaven,

---

[2] George Herbert (1593-1633) was an English poet and clergyman.

the face and will of his mother, recede farther and farther; a world of men, which he foolishly thinks a nobler as it is a larger world, draws him, claims him. More or less he yields. The example and influence of such as seem to him more than his mother like himself, grow strong upon him. His conscience speaks louder. And here, even at this early point in his history, what I might call his fourth birth *may* begin to take place: I mean the birth in him of the Will -- the real Will -- not the pseudo-will, which is the mere Desire, swayed of impulse, selfishness, or one of many a miserable motive. When the man, listening to his conscience, wills and does the right, irrespective of inclination as of consequence, then is the man free, the universe open before him. He is born from above. To him conscience needs never speak aloud, needs never speak twice; to him her voice never grows less powerful, for he never neglects what she commands. And when he becomes aware that he can will his will, that God has given him a share in essential life, in the causation of his own being, then is he a man indeed. I say, even here this birth may begin; but with most it takes years not a few to complete it. For, the power of the mother having waned, the power of the neighbour is waxing. If the boy be of common clay, that is, of clay willing to accept dishonour, this power of the neighbour over him will increase and increase, till individuality shall have vanished from him, and what his friends, what society, what the trade or the profession say, will be to him the rule of life. With such, however, I have to do no more than with the deaf dead, who sleep too deep for words to reach them.

My typical child of man is not of such. He is capable not of being influenced merely, but of influencing -- and first of all of influencing himself; of taking a share in his own making; of determining actively, not by mere passivity, what he shall be and become; for he never ceases to pay at least a little heed, however poor and intermittent, to the voice of his conscience, and to-day he pays more heed than he did yesterday.

Long ere now the joy of space, of room, has laid hold upon him -- the more powerfully if he inhabit a wild and broken region. The human animal delights in motion and change, motions of his members even violent, and swiftest changes of place. It is as if he would lay hold of the infinite by ceaseless abandonment and choice of a never -- abiding stand -- point, as if he would lay hold of strength by the consciousness of the strength he has. He is full of unrest. He must know what lies on the farther shore of every river, see how the world looks from every hill: *What is behind? What is beyond?* is his constant cry. To learn, to gather into himself, is his longing. Nor do many years pass thus, it may be not many months, ere the world begins to come alive around him. He begins to feel that the stars are strange, that the moon is sad, that the sunrise is mighty. He begins to see in them all the something men call beauty. He will lie on the sunny bank and gaze into the blue heaven till his soul seems to float abroad and mingle with the infinite made visible, with the boundless condensed into colour and shape. The rush of the water through the still twilight, under the faint gleam of the exhausted west, makes in his ears a melody he is almost aware he cannot understand. Dissatisfied with his emotions he desires a deeper waking, longs for a greater beauty, is troubled with the stirring in his bosom of an unknown ideal of Nature. Nor is it an ideal of Nature alone that is forming within him. A far more precious thing, a human ideal namely, is in his soul, gathering to itself shape and consistency. The wind that at night fills him with sadness -- he cannot tell why, in the daytime haunts him like a wild consciousness of strength which has neither difficulty nor danger enough to spend itself upon. He would be a champion of the weak, a friend to the great; for both he would fight -- a merciless foe to every oppressor of his kind. He would be rich that he might help, strong that he might rescue, brave -- that he counts himself already, for he has not proved his own weakness. In the first encounter he fails, and the bitter cup of shame and confusion of face, wholesome and saving, is handed him from the well of life. He is not yet capable of understanding that one such as he, filled with the glory and not the duty of victory, could not but fail, and therefore ought to fail; but his dismay and chagrin are soothed by the forgetfulness the days and nights bring, gently wiping out the sins that are past, that the young life may have a fresh chance, as we say, and begin again unburdened by the weight of a too much present failure.

And now, probably at school, or in the first months of his college -- life, a new phase of experience begins. He has wandered over the border of what is commonly called science, and the marvel of facts multitudinous, strung upon the golden threads of law, has laid hold upon him. His intellect is seized and possessed by a new spirit. For a time knowledge is pride; the mere consciousness of knowing is the reward of its labour; the ever recurring, ever passing contact of mind with a new fact is a joy full of excitement, and promises an endless delight. But ever the thing that is known sinks into insignificance, save as a step of the endless stair on which he is climbing -- whither he knows not; the unknown draws him; the new fact touches his mind, flames up in the contact, and drops dark, a mere fact, on the heap below. Even the grandeur of law as law, so far from adding fresh consciousness to his life, causes it no small suffering and loss. For at the entrance of Science, nobly and gracefully as she bears herself, young Poetry shrinks back startled, dismayed. Poetry is true as Science, and Science is holy as Poetry; but young Poetry is timid and Science is fearless, and bears with her a colder atmosphere than the other has yet learned to brave. It is not that Madam Science shows any antagonism to Lady Poetry; but the atmosphere and plane on which alone they can meet as friends who understand each other, is the mind and heart of the sage, not of the boy. The youth gazes on the face of Science, cold, clear, beautiful; then, turning, looks for his friend -- but, alas! Poetry has fled. With a great pang at the heart he rushes abroad to find her, but descries only the rainbow glimmer of her skirt on the far horizon. At night, in his dreams, she returns, but never for a season may he look on her face of loveliness. What, alas! have evaporation, caloric, atmosphere, refraction, the prism, and the second planet of our system, to do with "sad Hesper o'er the buried sun?"[3] From quantitative analysis how shall he turn again to "the rime of the ancient mariner," and "the moving moon" that "went up the sky, and nowhere did abide"?[4] From his window he gazes across the sands to the mightily troubled ocean: "What is the storm to me any more!" he cries; "it is but the clashing of countless water-drops!" He finds relief in the discovery that, the moment you place man in the midst of it, the clashing of water-drops becomes a storm, terrible to heart and brain: human thought and feeling, hope, fear, love, sacrifice, make the motions of nature alive with mystery and the shadows of destiny. The relief, however, is but partial, and may be but temporary; for what if this mingling of man and Nature in the mind of man be but the casting of a coloured shadow over her cold indifference? What if she means nothing -- never was meant to mean anything! What if in truth "we receive but what we give, and in our life alone doth Nature live!" What

---

[3] Alfred Tennyson, "In Memoriam A. H. H. OBIIT MDCCCXXXIII: 121," line 1.

[4] Samuel Taylor Coleridge, "The Rime of the Ancient Mariner," (1834), IV.40.

if the language of metaphysics as well as of poetry be drawn, not from Nature at all, but from human fancy concerning her!

At length, from the unknown, whence himself he came, appears an angel to deliver him from this horror -- this stony look -- ah, God! of soulless law. The woman is on her way whose part it is to meet him with a life other than his own, at once the complement of his, and the visible presentment of that in it which is beyond his own understanding. The enchantment of what we specially call *love* is upon him -- a deceiving glamour, say some, showing what is not, an opening of the eyes, say others, revealing that of which a man had not been aware: men will still be divided into those who believe that the horses of fire and the chariots of fire are ever present at their need of them, and those who class the prophet and the drunkard in the same category as the fools of their own fancies. But what this love is, he who thinks he knows least understands. Let foolish maidens and vulgar youths simper and jest over it as they please, it is one of the most potent mysteries of the living God. The man who can love a woman and remain a lover of his wretched self, is fit only to be cast out with the broken potsherds of the city, as one in whom the very salt has lost its savour. With this love in his heart, a man puts on at least the vision robes of the seer, if not the singing robes of the poet. Be he the paltriest human animal that ever breathed, for the time, and in his degree, he rises above himself. His nature so far clarifies itself, that here and there a truth of the great world will penetrate, sorely dimmed, through the fog-laden, self-shadowed atmosphere of his microcosm. For the time, I repeat, he is not a lover only, but something of a friend, with a reflex touch of his own far -- off childhood. To the youth of my history, in the light of his love -- a light that passes outward from the eyes of the lover -- the world grows alive again, yea radiant as an infinite face. He sees the flowers as he saw them in boyhood, recovering from an illness of all the winter, only they have a yet deeper glow, a yet fresher delight, a yet more unspeakable soul. He becomes pitiful over them, and not willingly breaks their stems, to hurt the life he more than half believes they share with him. He cannot think anything created only for him, any more than only for itself. Nature is no longer a mere contention of forces, whose heaven and whose hell in one is the dull peace of an equilibrium; but a struggle, through splendour of colour, graciousness of form, and evasive vitality of motion and sound, after an utterance hard to find, and never found but marred by the imperfection of the small and weak that would embody and set forth the great and mighty. The waving of the tree -- tops is the billowy movement of a hidden delight. The sun lifts his head with intent to be glorious. No day lasts too long, no night comes too soon: the twilight is woven of shadowy arms that draw the loving to the bosom of the Night. In the woman, the infinite after which he thirsts is given him for his own.

Man's occupation with himself turns his eyes from the great life beyond his threshold: when love awakes, he forgets himself for a time, and many a glimpse of strange truth finds its way through his windows, blocked no longer by the shadow of himself. He may now catch even a glimpse of the possibilities of his own being -- may dimly perceive for a moment the image after which he was made. But alas! too soon, self, radiant of darkness, awakes; every window becomes opaque with shadow, and the man is again a prisoner. For it is not the highest word alone that the cares of this world, the deceitfulness of riches, and the lust of other things entering in, choke, and render unfruitful. Waking from the divine vision, if that can be called waking which is indeed dying into the common day, the common man regards it straightway as a foolish dream; the wise man believes in it still, holds fast by the memory of the vanished glory, and looks to have it one day again a present portion of the light of his life. He knows that, because of the imperfection and dullness and weakness of his nature, after every vision follow the inclosing clouds, with the threat of an ever during dark; knows that, even if the vision could tarry, it were not well, for the sake of that which must yet be done with him, yet be made of him, that it should tarry. But the youth whose history I am following is not like the former, nor as yet like the latter.

From whatever cause, then, whether of fault, of natural law, or of supernal will, the flush that seemed to promise the dawn of an eternal day, shrinks and fades, though, with him, like the lagging skirt of the sunset in the northern west, it does not vanish, but travels on, a withered pilgrim, all the night, at the long last to rise the aureole of the eternal Aurora. And now new paths entice him -- or old paths opening fresh horizons. With stronger thews and keener nerves he turns again to the visible around him.[5] The changelessness amid change, the law

---

[5] "Thews" is a word that came to be understood in Middle English as "good bodily proportions, muscular development."

amid seeming disorder, the unity amid units, draws him again. He begins to descry the indwelling poetry of science. The untiring forces at work in measurable yet inconceivable spaces of time and room, fill his soul with an awe that threatens to uncreate him with a sense of littleness; while, on the other side, the grandeur of their operations fills him with such an informing glory, the mere presence of the mighty facts, that he no more thinks of himself, but in humility is great, and knows it not. Rapt spectator, seer entranced under the magic wand of Science, he beholds the billions of billions of miles of incandescent vapour begin a slow, scarce perceptible revolution, gradually grow swift, and gather an awful speed. He sees the vapour, as it whirls, condensing through slow eternities to a plastic fluidity. He notes ring after ring part from the circumference of the mass, break, rush together into a globe, and the glowing ball keep on through space with the speed of its parent bulk. It cools and still cools and condenses, but still fiercely glows. Presently -- after tens of thousands of years is the creative *presently* -- arises fierce contention betwixt the glowing heart and its accompanying atmosphere. The latter invades the former with antagonistic element. He listens in his soul, and hears the rush of ever descending torrent rains, with the continuous roaring shock of their evanishment in vapour -- to turn again to water in the higher regions, and again rush to the attack upon the citadel of fire. He beholds the slow victory of the water at last, and the great globe, now glooming in a cloak of darkness, covered with a wildly boiling sea -- not boiling by figure of speech, under contending forces of wind and tide, but boiling high as the hills to come, with veritable heat. He sees the rise of the wrinkles we call hills and mountains, and from their sides the avalanches of water to the lower levels. He sees race after race of living things appear, as the earth becomes, for each new and higher kind, a passing home; and he watches the succession of terrible convulsions dividing kind from kind, until at length the kind he calls his own arrives. Endless are the visions of material grandeur unfathomable, awaked in his soul by the bare facts of external existence.

But soon comes a change. So far as he can see or learn, all the motion, all the seeming dance, is but a rush for death, a panic flight

---

"Thew," *Merriam-Webster Dictionary*, accessed July 15, 2021, https://www.merriam-webster.com/dictionary/thew

into the moveless silence. The summer wind, the tropic tornado, the softest tide, the fiercest storm, are alike the tumultuous conflict of forces, rushing, and fighting as they rush, into the arms of eternal negation. On and on they hurry -- down and down, to a cold stirless solidity, where wind blows not, water flows not, where the seas are not merely tideless and beat no shores, but frozen cleave with frozen roots to their gulfy basin. All things are on the steep-sloping path to final evanishment, uncreation, non-existence. He is filled with horror -- not so much of the dreary end, as at the weary hopelessness of the path thitherward. Then a dim light breaks upon him, and with it a faint hope revives, for he seems to see in all the forms of life, innumerably varied, a spirit rushing upward from death -- a something in escape from the terror of the downward cataract, of the rest that knows not peace. "Is it not," he asks, "the soaring of the silver dove of life from its potsherd -- bed -- the heavenward flight of some higher and incorruptible thing? Is not vitality, revealed in growth, itself an unending resurrection?"

The vision also of the oneness of the universe, ever reappearing through the vapours of question, helps to keep hope alive in him. To find, for instance, the law of the relation of the arrangements of the leaves on differing plants, correspond to the law of the relative distances of the planets in approach to their central sun, wakes in him that hope of a central Will, which alone can justify one ecstatic throb at any seeming loveliness of the universe. For without the hope of such a centre, delight is unreason -- a mockery not such as the skeleton at the Egyptian feast, but such rather as a crowned corpse at a feast of skeletons. Life without the higher glory of the unspeakable, the atmosphere of a God, is not life, is not worth living. He would rather cease to be, than walk the dull level of the commonplace -- than live the unideal of men in whose company he can take no pleasure -- men who are as of a lower race, whom he fain would lift, who will not rise, but for whom as for himself he would cherish the hope they do their best to kill. Those who seem to him great, recognize the unseen -- believe the roots of science to be therein hid -- regard the bringing forth into sight of the things that are invisible as the end of all Art and every art -- judge the true leader of men to be him who leads them closer to the essential facts of their being. Alas for his love and his hope, alas for himself, if the visible should exist for its own sake only! -- if the face of a flower means nothing -- appeals to no region beyond the scope of the science that would unveil its growth. He cannot believe that its structure exists for the sake of its laws; that would be to build for the sake of its joints a scaffold where no house was to stand. Those who put their faith in Science are trying to live in the scaffold of the house invisible.

He finds harbour and comfort at times in the written poetry of his fellows. He delights in analyzing and grasping the thought that informs the utterance. For a moment, the fine figure, the delicate phrase, make him jubilant and strong; but the jubilation and the strength soon pass, for it is not any of the *forms*, even of the thought -- forms of truth that can give rest to his soul.

History attracts him little, for he is not able to discover by its records the operation of principles yielding hope for his race. Such there may be, but he does not find them. What hope for the rising wave that knows in its rise only its doom to sink, and at length be dashed on the low shore of annihilation?

But the time would fail me to follow the doubling of the soul coursed by the hounds of Death, or to set down the forms innumerable in which the golden Haemony springs in its path,[6]

> *Of sovran use*
> *'Gainst all enchantments,*
> *mildew blast, or damp.*[7]

And now the shadows are beginning to lengthen towards the night, which, whether there be a following morn or no, is the night, and spreads out the wings of darkness. And still as it approaches the more aware grows the man of a want that differs from any feeling I have already sought to describe -- a sense of insecurity, in no wise the same as the doubt of life beyond the grave -- a need more profound even than that which cries for a living Nature. And now he plainly knows, that, all his life, like a conscious duty unfulfilled, this sense has

---

[6] "Haemony" in John Milton's *Comus* is a "bright golden flower" that Hermes once gave to Ulysses. (*Comus*, lines 632-640) There has been much debate over the meaning of the flower as a symbol. It has been thought by various writers to symbolize Christian redemption, Christian temperance, and Christian knowledge. John Ulreich suggests that it is a symbol of transformation.

John C. Ulreich, ""A Bright Golden Flow'r: Haemony as a Symbol of Transformation," *Studies in English Literature, 1500-1900* 17, no. 1 (1977): 119.

[7] John Milton, *Comus*, lines 639-640.

haunted his path, ever and anon descending and clinging, a cold mist, about his heart. What if this lack was indeed the root of every other anxiety! Now freshly revived, this sense of not having, of something, he knows not what, for lack of which his being is in pain at its own incompleteness, never leaves him more. And with it the terror has returned and grows, lest there should be no Unseen Power, as his fathers believed, and his mother taught him, filling all things and *meaning* all things -- no Power with whom, in his last extremity, awaits him a final refuge. With the quickening doubt falls a tenfold blight on the world of poetry, both that in Nature and that in books. Far worse than that early chill which the assertions of science concerning what it knows, cast upon his inexperienced soul, is now the shivering death which its pretended denials concerning what it knows not, send through all his vital frame. The soul departs from the face of beauty, when the eye begins to doubt if there be any soul behind it; and now the man feels like one I knew, affected with a strange disease, who saw in the living face always the face of a corpse. What can the world be to him who lives for thought, if there be no supreme and perfect Thought, -- none but such poor struggles after thought as he finds in himself? Take the eternal thought from the heart of things, no longer can any beauty be real, no more can shape, motion, aspect of nature have significance in itself, or sympathy with human soul. At best and most the beauty he thought he saw was but the projected perfection of his own being, and from himself as the crown and summit of things, the soul of the man shrinks with horror: it is the more imperfect being who knows the least his incompleteness, and for whom, seeing so little beyond himself, it is easiest to imagine himself the heart and apex of things, and rejoice in the fancy. The killing power of a godless science returns upon him with tenfold force. The ocean -- tempest is once more a mere clashing of innumerable water -- drops; the green and amber sadness of the evening sky is a mockery of sorrow; his own soul and its sadness is a mockery of himself. There is nothing in the sadness, nothing in the mockery. To tell him as comfort, that in his own thought lives the meaning if nowhere else, is mockery worst of all; for if there be no truth in them, if these things be no embodiment, to make them serve as such is to put a candle in a death's -- head to light the dying through the place of tombs. To his former foolish fancy a primrose might preach a childlike trust; the untoiling lilies might from their field cast seeds of a higher growth into his troubled heart; now they are no better than the colour the painter leaves behind him on the doorpost of his workshop, when, the day's labour over, he wipes his brush on it ere he depart for the night.[8] The look in the eyes of his dog, happy in that he is short -- lived, is one of infinite sadness. All graciousness must henceforth be a sorrow: it has to go with the sunsets. That a thing must cease takes from it the joy of even an aeonian endurance -- for its *kind* is mortal; it belongs to the nature of things that cannot live.[9] The sorrow is not so much that it shall perish as that it could not live -- that it is not in its nature a real, that is, an eternal thing. His children are shadows -- their life a dance, a sickness, a corruption. The very element of unselfishness, which, however feeble and beclouded it may be, yet exists in all love, in giving life its only dignity adds to its sorrow. Nowhere at the root of things is love -- it is only a something that came after, some sort of fungous excrescence in the hearts of men grown helplessly superior to their origin.[10] Law, nothing but cold, impassive, material law, is the root of things -- lifeless happily, so not knowing itself, else were it a demon instead of a creative nothing. Endeavour is paralyzed in him. "Work for posterity," says he of the skyless philosophy; answers the man, "How can I work without hope? Little heart have I to labour, where labour is so little help. What can I do for my children that would render their life less hopeless than my own! Give me all you would secure for them, and my life would be to me but the worse mockery. The true end of labour would be, to lessen the number doomed to breathe the breath of this despair."

Straightway he develops another and a deeper mood. He turns and regards himself. Suspicion or sudden insight has directed the look. And there, in himself, he discovers such imperfection, such wrong, such shame, such weakness, as cause him to cry out, "It were well I should cease! Why should I mourn after life? Where were the good of prolonging it in a being like me? 'What should such fellows as I do

----

[8] The "untoiling lilies" is a reference to the words of Jesus to his followers about God's care for them found in Matthew 6:25-34 and Luke 12:22-32.

[9] Aeonian: "lasting for an immeasurably or indefinitely long period of time. "Aeonian," Merriam-Webster Dictionary, accessed July 15, 2021 https://www.merriam-webster.com/dictionary/aeonian

[10] Excrescence: "a projection or outgrowth especially when abnormal." "Excrescence," *Merriam-Webster Dictionary*, accessed July 15, 2021, https://www.merriam-webster.com/dictionary/excrescence.

crawling between heaven and earth!'" Such insights, when they come, the seers do their best, in general, to obscure; suspicion of themselves they regard as a monster, and would stifle. They resent the waking of such doubt. Any attempt at the raising in them of their buried best they regard as an offence against intercourse. A man takes his social life in his hand who dares it. Few therefore understand the judgment of Hamlet upon himself; the common reader is so incapable of imagining he could mean it of his own general character as a man, that he attributes the utterance to shame for the postponement of a vengeance, which indeed he must have been such as his critic to be capable of performing upon no better proof than he had yet had. When the man whose unfolding I would now represent, regards even his dearest love, he finds it such a poor, selfish, low-lived thing, that in his heart he shames himself before his children and his friends. How little labour, how little watching, how little pain has he endured for their sakes! He reads of great things in this kind, but in himself he does not find them. How often has he not been wrongfully displeased -- wrathful with the innocent! How often has he not hurt a heart more tender than his own! Has he ever once been faithful to the height of his ideal? Is his life on the whole a thing to regard with complacency, or to be troubled exceedingly concerning? Beyond him rise and spread infinite seeming possibilities -- height beyond height, glory beyond glory, each rooted in and rising from his conscious being, but alas! where is any hope of ascending them? These hills of peace, "in a season of calm weather," seem to surround and infold him, as a land in which he could dwell at ease and at home: surely among them lies the place of his birth![11] -- while against their purity and grandeur the being of his consciousness shows miserable -- dark, weak, and undefined -- a shadow that would fain be substance -- a dream that would gladly be born into the light of reality. But alas if the whole thing be only in himself -- if the vision be a dream of nothing, a revelation of lies, the outcome of that which, helplessly existent, is yet not created, therefore cannot create -- if not the whole thing only be a dream of the impotent, but the impotent be himself but a dream -- a dream of his own -- a self-dreamed dream -- with no master of dreams to whom to cry! Where then the cherished

---

[11] William Wordsworth, "Ode: Intimations of Immortality from Recollections of Early Childhood" in *Poems* (1807).

hope of one day atoning for his wrongs to those who loved him! -- they are nowhere -- vanished for ever, upmingled and dissolved in the primeval darkness! If truth be but the hollow of a sphere, ah, never shall he cast himself before them, to tell them that now at last, after long years of revealing separation, he knows himself and them, and that now the love of them is a part of his very being -- to implore their forgiveness on the ground that he hates, despises, contemns, and scorns the self that showed them less than absolute love and devotion! Never thus shall he lay his being bare to their eyes of love! They do not even rest, for they do not and will not know it. There is no voice nor hearing in them, and how can there be in him any heart to live! The one comfort left him is, that, unable to follow them, he shall yet die and cease, and fare as they -- go also nowhither!

To a man under the dismay of existence dissociated from power, unrooted in, unshadowed by a creating Will, who is Love, the Father of Man -- to him who knows not being and God together, the idea of death -- a death that knows no reviving, must be, and ought to be the blessedest thought left him. "O land of shadows!" well may such a one cry! "land where the shadows love to ecstatic self-loss, yet forget, and love no more! land of sorrows and despairs, that sink the soul into a deeper Tophet than death has ever sounded![12] broken kaleidoscope! shaken camera! promiser, speaking truth to the ear, but lying to the sense! land where the heart of my friend is sorrowful as my heart -- the more sorrowful that I have been but a poor and far -- off friend! land where sin is strong and righteousness faint! where love dreams mightily and walks abroad so feeble! land where the face of my father is dust, and the hand of my mother will never more caress! where my children will spend a few years of like trouble to mine, and then drop from the dream into the no -- dream! gladly, O land of sickliest shadows -- gladly, that is, with what power of gladness is in me, I take my leave of thee! Welcome the cold, pain -- soothing embrace of immortal Death! Hideous are his looks, but I love him better than Life: he is true, and will not deceive us. Nay, he only is our saviour, setting us free from the tyranny of the false that ought to be true, and sets us longing in vain."

---

[12] Tophet: another word for hell. It was the name of a shrine south of Jerusalem referred to in Jeremiah 7:31 where sacrifices were made to Moloch. "Tophet," *Merriam-Webster Dictionary*, accessed July 15, 2021 https://www.merriam-webster.com/dictionary/Tophet

But through all the man's doubts, fears, and perplexities, a certain whisper, say rather, an uncertain rumour, a vague legendary murmur, has been at the same time about, rather than in, his ears -- never ceasing to haunt his air, although hitherto he has hardly heeded it. He knows it has come down the ages, and that some in every age have been more or less influenced by a varied acceptance of it. Upon those, however, with whom he has chiefly associated, it has made no impression beyond that of a remarkable legend. It is the story of a man, represented as at least greater, stronger, and better than any other man. With the hero of this tale he has had a constantly recurring, though altogether undefined suspicion that he has something to do. It is strongest, though not even then strong, at such times when he is most aware of evil and imperfection in himself. Betwixt the two, the idea of this man and his knowledge of himself, seems to lie, dim -- shadowy, some imperative duty. He knows that the whole matter concerning the man is commemorated in many of the oldest institutions of his country, but up to this time he has shrunk from the demands which, by a kind of spiritual insight, he foresaw would follow, were he once to admit certain things to be true. He has, however, known some and read of more who by their faith in the man conquered all anxiety, doubt, and fear, lived pure, and died in gladsome hope. On the other hand, it seems to him that the faith which was once easy has now become almost an impossibility. And what is it he is called upon to believe? One says one thing, another another. Much that is asserted is simply unworthy of belief, and the foundation of the whole has in his eyes something of the look of a cunningly devised fable. Even should it be true, it cannot help him, he thinks, for it does not even touch the things that make his woe: the God the tale presents is not the being whose very existence can alone be his cure.

But he meets one who says to him, "Have you then come to your time of life, and not yet ceased to accept hearsay as ground of action -- for there is action in abstaining as well as in doing? Suppose the man in question to have taken all possible pains to be understood, does it follow of necessity that he is now or ever was fairly represented by the bulk of his followers? With such a moral distance between him and them, is it possible?"

"But the whole thing has from first to last a strange aspect!" our thinker replies.

"As to the *last* that is not yet come. And as to its *aspect*, its reality must be such as human eye could never convey to reading heart. Every human idea of it *must* be more or less wrong. And yet perhaps the truer the aspect the stranger it would be. But is it not just with ordinary things you are dissatisfied? And should not therefore the very strangeness of these to you little better than rumours incline you to examine the object of them? Will you assert that nothing strange can have to do with human affairs? Much that was once scarce credible is now so ordinary that men have grown stupid to the wonder inherent in it. Nothing around you serves your need: try what is at least of another class of phenomena. What if the things rumoured belong to a *more* natural order than these, lie nearer the roots of your dissatisfied existence, and look strange only because you have hitherto been living in the outer court, not in the *penetralia* of life?[13] The rumour has been vital enough to float down the ages, emerging from every storm: why not see for yourself what may be in it? So powerful an influence on human history, surely there will be found in it signs by which to determine whether the man understood himself and his message, or owed his apparent greatness to the deluded worship of his followers! That he has always had foolish followers none will deny, and none but a fool would judge any leader from such a fact. Wisdom as well as folly will serve a fool's purpose; he turns all into folly. I say nothing now of my own conclusions, because what you imagine my opinions are as hateful to me as to you disagreeable and foolish."

So says the friend; the man hears, takes up the old story, and says to himself, "Let me see then what I can see!"

I will not follow him through the many shadows and slow dawns by which at length he arrives at this much: A man claiming to be the Son of God says he has come to be the light of men; says, "Come to me, and I will give you rest;" says, "Follow me, and you shall find my Father; to know him is the one thing you cannot do without, for it is eternal life." He has learned from the reported words of the man, and from the man himself as in the tale presented, that the bliss of his conscious being is his Father; that his one delight is to do the will of that Father -- the only thing in his eyes worthy of being done, or worth

---

[13] "Penetralia: the innermost or most private parts." "Penetralia," *Merriam-Webster Dictionary*, accessed July 15, 2021 https://www.merriam-webster.com/dictionary/penetralia.

having done; that he would make men blessed with his own blessedness; that the cry of creation, the cry of humanity shall be answered into the deepest soul of desire; that less than the divine mode of existence, the godlike way of being, can satisfy no man, that is, make him content with his consciousness; that not this world only, but the whole universe is the inheritance of those who consent to be the children of their Father in heaven, who put forth the power of their will to be of the same sort as he; that to as many as receive him he gives power to become the sons of God; that they shall be partakers of the divine nature, of the divine joy, of the divine power -- shall have whatever they desire, shall know no fear, shall love perfectly, and shall never die; that these things are beyond the grasp of the knowing ones of the world, and to them the message will be a scorn; but that the time will come when its truth shall be apparent, to some in confusion of face, to others in joy unspeakable; only that we must beware of judging, for many that are first shall be last, and there are last that shall be first.

To find himself in such conscious as well as vital relation with the source of his being, with a Will by which his own will exists, with a Consciousness by and through which he is conscious, would indeed be the the end of all the man's ills! nor can he imagine any other, not to say better way, in which his sorrows could be met, understood and annihilated. For the ills that oppress him are both within him and without, and over each kind he is powerless. If the message were but a true one! If indeed this man knew what he talked of! But if there should be help for man from anywhere beyond him, some *one* might know it first, and may not this be the one? And if the message be so great, so perfect as this man asserts, then only a perfect, an eternal man, at home in the bosom of the Father, could know, or bring, or tell it. According to the tale, it had been from the first the intent of the Father to reveal himself to man as man, for without the knowledge of the Father after man's own modes of being, he could not grow to real manhood. The grander the whole idea, the more likely is it to be what it claims to be! and if not high as the heavens above the earth, beyond us yet within our reach, it is not for us, it cannot be true. Fact or not, the existence of a God such as Christ, a God who is a good man infinitely, is the only idea containing hope enough for man! If such a God has come to be known, marvel must surround the first news at least of the revelation of him. Because of its marvel, shall men find it in reason to turn from the gracious rumour of what, if it be true, must be the event of all events? And could marvel be lovelier than the marvel reported? But the humble men of heart alone can believe in the high -- they alone can perceive, they alone can embrace grandeur. Humility is essential greatness, the inside of grandeur.

Something of such truths the man glimmeringly sees. But in his mind awake, thereupon, endless doubts and questions. What if the whole idea of his mission was a deception born of the very goodness of the man? What if the whole matter was the invention of men pretending themselves the followers of such a man? What if it was a little truth greatly exaggerated? Only, be it what it may, less than its full idea would not be enough for the wants and sorrows that weaken and weigh him down!

He passes through many a thorny thicket of inquiry; gathers evidence upon evidence; reasons upon the goodness of the men who wrote: they might be deceived, but they dared not invent; holds with himself a thousand arguments, historical, psychical, metaphysical -- which for their setting -- forth would require volumes; hears many an opposing, many a scoffing word from men "who surely know, else would they speak?" and finds himself much where he was before. But at least he is haunting the possible borders of discovery, while those who turn their backs upon the idea are divided from him by a great gulf -- it may be of moral difference. To him there is still a grand auroral hope about the idea, and it still draws him; the others, taking the thing from merest report of opinion, look anywhere but thitherward. He who would not trust his best friend to set forth his views of life, accepts the random judgements of unknown others for a sufficing disposal of what the highest of the race have regarded as a veritable revelation from the Father of men. He sees in it therefore nothing but folly; for what he takes for the thing nowhere meets his nature. Our searcher at least holds open the door for the hearing of what voice may come to him from the region invisible: if there be truth there, he is where it will find him.

As he continues to read and reflect, the perception gradually grows clear in him, that, if there be truth in the matter, he must, first of all, and beyond all things else, give his best heed to the reported words of the man himself -- to what he says, not what is said about him, valuable as that may afterwards prove to be. And he finds that concerning these words of his, the man says, or at least plainly implies, that only the obedient, childlike soul can understand them. It follows

49

that the judgement of no man who does not obey can be received concerning them or the speaker of them -- that, for instance, a man who hates his enemy, who tells lies, who thinks to serve God and Mammon, whether he call himself a Christian or no, has not the right of an opinion concerning the Master or his words -- at least in the eyes of the Master, however it may be in his own.[14] This is in the very nature of things: obedience alone places a man in the position in which he can see so as to judge that which is above him. In respect of great truths investigation goes for little, speculation for nothing; if a man would know them, he must obey them.[15] Their nature is such that the only door into them is obedience. And the truth-seeker perceives -- which allows him no loophole of escape from life -- that what things the Son of Man requires of him, are either such as his conscience backs for just, or such as seem too great, too high for any man. But if there be help for him, it must be a help that recognizes the highest in him, and urges him to its use. Help cannot come to one made in the image of God, save in the obedient effort of what life and power are in him, for God is action. In such effort alone is it possible for need to encounter help. It is the upstretched that meets the downstretched hand. He alone who obeys can with confidence pray -- to him alone does an answer seem a thing that may come. And should anything spoken by the Son of Man seem to the seeker unreasonable, he feels in the rest such a majesty of duty as compels him to judge with regard to the other, that he has not yet perceived its true nature, or its true relation to life.

And now comes the crisis: if here the man sets himself honestly to do the thing the Son of Man tells him, he so, and so first, sets out positively upon the path which, if there be truth in these things, will conduct him to a knowledge of the whole matter; not until then is he a disciple. If the message be a true one, the condition of the knowledge of its truth is not only reasonable but an unavoidable necessity. If there be help for him, how otherways should it draw nigh? He has to be assured of the highest truth of his being: there can be no other

---

[14] Mammon is wealth and worldly possessions. Jesus warns his followers in Matthew 6:24 that they "cannot serve God and Mammon."

[15] This connection of knowing and doing as a characteristic of true faith is the topic of MacDonald's 1882 sermon titled "Faith: the Proof of the Unseen." A reading of the sermon: https://youtu.be/oyCfnOLkn1w The text available online at http://www.george-macdonald.com/etexts/faith_proof_unseen.html

assurance than that to be gained thus, and thus alone; for not only by obedience does a man come into such contact with truth as to know what it is, and in regard to truth knowledge and belief are one. That things which cannot appear save to the eye capable of seeing them, that things which cannot be recognized save by the mind of a certain development, should be examined by eye incapable, and pronounced upon by mind undeveloped, is absurd. The deliverance the message offers is a change such that the man shall *be* the rightness of which he talked: while his soul is not a hungered, athirst, aglow, a groaning after righteousness -- that is, longing to be himself honest and upright, it is an absurdity that he should judge concerning the way to this rightness, seeing that, while he walks not in it, he is and shall be a dishonest man: he knows not whither it leads and how can he know the way! What he *can* judge of is, his duty at a given moment -- and that not in the abstract, but as something to be by him *done*, neither more, nor less, nor other than *done*. Thus judging and doing, he makes the only possible step nearer to righteousness and righteous judgement; doing otherwise, he becomes the more unrighteous, the more blind. For the man who knows not God, whether he believes there is a God or not, there can be, I repeat, no judgement of things pertaining to God. To our supposed searcher, then, the crowning word of the Son of Man is this, "If any man is willing to do the will of the Father, he shall know of the doctrine, whether it be of God, or whether I speak of myself."[16]

Having thus accompanied my type to the borders of liberty, my task for the present is over. The rest let him who reads prove for himself. Obedience alone can convince. To convince without obedience I would take no bootless labour; it would be but a gain for hell. If any man call these things foolishness, his judgement is to me insignificant. If any man say he is open to conviction, I answer him he can have none but on the condition, by the means of obedience. If a man say, "The thing is not interesting to me," I ask him, "Are you following your conscience? By that, and not by the interest you take or do not take in a thing, shall you be judged. Nor will anything be said to you, or of you, in that day, whatever *that day* mean, of which your conscience will not echo every syllable."

---

[16] John 7:17

Oneness with God is the sole truth of humanity. Life parted from its causative life would be no life; it would at best be but a barrack of corruption, an outpost of annihilation. In proportion as the union is incomplete, the derived life is imperfect. And no man can be one with neighbour, child, dearest, except as he is one with his origin; and he fails of his perfection so long as there is one being in the universe he could not love.

Of all men he is bound to hold his face like a flint in witness of this truth who owes everything that makes for eternal good, to the belief that at the heart of things and causing them to be, at the centre of monad, of world, of protoplastic mass, of loving dog, and of man most cruel, is an absolute, perfect love; and that in the man Christ Jesus this love is with us men to take us home. To nothing else do I for one owe any grasp upon life. In this I see the setting right of all things. To the man who believes in the Son of God, poetry returns in a mighty wave; history unrolls itself in harmony; science shows crowned with its own aureole of holiness. There is no enlivener of the imagination, no enabler of the judgment, no strengthener of the intellect, to compare with the belief in a live Ideal, at the heart of all personality, as of every law. If there be no such live Ideal, then a falsehood can do more for the race than the facts of its being; then an unreality is needful for the development of the man in all that is real, in all that is in the highest sense true; then falsehood is greater than fact, and an idol necessary for lack of a God. They who deny cannot, in the nature of things, know what they deny. When one sees a chaos begin to put on the shape of an ordered world, he will hardly be persuaded it is by the power of a foolish notion bred in a diseased fancy.

Let the man then who would rise to the height of his being, be persuaded to test the Truth by the deed -- the highest and only test that can be applied to the loftiest of all assertions. To every man I say, "Do the truth you know, and you shall learn the truth you need to know."

St. George's Day 1564

All England knows that this year (1864) is the three hundredth since Shakspere was born. The strong probability is likewise that this month of April is that in which he first saw the earthly light. On the twenty -- sixth of April he was baptized. Whether he was born on the twenty -- third, to which effect there may once have been a tradition, we do not know; but though there is nothing to corroborate that statement, there are two facts which would incline us to believe it if we could: the one that he *died* on the twenty -- third of April, thus, as it were, completing a cycle; and the other that the twenty -- third of April is St. George's Day.[1] If there is no harm in indulging in a little fanciful sentiment about such a grand fact, we should say that certainly it was *St. George for merry England* when Shakspere was born. But had St. George been the best saint in the calendar -- which we have little enough ground for supposing he was -- it would better suit our subject to say that the Highest was thinking of his England when he sent Shakspere into it, to be a strength, a wonder, and a gladness to the nations of his earth.

But if we write thus about Shakspere, influenced only by the fashion of the day, we shall be much in the condition of those *fashionable* architects who with their vain praises built the tombs of the prophets, while they had no regard to the lessons they taught. We hope to be able to show that we have good grounds for our rejoicing in the birth of that child whom after -- years placed highest on the rocky steep of Art, up which so many of those who combine feeling and thought are always striving.

---

[1] St. George was a saint who lived in the second century. The patron saint of England, he is honored the world over for military valor and selflessness. He is perhaps best known from Jacob de Voragine's tale of St. George rescuing a princess from a dragon.

"Saint George | Facts, Legends, & Feast Day," *Encyclopedia Britannica*, accessed August 18, 2021, https://www.britannica.com/biography/Saint-George.

We can see in MacDonald's essay that the nation's affinity for both St. George and Shakespeare are so strong that both figures help define who they are as a people.

First, however, let us look at some of the more powerful of the influences into the midst of which he was born. For a child is born into the womb of the time, which indeed enclosed and fed him before he was born. Not the least subtle and potent of those influences which tend to the education of the child (in the true sense of the word *education*) are those which are brought to bear upon him *through* the mind, heart, judgement of his parents. We mean that those powers which have operated strongly upon them, have a certain concentrated operation, both antenatal and psychological, as well as educational and spiritual, upon the child. Now Shakspere was born in the sixth year of Queen Elizabeth.[2] He was the eldest son, but the third child. His father and mother must have been married not later than the year 1557, two years after Cranmer was burned at the stake, one of the two hundred who thus perished in that time of pain, resulting in the firm establishment of a reformation which, like all other changes for the better, could not be verified and secured without some form or other of the *trial by fire*.[3] Events such as then took place in every part of the country could not fail to make a strong impression upon all thinking people, especially as it was not those of high position only who were thus called upon to bear witness to their beliefs. John Shakspere and Mary Arden were in all likelihood themselves of the Protestant party; and although, as far as we know, they were never in any especial danger of being denounced, the whole of the circumstances must have tended to produce in them individually, what seems to have been characteristic of the age in which they lived, earnestness. In times such as those, people are compelled to think.

---

[2] Queen Elizabeth I (1533-1603) was queen of England from 1558-1603. Her reign was a time of ascendancy for England and it was known as the "Elizabethan Age." She was the daughter of the notorious Henry VIII and his unfortunate second wife, Anne Boleyn.

"Elizabeth I | Biography, Facts, Mother, & Death," *Encyclopedia Britannica*, accessed August 18, 2021, https://www.britannica.com/biography/Elizabeth-I.

[3] Thomas Cranmer (1489-1556) was the one of the leaders of the Reformation in England and the first archbishop of Canterbury, the leader of the Church of England. Integral in Henry VIII's break with the Roman Catholic Church and in establishing the Church of England, Cranmer was burned at the stake as a heretic by Henry's Catholic daughter, Mary I.

"Thomas Cranmer | Archbishop of Canterbury," *Encyclopedia Britannica*, accessed August 18, 2021, https://www.britannica.com/biography/Thomas-Cranmer-archbishop-of-Canterbury.

And here an interesting question occurs: Was it in part to his mother that Shakspere was indebted for that profound knowledge of the Bible which is so evident in his writings? A good many copies of the Scriptures must have been by this time, in one translation or another, scattered over the country.[4] No doubt the word was precious in those days, and hard to buy; but there might have been a copy, notwithstanding, in the house of John Shakspere, and it is possible that it was from his mother's lips that the boy first heard the Scripture tales. We have called his acquaintance with Scripture *profound*, and one peculiar way in which it manifests itself will bear out the assertion; for frequently it is the very spirit and essential aroma of the passage that he reproduces, without making any use of the words themselves. There are passages in his writings which we could not have understood but for some acquaintance with the New Testament. We will produce a few specimens of the kind we mean, confining ourselves to one play, "Macbeth."

Just mentioning the phrase, "temple-haunting martlet" (act i. scene 6), as including in it a reference to the verse, "Yea, the sparrow hath found an house, and the swallow a nest for herself, where she may lay her young, even thine altars, O Lord of hosts," we pass to the following passage, for which we do not believe there is any explanation but that suggested to us by the passage of Scripture to be cited.

Macbeth, on his way to murder Duncan, says, --

Thou sure and firm -- set earth,

Hear not my steps, which way they walk, for fear

Thy very stones prate of my whereabout,

And take the present horror from the time

Which now suits with it.[5]

---

[4] * And it seems to us probable that this diffusion of the Bible, did more to rouse the slumbering literary power of England, than any influences of foreign literature whatever.

[5] "Macbeth," Act 2, scene 1, lines 57-60.

What is meant by the last two lines? It seems to us to be just another form of the words, "For there is nothing covered, that shall not be revealed; neither hid, that shall not be known. Therefore whatsoever ye have spoken in darkness shall be heard in the light; and that which ye have spoken in the ear in closets shall be proclaimed upon the house -- tops."[6] Of course we do not mean that Macbeth is represented as having this passage in his mind, but that Shakspere had the feeling of it when he wrote thus. What Macbeth means is, "Earth, do not hear me in the dark, which is suitable to the present horror, lest the very stones prate about it in the daylight, which is not suitable to such things; thus taking 'the present horror *from* the time which now suits with it.'"[7]

Again, in the only piece of humour in the play -- if that should be called humour which, taken in its relation to the consciousness of the principal characters, is as terrible as anything in the piece -- the porter ends off his fantastic soliloquy, in which he personates the porter of hell-gate, with the words, "But this place is too cold for hell: I'll devil-porter it no further. I had thought to have let in some of all professions, that go the primrose way to the everlasting bonfire."[8] Now what else had the writer in his mind but the verse from the Sermon on the Mount, "For wide is the gate, and broad is the way, that leadeth to destruction, and many there be which go in thereat"?[9]

It may be objected that such passages as these, being of the most commonly quoted, imply no profound acquaintance with Scripture, such as we have said Shakspere possessed. But no amount of knowledge of the *words* of the Bible would be sufficient to justify the use of the word *profound.* What is remarkable in the employment of these passages, is not merely that they are so present to his mind that they come up for use in the most exciting moments of composition, but that he embodies the spirit of them in such a new form as reveals to minds saturated and deadened with the *sound* of the words, the very visual image and spiritual meaning involved in them. "*The primrose way!*" And to what?

---

[6] Luke 12:2-3

[7] This appears to be a rendition of "Macbeth," Act 2, scene 1, lines 24-28.

[8] "Macbeth," Act 2, scene 3, lines 15-18.

[9] Matthew 7:13.

We will confine ourselves to one passage more: -- --

Macbeth
Is ripe for shaking, and the powers above
Put on their instruments.[10]

In the end of the 14th chapter of the Revelation we have the words, "Thrust in thy sickle, and reap: for the time is come for thee to reap; for the harvest of the earth is ripe."[11] We suspect that Shakspere wrote, ripe *to* shaking.

The instances to which we have confined ourselves do not by any means belong to the most evident kind of proof that might be adduced of Shakspere's acquaintance with Scripture. The subject, in its ordinary aspect, has been elsewhere treated with far more fulness than our design would permit us to indulge in, even if it had not been done already. Our object has been to bring forward a few passages which seem to us to breathe the very spirit of individual passages in sacred writ, without direct use of the words themselves; and, of course, in such a case we can only appeal to the (no doubt) very various degrees of conviction which they may rouse in the minds of our readers.

But there is one singular correspondence in another *almost* literal quotation from the Gospel, which is to us wonderfully interesting. We are told that the words "eye of a needle," in the passage about a rich man entering the kingdom of heaven, mean the small side entrance in a city gate. Now, in "Richard II," act v. scene 5, *Richard* quotes the passage thus: -- --

It is as hard to come as for a camel
To thread the postern of a needle's eye;[12]

showing that either the imagination of Shakspere suggested the real explanation, or he had taken pains to acquaint himself with the significance of the simile. We can hardly say that the correspondence might be *merely* fortuitous; because, at the least, Shakspere looked for and found a suitable figure to associate with the words *eye of a needle,*

---

[10] "Macbeth," Act 4, scene 3, lines 287-289.

[11] Revelation 14:15

[12] Matthew 19:24

and so fell upon the real explanation; except, indeed, he had no particular significance in using the word that meant a *little* gate, instead of a word meaning any kind of entrance, which, with him, seems unlikely.

We have not by any means proven that Shakspere's acquaintance with the Scriptures had an early date in his history; but certainly the Bible must have had a great influence upon him who was the highest representative mind of the time, its influence on the general development of the nation being unquestionable. This, therefore, seeing the Bible itself was just dawning full upon the country while Shakspere was becoming capable of understanding it, seems the suitable sequence in which to take notice of that influence, and of some of those passages in his works which testify to it.

But, besides *the* Bible, every nation has *a* Bible, or at least *an* Old Testament, in its own history; and that Shakspere paid especial attention to this, is no matter of conjecture. We suspect his mode of writing historical plays is more after the fashion of the Bible histories than that of most writers of history. Indeed, the development and consequences of character and conduct are clear to those that read his histories with open eyes. Now, in his childhood Shakspere may have had some special incentive to the study of history springing out of the fact that his mother's grandfather had been "groom of the chamber to Henry VII.," while there is sufficient testimony that a further removed ancestor of his father, as well, had stood high in the favour of the same monarch. Therefore the history of the troublous times of the preceding century, which were brought to a close by the usurpation of Henry VII., would naturally be a subject of talk in the quiet household, where books and amusements such as now occupy our boys, were scarce or wanting altogether. The proximity of such a past of strife and commotion, crowded with eventful change, must have formed a background full of the material of excitement to an age which lived in the midst of a peculiarly exciting history of its own.

Perhaps the chief intellectual characteristic of the age of Elizabeth was *activity*; this activity accounting even for much that is objectionable in its literature. Now this activity must have been growing in the people throughout the fifteenth century; the wars of the Roses,[13] although they

---

[13] The wars of the Roses refers to a period of conflict in England during the fifteenth century between the noble houses of York (symbolized by a white rose) and

stifled literature, so that it had, as it were, to be born again in the beginning of the following century, being, after all, but as the "eager strife" of the shadow -- leaves above the "genuine life" of the grass, --

And the mute repose

Of sweetly breathing flowers.[14]

But when peace had fallen on the land, it would seem as if the impulse to action springing from strife still operated, as the waves will go on raving upon the shore after the wind has ceased, and found one outlet, amongst others, in literature, and peculiarly in dramatic literature. Peace, rendered yet more intense by the cessation of the cries of the tormentors, and the groans of the noble army of suffering martyrs, made, as it were, a kind of vacuum; and into that vacuum burst up the torrent -- springs of a thousand souls -- the thoughts that were no longer repressed -- in the history of the past and the Utopian speculation on the future; in noble theology, capable statesmanship, and science at once brilliant and profound; in the voyage of discovery, and the change of the swan -- like merchantman into a very fire -- drake of war for the defence of the threatened shores; in the first brave speech of the Puritan in Elizabeth's Parliament, the first murmurs of the voice of liberty, soon to thunder throughout the land; in the naturalizing of foreign genius by translation, and the invention, or at least adoption, of a new and transcendent rhythm; in the song, in the epic, in the drama.

So much for the general. Let us now, following the course of his life, recall, in a few sentences, some of the chief events which must have impressed the all -- open mind of Shakspere in the earlier portion of his history.

Perhaps it would not be going back too far to begin with the Massacre of Paris, which took place when he was eight years old.[15] It

---

Lancaster (symbolized by a red rose.) "Wars of the Roses | Homepage," *Wars of the Roses*, accessed August 18, 2021, https://www.warsoftheroses.com.

14 William Wordsworth, "XXIX," lines 17-18.

15 "The Massacre at Paris" is the name of two different English plays: one by Christopher Marlowe and the other by Nathaniel Lee. Both refer to the Saint Bartholomew's Day Massacre, which began August 23-24, 1572. The Catholic French Queen, Catherine de Medici, ordered the assassination of a group of Protestant French Huguenots. The massacre lasted several weeks and spread across France. History com Editors, "Saint Bartholomew's Day Massacre," *HISTORY*, accessed

caused so much horror in England, that it is not absurd to suppose that some black rays from the deed of darkness may have fallen on the mind of such a child as Shakspere.

In strong contrast with the foregoing is the next event to which we shall refer.

When he was eleven years old, Leicester gave the Queen that magnificent reception at Kenilworth which is so well known from its memorials in our literature.[16] It has been suggested as probable, with quite enough of likelihood to justify a conjecture, that Shakspere may have been present at the dramatic representations then so gorgeously accumulated before her Majesty. If such was the fact, it is easy to imagine what an influence the shows must have had on the mind of the young dramatic genius, at a time when, happily, the critical faculty is not by any means so fully awake as are the receptive and exultant faculties, and when what the nature chiefly needs is excitement to growth, without which all pruning, the most artistic, is useless, as having nothing to operate upon.

When he was fifteen years old, Sir Thomas North's translation of Plutarch (through the French) was first published.[17] Any reader who

---

August 18, 2021, https://www.history.com/this-day-in-history/saint-bartholomews-day-massacre.

[16] In 1575, Robert Dudley, Earl of Leicester, threw a 19 day banquet at Kenilworth Castle for Queen Elizabth. George Gascoigne published an account of the event in *The Princely Pleasures, at the Court at Kenilworth* in 1576. Kevin Sanders, "The Real Story of Queen Elizabeth and Robert Dudley," *English Heritage Blog*, last modified February 6, 2018, accessed August 18, 2021, https://blog.english-heritage.org.uk/queen-elizabeth-and-robert-dudley/.

[17] Plutarch (45-120 AD) was a Greek philosopher who is most well-known today for his "Parallel Lives" recording the histories of prominent Greek and Roman leaders.

"Plutarch | Biography, Works, & Facts," *Encyclopedia Britannica*, accessed August 18, 2021, https://www.britannica.com/biography/Plutarch.

George Karamanolis, "Plutarch," in *The Stanford Encyclopedia of Philosophy*, ed. Edward N. Zalta, Summer 2020. (Metaphysics Research Lab, Stanford University, 2020), accessed August 18, 2021, https://plato.stanford.edu/archives/sum2020/entries/plutarch/.

MacDonald's belief that Shakespeare based his plays on North's translation of Plutarch's Parallel Lives is a common one among Shakespeare scholars. A recent book suggests that Shakespeare based his plays not only on the translation of this ancient work, but North's own plays.

has compared one of Shakspere's Roman plays with the corresponding life in Plutarch, will not be surprised that we should mention this as one of those events which must have been of paramount influence upon Shakspere. It is not likely that he became acquainted with the large folio with its medallion portraits first placed singly, and then repeated side by side for comparison, as soon as it made its appearance, but as we cannot tell when he began to read it, it seems as well to place it in the order its publication would assign to it. Besides, it evidently took such a hold of the man, that it is most probable his acquaintance with it began at a very early period of his history. Indeed, it seems to us to have been one of the most powerful aids to the development of that perception and discrimination of character with which he was gifted to such a remarkable degree. Nor would it be any derogation from the originality of his genius to say, that in a very pregnant sense he must have been a disciple of Plutarch. In those plays founded on Plutarch's stories he picked out every dramatic point, and occasionally employed the very phrases of North's nervous, graphic, and characteristic English. He seems to have felt that it was an honour to his work to embody in it the words of Plutarch himself, as he knew them first. From him he seems especially to have learned how to bring out the points of a character, by putting one man over against another, and remarking wherein they resembled each other and wherein they differed; after which fashion, in other plays as well as those, he partly arranged his dramatic characters.

Not long after he went to London, when he was - two, the death of Sir Philip Sidney at the age of thirty-two, must have had its unavoidable influence on him, seeing all Europe was in mourning for the death of its model, almost ideal man.[18] In England the general

---

"Sir Thomas North | English Translator," Encyclopedia Britannica, accessed August 18, 2021, https://www.britannica.com/biography/Thomas-North.

David Kindy, "Did Shakespeare Base His Masterpieces on Works by an Obscure Elizabethan Playwright?," Smithsonian Magazine, accessed August 18, 2021, https://www.smithsonianmag.com/arts-culture/did-shakespeare-base-his-literary-masterpieces-works-obscure-elizabethan-playwright-180977424/.

[18] Philip Sidney was a well-connected English poet during the Elizabethan age. The nephew of Robert Dudley, his family had a flair for extravagant events. When Sidney died at age 31, his father-in=law threw an elaborate funeral procession. "Sir Philip Sidney | English Author and Statesman," *Encyclopedia Britannica*, accessed August 18, 2021, https://www.britannica.com/biography/Philip-Sidney.

mourning, both in the court and the city, which lasted for months, is supposed by Dr. Zouch to have been the first instance of the kind; that is, for the death of a private person.[19] Renowned over the civilized world for everything for which a man could be renowned, his literary fame must have had a considerable share in the impression his death would make on such a man as Shakspere. For although none of his works were published till after his death, the first within a few months of that event, his fame as a writer was widely spread in private, and report of the same could hardly fail to reach one who, although he had probably no friends of rank as yet, kept such keen open ears for all that was going on around him. But whether or not he had heard of the literary greatness of Sir Philip before his death, the "Arcadia," which was first published four years after his death (1590), and which in eight years had reached the third edition -- with another still in Scotland the following year -- must have been full of interest to Shakspere. This book is very different indeed from the ordinary impression of it which most minds have received through the confident incapacity of the critics of last century. Few books have been published more fruitful in the results and causes of thought, more sparkling with fancy, more evidently the outcome of rich and noble habit, than this "Arcadia" of Philip Sidney. That Shakspere read it, is sufficiently evident from the fact that from it he has taken the secondary but still important plots in two of his plays.

Although we are anticipating, it is better to mention here another book, published in the same year, namely, 1590, when Shakspere was six-and-twenty: the first three books of Spenser's "Faery Queen."[20] Of its reception and character it is needless here to say anything further than, of the latter, that nowadays the depths of its teaching, heartily prized as that was by no less a man than Milton, are seldom explored.[21] But it would be a labour of months to set out the known and imagined

---

[19] Richard Zouch (1590-1661) was an English judge and member of parliament who is known for his legal writing. "Richard Zouch - 1911 Encyclopedia Britannica -," *StudyLight.org*, accessed August 18, 2021, https://www.studylight.org/encyclopedias/eng/bri/r/richard-zouch.html.

[20] Edmund Spenser (1552-1599) was an Elizabethan poet best known for his epic "The Faerie Queen."

[21] John Milton (1608-1674) was an English intellectual who wrote commentaries on political issues of his day, but is best known for his epic poem *Paradise Lost* (1667).

sources of the knowledge and spiritual pabulum of the man who laid every mental region so under contribution, that he has been claimed by almost every profession as having been at one time or another a student of its peculiar science, so marvellously in him was the power of assimilation combined with that of reproduction.

To go back a little: in 1587, when he was three-and-twenty, Mary Queen of Scots was executed.[22] In the following year came that mighty victory of England, and her allies the winds and the waters, over the towering pride of the Spanish Armada.[23] Out from the coasts, like the birds from their cliffs to defend their young, flew the little navy, many of the vessels only able to carry a few guns; and fighting, fire-ships and tempest left this island, --

This precious stone set in the silver sea,[24]

still a "blessed plot," with an accumulated obligation to liberty which can only be paid by helping others to be free; and when she utterly forgets which, her doom is sealed, as surely as that of the old empires which passed away in their self- indulgence and wickedness.

When Shakspere was about thirty-two, Sir Walter Raleigh published his glowing account of Guiana, which instantly provided the English mind with an earthly paradise or fairy-land.[25] Raleigh himself seems to have been too full of his own reports for us to be able to

---

[22] Mary, Queen of Scots (1542-1587) was the queen of Scotland from 1542 to 1567. Mary, was seen by many to have a claim to the English throne through her great-grandfather, Henry VII. She was beheaded in 1567 after being convicted of plotting against Elizabeth I. Emma Goodrey, "Mary, Queen of Scots (r.1542-1567)," *The Royal Family*, last modified February 3, 2016, accessed August 18, 2021, https://www.royal.uk/mary-queen-scots-r1542-1567.

[23] In 1588, Phillip II of Spain sent the "Spanish Armada," a 130-ship fleet of ships, to invade England with the intent of overthrowing Protestant Elizabeth I and reestablishing the Catholic faith as the religion of England. History com Editors, "Spanish Armada," *HISTORY*, accessed August 18, 2021, https://www.history.com/topics/british-history/spanish-armada.

[24] William Shakespeare, "Richard II," Act 2, scene 1, line 46.

[25] Sir Walter Raleigh (1554-1618) was an English statesman, explorer, and military leader. He was given a charter by Elizabeth I to explore the New World. He explored Guyana in a search for the mythical city, El Dorado, the "city of gold." "Sir Walter Raleigh | Biography, Accomplishments, Roanoke, Death, & Facts," *Encyclopedia Britannica*, accessed August 18, 2021, https://www.britannica.com/biography/Walter-Raleigh-English-explorer.

suppose that he either invented or disbelieved them; especially when he represents the heavenly country to which, in expectation of his execution, he is looking forward, after the fashion of those regions of the wonderful West: --

Then the blessed Paths wee'l travel,

Strow'd with Rubies thick as gravel;

Sealings of Diamonds, Saphire floors,

High walls of Coral, and Pearly Bowers.[26]

Such were some of the influences which widened the region of thought, and excited the productive power, in the minds of the time. After this period there were fewer of such in Shakspere's life; and if there had been more of them they would have been of less import as to their operation on a mind more fully formed and more capable of choosing its own influences. Let us now give a backward glance at the history of the art which Shakspere chose as the means of easing his own mind of that wealth which, like the gold and the silver, has a moth and rust of its own, except it be kept in use by being sent out for the good of our neighbours.

It was a mighty gain for the language and the people when, in the middle of the fourteenth century, by permission of the Pope, the miracle-plays, most probably hitherto represented in Norman-French, as Mr. Collier supposes, began to be represented in English.[27] Most

---

[26] Sir Walter Raleigh, "Pilgrimage," lines 29-32.

[27] MacDonald may be referring to John Payne Collier (1789-1883), a journalist and Shakespeare scholar who best known for his Shakespeare forgeries. "John Payne Collier | Encyclopedia Britannica," Theodora, accessed August 18, 2021, https://theodora.com/encyclopedia/c2/john_payne_collier.html.

The pope MacDonald refers to is Clement V who instituted the feast of Corpus Christi to celebrate the real presence of Christ in mass. This feast included a procession with the communion elements carried through the streets. This launched the development of "mystery plays" or "miracle plays" that were designed to teach the doctrine and liturgy of the church in "living pictures."

Wayne Narey, "Miracle Plays," Religious Studies program, Arkansas State University, accessed August 18, 2021, http://www.clt.astate.edu/wnarey/Religious%20Studies%20Program/Religion%20S tudies%20Program/Religious%20Studies%20Program%20Files/The_Miracle_Plays. htm

likely there had been dramatic representations of a sort from the very earliest period of the nation's history; for, to begin with the lowest form, at what time would there not, for the delight of listeners, have been the imitation of animal sounds, such as the drama of the conversation between an attacking poodle and a fiercely repellent puss? Through innumerable gradations of childhood would the art grow before it attained the first formal embodiment in such plays as those, so-called, of miracles, consisting just of Scripture stories, both canonical and apocryphal, dramatized after the rudest fashion. Regarded from the height which the art had reached two hundred and fifty years after, "how dwarfed a growth of cold and night" do these miracle-plays show themselves! But at a time when there was no printing, little preaching, and Latin prayers, we cannot help thinking that, grotesque and ill-imagined as they are, they must have been of unspeakable value for the instruction of a people whose spiritual digestion was not of a sort to be injured by the presence of a quite abnormal quantity of husk and saw-dust in their food. And occasionally we find verses of true poetic feeling, such as the following, in "The Fall of Man:" -- --

> *Deus. Adam, that with myn handys I made,*
> *Where art thou now? What hast thou wrought?*
>
> *Adam. A! lord, for synne oure floures do ffade,*
> *I here thi voys, but I se the nought;*[28]

implying that the separation between God and man, although it had destroyed the beatific vision, was not yet so complete as to make the creature deaf to the voice of his Maker. Nor are the words of Eve, with which she begs her husband, in her shame and remorse, to strangle her, odd and quaint as they are, without an almost overpowering pathos: --

> *Now stomble we on stalk and ston;*
> *My wyt awey is fro me gon:*

---

[28] "The Fall of Man" is part of the *N-Town Plays*, a collection of medieval mystery plays. Lines 191-194.

> *Wrythe on to my necke bon*
> *With, hardnesse of thin honde.*[29]

To this Adam commences his reply with the verses, --

> *Wyff, thi wytt is not wurthe a rosche.*
> *Leve woman, turn thi thought.*[30]

And this portion of the general representation ends with these verses, spoken by Eve: --

> *Alas! that ever we wrought this synne.*
> *Oure bodely sustenauns for to wynne,*
> *Ye must delve and I xal spynne,*
> *In care to ledyn oure lyff.*[31]

In connexion with these plays, one of the contemplations most interesting to us is, the contrast between them and the places in which they were occasionally represented. For though the scaffolds on which they were shown were usually erected in market-places or churchyards, sometimes they rose in the great churches, and the plays were represented with the aid of ecclesiastics. Here, then, we have the rude beginnings of the dramatic art, in which the devil is the unfortunate buffoon, giving occasion to the most exuberant laughter of the people -- here is this rude boyhood, if we may so say, of the one art, roofed in with the perfection of another, of architecture; a perfection which now we can only imitate at our best: below, the clumsy contrivance and the vulgar jest; above, the solemn heaven of uplifted arches, their mysterious glooms ringing with the delight of the multitude: the play of children enclosed in the heart of prayer aspiring in stone. But it was not by any means all laughter; and so much, nearer than architecture is the drama to the ordinary human heart, that we cannot help thinking these grotesque representations did far more to arouse the inward life and conscience of the people than all the glory into which the out --

---

[29] "Fall of Man," lines 305-308.

[30] Ibid., lines 309-310.

[31] Ibid., lines 331-334.

working spirit of the monks had compelled the stubborn stone to bourgeon and blossom.

But although, no doubt, there was some kind of growth going on in the drama even during the dreary fifteenth century, we must not suppose that it was by any regular and steady progression that it arrived at the grandeur of the Elizabethan perfection. It was rather as if a dry, knotty, uncouth, but vigorous plant suddenly opened out its inward life in a flower of surpassing splendour and loveliness. When the representation of real historical persons in the miracle-plays gave way before the introduction of unreal allegorical personages, and the miracle-play was almost driven from the stage by the "play of morals" as it was called, there was certainly no great advance made in dramatic representation. The chief advantage gained was room for more variety; while in some important respects these plays fell off from the merits of the preceding kind. Indeed, any attempt to teach morals allegorically must lack that vivifying fire of faith working in the poorest representations of a history which the people heartily believed and loved. Nor when we come to examine the favourite amusement of later royalty, do we find that the interludes brought forward in the pauses of the banquets of Henry VIII. have a claim to any refinement upon those old miracle-plays. They have gained in facility and wit; they have lost in poetry. They have lost pathos too, and have gathered grossness. In the comedies which soon appear, there is far more of fun than of art; and although the historical play had existed for some time, and the streams of learning from the inns of court had flowed in to swell that of the drama, it is not before the appearance of Shakspere that we find any *whole* of artistic or poetic value. And this brings us to another branch of the subject, of which it seems to us that the importance has never been duly acknowledged. We refer to the use, if not invention, of *blank verse* in England, and its application to the purposes of the drama. It seems to us that in any contemplation of Shakspere and his times, the consideration of these points ought not to be omitted.

We have in the present day one grand master of blank verse, the Poet Laureate.[32] But where would he have been if Milton had not gone before him; or if the verse amidst which he works like an informing spirit had not existed at all? No doubt he might have invented it

---

[32] England's Poet Laureate was Lord Alfred Tennyson.

himself; but how different would the result have been from the verse which he will now leave behind him to lie side by side for comparison with that of the master of the epic! All thanks then to Henry Howard, Earl of Surrey! who, if, dying on the scaffold at the early age of thirty, he has left no poetry in itself of much value, yet so wrote that he refined the poetic usages of the language, and, above all, was the first who ever made blank verse in English.[33] He used it in translating the second and fourth books of Virgil's "Aeneid." This translation he probably wrote not long before his execution, which took place in 1547, seventeen years before the birth of Shakspere. There are passages of excellence in the work, and very rarely does a verse quite fail. But, as might be expected, it is somewhat stiff, and, as it were, stunted in sound; partly from the fact that the lines are too much divided, where *distinction* would have been sufficient. It would have been strange, indeed, if he had at once made a free use of a rhythm which every boy -- poet now thinks he can do what he pleases with, but of which only a few ever learn the real scope and capabilities. Besides, the difficulty was increased by the fact that the nearest approach to it in measure was the heroic couplet, so well known in our language, although scarce one who has used it has come up to the variousness of its modelling in the hands of Chaucer, with whose writings Surrey was of course familiar.[34] But various as is its melody in Chaucer, the fact of there being always an anticipation of the perfecting of a rhyme at the end of the couplet would make one accustomed to heroic verse ready to introduce a rhythmical fall and kind of close at the end of every blank verse in trying to write that measure for the first time. Still, as we say, there is good verse in Surrey's translation. Take the following lines for a specimen, in which the fault just mentioned is scarcely perceptible. Mercury is the subject of them.

---

[33] Henry Howard (1517-1547) was one of the founders of English Renaissance poetry. This is the foundation to which MacDonald refers. Howard's family was well connected in court, but was beheaded by Henry VIII for his hubris. "Henry Howard, Earl of Surrey | English Poet," *Encyclopedia Britannica*, accessed August 18, 2021, https://www.britannica.com/biography/Henry-Howard-Earl-of-Surrey.

[34] Geoffrey Chaucer (1342-1400) was an medieval poet and author and is considered "the father of English literature." He is most well known for *The Canterbury Tales*. "Geoffrey Chaucer | Biography, Poems, *Canterbury Tales*, & Facts," *Encyclopedia Britannica*, accessed August 18, 2021, https://www.britannica.com/biography/Geoffrey-Chaucer.

His golden wings he knits, which him transport,

With a light wind above the earth and seas;

And then with him his wand he took, whereby

He calls from hell pale ghosts.

'By power whereof he drives the winds away,

And passeth eke amid the troubled clouds,

Till in his flight he 'gan descry the top

And the steep flanks of rocky Atlas' hill

That with his crown sustains the welkin up;

Whose head, forgrown with pine, circled always

With misty clouds, is beaten with wind and storm;

His shoulders spread with snow; and from his chin

The springs descend; his beard frozen with ice.

Here Mercury with equal shining wings

First touched.[35]

In all comparative criticism justice demands that he who began any mode should not be compared with those who follow only on the ground of absolute merit in the productions themselves; for while he may be inferior in regard to quality, he stands on a height, as the inventor, to which they, as imitators, can never ascend, although they may climb other and loftier heights, through the example he has set them. It is doubtful, however, whether Surrey himself invented this verse, or only followed the lead of some poet of Italy or Spain; in both which countries it is said that blank verse had been used before Surrey wrote English in that measure.

---

[35] Virgil, *Aeneid*, trans Henry Howard. (1880) Book 4, lines 309-323.

Here then we have the low beginnings of blank verse. It was nearly a hundred and twenty years before Milton took it up, and, while it served him well, glorified it; nor are we aware of any poem of worth written in that measure between. Here, of course, we speak of the epic form of the verse, which, as being uttered *ore rotundo*, is necessarily of considerable difference from the form it assumes in the drama.

Let us now glance for a moment at the forms of composition in use for dramatic purposes before blank verse came into favour with play-writers. The nature of the verse employed in the miracle-plays will be sufficiently seen from the short specimens already given. These plays were made up of carefully measured and varied lines, with correct and superabundant rhymes, and no marked lack of melody or rhythm. But as far as we have made acquaintance with the moral and other rhymed plays which followed, there was a great falling off in these respects. They are in great measure composed of long, irregular lines, with a kind of rhythmical progress rather than rhythm in them. They are exceedingly difficult to read musically, at least to one of our day. Here are a few verses of the sort, from the dramatic poem, rather than drama, called somewhat improperly "The Moral Play of God's Promises," by John Bale, who died the year before Shakspere was born. It is the first in Dodsley's collection.[36] The verses have some poetic merit. The rhythm will be allowed to be difficult at least. The verses are arranged in stanzas, of which we give two. In most plays the verses are arranged in rhyming couplets only.

Pater Coelestis.

I have with fearcenesse mankynde oft tymes corrected,

And agayne, I have allured hym by swete promes.

I have sent sore plages, when he hath me neglected,

And then by and by, most comfortable swetnes.

---

[36] Robert Dodsley published *A Select Collection of Old Plays* which included works from John Bale. John Bale (1494-1563) was a Protestant convert from Catholicism and a contemporary of Thomas Cromwell. He was a controversial and contentious person and this was often reflected in his writing. "Life of John Bale (1495-1563) [Biography of the Tudor Dramatist and Theologian]," accessed August 18, 2021, http://www.luminarium.org/renlit/balebio.htm.

To wynne hym to grace, bothe mercye and ryghteousnes

I have exercysed, yet wyll he not amende.

Shall I now lose hym, or shall I him defende?

In hys most myschefe, most hygh grace will I sende,

To overcome hym by favoure, if it may be.

With hys abusyons no longar wyll I contende,

But now accomplysh my first wyll and decre.

My worde beynge flesh, from hens shall set hym fre,

Hym teachynge a waye of perfyght ryhteousnesse,

That he shall not nede to perysh in hys weaknesse.

To our ears, at least, the older miracle -- plays were greatly superior. It is interesting to find, however, in this apparently popular mode of "building the rhyme" -- certainly not the *lofty* rhyme, for no such crumbling foundation could carry any height of superstructure -- the elements of the most popular rhythm of the present day; a rhythm admitting of any number of syllables in the line, from four up to twelve, or even more, and demanding only that there shall be not more than four accented syllables in the line. A song written with any spirit in this measure has, other things *not* being quite equal, yet almost a certainty of becoming more popular than one written in any other measure. Most of Barry Cornwall's and Mrs. Heman's songs are written in it.[37] Scott's "Lay of the Last Minstrel," Coleridge's "Christabel," Byron's "Siege of Corinth," Shelley's "Sensitive Plant," are examples of the rhythm.[38] Spenser is the first who has made good use of it. One of the months in the "Shepherd's Calendar" is composed in it. We quote a few lines from this poem, to show at once the kind we mean: --

---

[37] Barry Cornall (1787-1874) was the pseudonym for the English poet Bryan Waller Procter. Felicia Hemans (1793-1835) was a prolific Victorian poet.

[38] The poets MacDonald refers to are Sir Walter Scott (1771-1832), Samuel Taylor Coleridge (1772-1834), Lord George Gordon Byron (1788-1834), and Percy Bysshe Shelley (1792-1822).

No marvel, Thenot, if thou can bear

Cheerfully the winter's wrathful cheer;

For age and winter accord full nigh;

This chill, that cold; this crooked, that wry;

And as the lowering weather looks down,

So seemest thou like Good Friday to frown:

But my flowering youth is foe to frost;

My ship unwont in storms to be tost.

We can trace it slightly in Sir Thomas Wyatt, and we think in others who preceded Spenser. There is no sign of it in Chaucer. But we judge it to be the essential rhythm of Anglo-Saxon poetry, which will quite harmonize with, if it cannot explain, the fact of its being the most popular measure still. Shakspere makes a little use of it in one, if not in more, of his plays, though it there partakes of the irregular character of that of the older plays which he is imitating. But we suspect the clowns of the authorship of some of the rhymes, "speaking more than was set down for them," evidently no uncommon offence.

Prose was likewise in use for the drama at an early period.

But we must now regard the application of blank verse to the use of the drama. And in this part of our subject we owe most to the investigations of Mr. Collier, than whom no one has done more to merit our gratitude for such aids. It is universally acknowledged that "Ferrex and Porrex" was the first drama in blank verse. But it was never represented on the public stage. It was the joint production of Thomas Sackville, afterwards Lord Buckhurst and Earl of Dorset, and Thomas Norton, both gentlemen of the Inner Temple, by the members of which it was played before the Queen at Whitehall in 1561, three years before Shakspere was born.[39] As to its merits, the impression left by it upon our minds is such that, although the verse is decent, and in some respects irreproachable, we think the time spent in reading it must be

---

[39] The Inner Temple is a professional organization that is, along with the other three Inns of Court, is responsible for training and regulating barristers in England and Wales. Whitehall Palace was one of Elizabeth I's favorite residences. https://www.innertemple.org.uk/who-we-are/history/

all but lost to any but those who must verify to themselves their literary profession; a profession which, like all other professions, involves a good deal of disagreeable duty. We spare our readers all quotation, there being no occasion to show what blank verse of the commonest description is. But we beg to be allowed to state that this drama by no means represents the poetic powers of Thomas Sackville.[40] For although we cannot agree with Hallam's general criticism, either for or against Sackville, and although we admire Spenser, we hope, as much as that writer could have admired him, we yet venture to say that not only may some of Sackville's personifications "fairly be compared with some of the most poetical passages in Spenser," but that there is in this kind in Sackville a strength and simplicity of representation which surpasses that of Spenser in passages in which the latter probably imitated the former.[41] We refer to the allegorical personages in Sackville's "Induction to the Mirrour of Magistrates," and in Spenser's description of the "House of Pride."

Mr. Collier judges that the play in blank verse first represented on the public stage was the "Tamburlaine" of Christopher Marlowe, and that it was acted before 1587, at which date Shakspere would be twenty -- three.[42] This was followed by other and better plays by the same author. Although we cannot say much for the dramatic art of Marlowe, he has far surpassed every one that went before him in dramatic *poetry*. The passages that might worthily be quoted from Marlowe's writings for the sake of their poetry are innumerable, notwithstanding that there are many others which occupy a border land between poetry and bombast, and are such that it is to us impossible to say to which class they rather belong. Of course it is easy for a critic to gain the credit of common -- sense at the same time that he saves himself the trouble of doing what he too frequently shows himself incapable of doing to any good purpose -- we mean -- by classing all such passages together as bombastical nonsense; but even in the matter of poetry and bombast, a wise reader will recognize that extremes so entirely meet, without being in the least identical, that they are capable of a sort of - literary

---

[40] Thomas Sackville (1599-1608) was a British statesman and poet.

[41] Henry Hallam (1777-1859) was an English historian who wrote on a commentary on the influences of Thomas Sackville in *The Works of Henry Hallam, Introduction to the Literature of Europe* (1866), Chapter V: Sackville's Induction.

[42] Christopher Marlowe (1564-1593) was an English poet and playwright.

admixture, if not of combination. Goethe himself need not have been ashamed to have written one or two of the scenes in Marlowe's "Faust;" not that we mean to imply that they in the least resemble Goethe's handiwork.[43] His verse is, for dramatic purposes, far inferior to Shakspere's; but it was a great matter for Shakspere that Marlowe preceded him, and helped to prepare to his hand the tools and fashions he needed. The provision of blank verse for Shakspere's use seems to us worthy of being called providential, even in a system in which we cannot believe that there is any chance. For as the stage itself is elevated a few feet above the ordinary level, because it is the scene of a *representation*, just so the speech of the drama, dealing not with unreal but with ideal persons, the fool being a worthy fool, and the villain a worthy villain, needs to be elevated some tones above that of ordinary life, which is generally flavoured with so much of the *commonplace*. Now the commonplace has no place at all in the drama of Shakspere, which fact at once elevates it above the tone of ordinary life. And so the mode of the speech must be elevated as well; therefore from prose into blank verse. If we go beyond this, we cease to be natural for the stage as well as life; and the result is that kind of composition well enough known in Shakspere's time, which he ridicules in the recitations of the player in "Hamlet," about *Priam* and *Hecuba*.[44] We could show the very passages of the play-writer Nash which Shakspere imitates in these.[45] To use another figure, Shakspere, in the same play, instructs the players "to hold, as 'twere, the mirror up to nature." Now every one must have felt that somehow there is a difference between the appearance of any object or group of objects immediately presented to the eye, and the appearance of the same object or objects in a mirror. Nature herself is not the same in the mirror held up to her. Everything changes sides in this representation; and the room which is an ordinary, well-known, homely room, gains something of the strange and poetic when regarded in the mirror over the fire. Now for this representation, for

---

[43] Johan Wolfgang von Goethe (1749-1832) was a German poet and scholar. He wrote on a wide range of topics from his scientific work, the *Metamorphosis of Plants*, to his most famous play *Faust*.

[44] Shakespeare references Homer's *Illiad* in "Hamlet" when he refers to Priam, the king of Troy, and Hecuba his wife.

[45] Thomas Nash (1567-1601) was an Elizabethan playwright.

this mirror-reflection on the stage, blank verse is just the suitable glass to receive the silvering of the genius-mind behind it.

But if Shakspere had had to sit down and make his tools first, and then quarry his stone and fell his timber for the building of his house, instead of finding everything ready to his hand for dressing his stone already hewn, for sawing and carving the timber already in logs and planks beside him, no doubt his house would have been built; but can we with any reason suppose that it would have proved such "a lordly pleasure-house"? Not even Shakspere could do without his poor little brothers who preceded him, and, like the goblins and gnomes of the drama, got everything out of the bowels of the dark earth, ready for the master, whom it would have been a shame to see working in the gloom and the dust instead of in the open eye of the day. Nor is anything so helpful to the true development of power as the possibility of free action for as much of the power as is already operative. This room for free action was provided by blank verse.

Yet when Shakspere came first upon the scene of dramatic labour, he had to serve his private apprenticeship, to which the apprenticeship of the age in the drama, had led up. He had to act first of all. Driven to London and the drama by an irresistible impulse, when the choice of some profession was necessary to make him independent of his father, seeing he was himself, though very young, a married man, the first form in which the impulse to the drama would naturally show itself in him would be the desire to act; for the outside relations would first operate. As to the degree of merit he possessed as an actor we have but scanty means of judging; for afterwards, in his own plays, he never took the best characters, having written them for his friend Richard Burbage.[46] Possibly the dramatic impulse was sufficiently appeased by the writing of the play, and he desired no further satisfaction from personal representation; although the amount of study spent upon the higher department of the art might have been more than sufficient to render him unrivalled as well in the presentation of his own conceptions. But the dramatic spring, having once broken the upper surface, would scoop out a deeper and deeper well for itself to play in, and the actor would soon begin to work upon the parts he had himself to study for

---

[46] Richard Burbage (1567-1619) was an English stage actors with the Globe Theatre.

presentation. It being found that he greatly bettered his own parts, those of others would be submitted to him, and at length whole plays committed to his revision, of which kind there may be several in the collection of his works. If the feather -- end of his pen is just traceable in "Titus Andronicus," the point of it is much more evident, and to as good purpose as Beaumont or Fletcher could have used his to, at the best, in "Pericles, Prince of Tyre."[47] Nor would it be long before he would submit one of his own plays for approbation; and then the whole of his dramatic career lies open before him, with every possible advantage for perfecting the work, for the undertaking of which he was better qualified by nature than probably any other man whosoever; for he knew everything about acting, practically -- about the play-house and its capabilities, about stage necessities, about the personal endowments and individual qualifications of each of the company -- so that, when he was writing a play, he could distribute the parts before they even appeared upon paper, and write for each actor with the very living form of the ideal person present "in his mind's eye," and often to his bodily sight; so that the actual came in aid of the ideal, as it always does if the ideal be genuine, and the loftiest conceptions proved the truest to visible nature.

This close relation of Shakspere to the actual leads us to a general and remarkable fact, which again will lead us back to Shakspere. All the great writers of Queen Elizabeth's time were men of affairs; they were not literary men merely, in the general acceptation of the word at present. Hooker was a hard-working, sheep-keeping, cradle-rocking pastor of a country parish.[48] Bacon's legal duties were innumerable before he became Lord Keeper and Lord Chancellor.[49] Raleigh was soldier, sailor, adventurer, courtier, politician, discoverer: indeed, it is to his imprisonment that we are indebted for much the most ambitious of his literary undertakings, "The History of the World," a work which for simple majesty of subject and style is hardly to be surpassed in prose. Sidney, at the age of three-and-twenty, received the highest praise for the management of a secret embassy to the Emperor of

---

[47] Francis Beaumont (1584-1616) and John Fletcher (1579-1625) were popular English playwrights that collaborated in their work.

[48] Richard Hooker (1554-1600) was an English priest and Protestant theologian.

[49] Lord Francis Bacon (1561-1626).

Germany; took the deepest and most active interest in the political affairs of his country; would have sailed with Sir Francis Drake for South American discovery; and might probably have been king of poor Poland, if the queen had not been too selfish or wise to spare him. The whole of his literary productions was the work of his spare hours. Spenser himself, who was, except Shakspere, the most purely a literary man of them all, was at one time Secretary to the Lord Deputy of Ireland, and, later in life, Sheriff of Cork. Nor is the remark true only of the writers of Elizabeth's period, or of the country of England.

It seems to us one of the greatest advantages that can befall a poet, to be drawn out of his study, and still more out of the chamber of imagery in his own thoughts, to behold and speculate upon the embodiment of Divine thoughts and purposes in men and their affairs around him. Now Shakspere had no public appointment, but he reaped all the advantage which such could have given him, and more, from the perfection of his dramatic position. It was not with making plays alone that he had to do; but, himself an actor, himself in a great measure the owner of more than one theatre, with a little realm far more difficult to rule than many a kingdom -- -- a company, namely, of actors -- -- although possibly less difficult from the fact that they were only men and boys; with the pecuniary affairs of the management likewise under his supervision -- -- he must have found, in the relations and necessities of his own profession, not merely enough of the actual to keep him real in his representations, but almost sufficient opportunity for his one great study, that of mankind, independently of social and friendly relations, which in his case were of the widest and deepest.

But Shakspere had not business relations merely: he was a man of business. There is a common blunder manifested, both in theory on the one side, and in practice on the other, which the life of Shakspere sets full in the light. The theory is, that genius is a sort of abnormal development of the imagination, to the detriment and loss of the practical powers, and that a genius is therefore a kind of incapable, incompetent being, as far as worldly matters are concerned. The most complete refutation of this notion lies in the fact that the greatest genius the world has known was a successful man in common affairs. While his genius grew in strength, fervour, and executive power, his worldly condition rose as well; he became a man of importance in the eyes of his townspeople, by whom he would not have been honoured if he had not made money; and he purchased landed property in his native place with the results of his management of his theatres.

The practical blunder lies in the notion cherished occasionally by young people ambitious of literary distinction, that in the pursuit of such things they must be content with the poverty to which the world dooms its greatest men; accepting their very poverty as an additional proof of their own genius. If this means that the poet is not to make money his object, it means well: no man should. But if it means either that the world is unkind, or that the poet is not to "gather up the fragments, that nothing be lost," it means ill. Shakspere did not make haste to be rich. He neither blamed, courted, nor neglected the world: he was friendly with it. He *could* not have pinched and scraped; but neither did he waste or neglect his worldly substance, which is God's gift too. Many immense fortunes have been made, not by absolute dishonesty, but in ways to which a man of genius ought to be yet more ashamed than another to condescend; but it does not therefore follow that if a man of genius will do honest work he will not make a fair livelihood by it, which for all good results of intellect and heart is better than a great fortune. But then Shakspere began with doing what he could. He did not consent to starve until the world should recognize his genius, or grumble against the blindness of the nation in not seeing what it was impossible it should see before it was fairly set forth. He began at once to supply something which the world wanted; for it wants many an honest thing. He went on the stage and acted, and so gained power to reveal the genius which he possessed; and the world, in its possible measure, was not slow to recognize it. Many a young fellow who has entered life with the one ambition of being a poet, has failed because he did not perceive that it is better to be a man than to be a poet, that it is his first duty to get an honest living by doing some honest work that he can do, and for which there is a demand, although it may not be the most pleasant employment. Time would have shown whether he was meant to be a poet or not; and if he had been no poet he would have been no beggar; and if he had turned out a poet, it would have been partly in virtue of that experience of life and truth, gained in his case in the struggle for bread, without which, gained somehow, a man may be a sweet dreamer, but can be no strong maker, no poet. In a word, here is *the* Englishman of genius, beginning life with nothing, and dying, not rich, but easy and honoured; and this by doing what no one else could do, writing dramas in which the outward grandeur or beauty is but an exponent of the inward worth; hiding pearls for the wise even within the jewelled play of the variegated bubbles of fancy, which he blew while he wrought, for the innocent delight of his thoughtless brothers and sisters. Wherever the rainbow of Shakspere's genius stands, there lies, indeed, at the foot of its glorious arch, a golden key, which will open the secret doors of truth, and admit the humble seeker into the presence of Wisdom, who, having cried in the streets in vain, sits at home and waits for him who will come to find her. And Shakspere had cakes and ale, although he was virtuous.

But what do we know about the character of Shakspere? How can we tell the inner life of a man who has uttered himself in dramas, in which of course it is impossible that he should ever speak in his own person? No doubt he may speak his own sentiments through the mouths of many of his persons; but how are we to know in what cases he does so? -- At least we may assert, as a self-evident negative, that a passage treating of a wide question put into the mouth of a person despised and rebuked by the best characters in the play, is not likely to contain any cautiously formed and cherished opinion of the dramatist. At first sight this may seem almost a truism; but we have only to remind our readers that one of the passages oftenest quoted with admiration, and indeed separately printed and illuminated, is "The Seven Ages of Man," a passage full of inhuman contempt for humanity and unbelief in its destiny, in which not one of the seven ages is allowed to pass over its poor sad stage without a sneer; and that this passage is given by Shakspere to the *blasé* sensualist *Jaques* in "As You Like it," a man who, the good and wise *Duke* says, has been as vile as it is possible for man to be, so vile that it would be an additional sin in him to rebuke sin; a man who never was capable of seeing what is good in any man, and hates men's vices *because* he hates themselves, seeing in them only the reflex of his own disgust. Shakspere knew better than to say that all the world is a stage, and all the men and women merely players. He had been a player himself, but only on the stage: *Jaques* had been a player where he ought to have been a true man. The whole of his account of human life is contradicted and exposed at once by the entrance, the very moment when he has finished his wicked burlesque, of *Orlando*, the young master, carrying *Adam*, the old servant, upon his back. The song that immediately follows, sings true: "Most friendship is feigning, most loving mere folly." But between the *all* of *Jaques* and the *most* of the song, there is just the difference between earth and hell. -- Of

79

course, both from a literary and dramatic point of view, "The Seven Ages" is perfect.

Now let us make one positive statement to balance the other: that wherever we find, in the mouth of a noble character, not stock sentiments of stage virtue, but appreciation of a truth which it needs deep thought and experience united with love of truth, to discover or verify for one's self, especially if the truth be of a sort which most men will fail not merely to recognize as a truth, but to understand at all, because the understanding of it depends on the foregoing spiritual perception -- then we think we may receive the passage as an expression of the inner soul of the writer. He must have seen it before he could have said it; and to see such a truth is to love it; or rather, love of truth in the general must have preceded and enabled to the discovery of it. Such a passage is the speech of the *Duke*, opening the second act of the play just referred to, "As You Like it." The lesson it contains is, that the well-being of a man cannot be secured except he partakes of the ills of life, "the penalty of Adam." And it seems to us strange that the excellent editors of the Cambridge edition, now in the course of publication -- a great boon to all students of Shakspere -- should not have perceived that the original reading, that of the folios, is the right one, -- --

"Here feel we not the penalty of Adam?"

which, with the point of interrogation supplied, furnishes the true meaning of the whole passage; namely, that the penalty of Adam is just what makes the "wood more free from peril than the envious court," teaching each "not to think of himself more highly than he ought to think."

But Shakspere, although everywhere felt, is nowhere seen in his plays. He is too true an artist to show his own face from behind the play of life with which he fills his stage. What we can find of him there we must find by regarding the whole, and allowing the spiritual essence of the whole to find its way to our brain, and thence to our heart. The student of Shakspere becomes imbued with the idea of his character. It exhales from his writings. And when we have found the main drift of any play -- the grand rounding of the whole -- then by that we may interpret individual passages. It is alone in their relation to the whole that we can do them full justice, and in their relation to the whole that we discover the mind of the master.

But we have another source of more direct enlightenment as to Shakspere himself. We only say more *direct*, not more certain or extended enlightenment. We have one collection of poems in which he speaks in his own person and of himself. Of course we refer to his sonnets. Though these occupy, with their presentation of himself, such a small relative space, they yet admirably round and complete, to our eyes, the circle of his individuality. In them and the plays the common saying -- one of the truest -- that extremes meet, is verified. No man is complete in whom there are no extremes, or in whom those extremes do not meet. Now the very individuality of Shakspere, judged by his dramas alone, has been declared nonexistent; while in the sonnets he manifests some of the deepest phases of a healthy self-consciousness. We do not intend to enter into the still unsettled question as to whether these sonnets were addressed to a man or a woman. We have scarcely a doubt left on the question ourselves, as will be seen from the argument we found on our conviction. We cannot say we feel much interest in the other question, *If a man, what man?* A few placed at the end, arranged as they have come down to us, are beyond doubt addressed to a woman. But the difference in tone between these and the others we think very remarkable. Possibly at the time they were written -- most of them early in his life, as it appears to us, although they were not published till the year 1609, when he was forty -- five years of age, Meres referring to them in the year 1598, eleven years before, as known "among his private friends" -- he had not known such women as he knew afterwards, and hence the true devotion of his soul is given to a friend of his own sex.[50] Gervinus, whose lectures on Shakspere, profound and lofty to a degree unattempted by any other interpreter, we are glad to find have been done into a suitable English translation, under the superintendence of the author himself -- Gervinus says somewhere in them that, as Shakspere lived and wrote, his ideal of womanhood grew nobler and purer.[51] Certainly the woman

---

[50] Frances Meres (1565-1647) published *Palladis Tamia, Wits Treasury* in 1598, which is considered the first critical commentary that includes the works of Shakespeare.

[51] Georg Gottfried Gervinus (1805-1871) was a German historian who wrote on literature and politics.

to whom the last few of these sonnets are addressed was neither noble nor pure. We think, in this matter at least, they record one of his early experiences.

We shall briefly indicate what we find in these sonnets about the man himself, and shall commence with what is least pleasing and of least value.

We must confess, then, that, probably soon after he came first to London, he, then a married man, had an intrigue with a married woman, of which there are indications that he was afterwards deeply ashamed. One little incident seems curiously traceable: that he had given her a set of tablets which his friend had given him; and the sonnet in which he excuses himself to his friend for having done so, seems to us the only piece of special pleading, and therefore ungenuine expression, in the whole. This friend, to whom the rest of the sonnets are addressed, made the acquaintance of this woman, and both were false to Shakspere. Even Shakspere could not keep the love of a worthless woman. So much the better for him; but it is a sad story at best. Yet even in this environment of evil we see the nobility of the man, and his real self. The sonnets in which he mourns his friend's falsehood, forgives him, and even finds excuses for him, that he may not lose his own love of him, are, to our minds, amongst the most beautiful, as they are the most profound. Of these are the 33rd and 34th. Nor does he stop here, but proceeds in the following, the 35th, to comfort his friend in his grief for his offence, even accusing himself of offence in having made more excuse for his fault than the fault needed! But to leave this part of his history, which, as far as we know, stands alone, and yet cannot with truth be passed by, any more than the story of the crime of David, though in this case there is no comparison to be made between the two further than the primary fact, let us look at the one reality which, from a spiritual point of view, independently of the literary beauties of these poems, causes them to stand all but alone in literature.[52] We mean what has been unavoidably touched upon already, the devotion of his friendship. We have said this makes the poems stand *all but alone*; for we ought to be better able to understand these poems of Shakspere, from the fact that in our day has

---

[52] The "story of the crime of David" refers to David's adulterous affair with Bathsheba in 2 Samuel 11.

appeared the only other poem which is like these, and which casts back a light upon them.

> *Yet turn thee to the doubtful shore,*
>
> *Where thy first form was made a man:*

> *I loved thee, spirit, and love; nor can*
>
> *The soul of Shakspeare love thee more.*

So sings the Poet of our day, in the loftiest of his poems -- "In Memoriam" -- addressing the spirit of his vanished friend.[53] In the midst of his song arises the thought of *the Poet* of all time, who loved his friend too, and would have lost him in a way far worse than death, had not his love been too strong even for that death, alone ghastly, which threatened to cut the golden chain that bound them, and part them by the gulf impassable. Tennyson's friend had never wronged him; and to the divineness of Shakspere's love is added that of forgiveness. Such love as this between man and man is rare, and therefore to the mind which is in itself no way rare, incredible, because unintelligible. But though all the commonest things are very divine, yet divine individuality is and will be a rare thing at any given period on the earth. Faith, in its ideal sense, will always be hard to find on the earth. But perhaps this kind of affection between man and man may, as Coleridge indicates in his "Table Talk," have been more common in the reigns of Elizabeth and James than it is now. There is a certain dread of the demonstrative in the present day, which may, perhaps, be carried into regions where it is out of place, and hinder the development of a devotion which must be real, and grand, and divine, if one man such as Shakspere or Tennyson has ever felt it. If one has felt it, humanity may claim it. And surely He who is *the* Son of man has verified the claim. We believe there are indeed few of us who know what *to love our neighbour as ourselves* means; but when we find a man here and there in the course of centuries who does, we may take this man

---

[53] The "Poet of our day" was Alfred Tennyson who wrote "In Memoriam" in honor of Arthur Henry Hallam.

as the prophet of coming good for his race, his prophecy being himself.[54]

But next to the interest of knowing that a man could love so well, comes the association of this fact with his art. He who could look abroad upon men, and understand them all -- who stood, as it were, in the wide-open gates of his palace, and admitted with welcome every one who came in sight -- had in the inner places of that palace one chamber in which he met his friend, and in which his whole soul went forth to understand the soul of his friend. The man to whom nothing in humanity was common or unclean; in whom the most remarkable of his artistic morals is fair-play; who fills our hearts with a saintly love for *Cordelia* and an admiration of *Sir John Falstaff* the lost gentleman, mournful even in the height of our laughter; who could make an *Autolycus* and a *Macbeth* both human, and an *Ariel* and a *Puck* neither human -- this is the man who loved best. And we believe that this depth of capacity for loving lay at the root of all his knowledge of men and women, and all his dramatic pre-eminence. The heart is more intelligent than the intellect. Well says the poet Matthew Raydon, who has hardly left anything behind him but the lamentation over Sir Philip Sidney in which the lines occur, --

He that hath love and judgment too

Sees more than any other do.[55]

Simply, we believe that this, not this only, but this more than any other endowment, made Shakspere the artist he was, in providing him all the material of humanity to work upon, and keeping him to the true spirit of its use. Love looking forth upon strife, understood it all. Love is the true revealer of secrets, because it makes one with the object regarded.

"But," say some impatient readers, "when shall we have done with Shakspere? There is no end to this writing about him." It will be a bad day for England when we have done with Shakspere; for that will imply, along with the loss of him, that we are no longer capable of

---

[54] Mark 12:30-31.

[55] Matthew Roydon (d 1622), "An Elegy; or, Friend's Passion for his Astrophel" (1595).

understanding him. Should that time ever come, Heaven grant the generation which does not understand him at least the grace to keep its pens off him, which will by no means follow as a necessary consequence of the non-intelligence! But the writing about Shakspere which has been hitherto so plentiful must do good just in proportion as it directs attention to him and gives aid to the understanding of him. And while the utterances of to-day pass away, the children of to-morrow are born, and require a new utterance for their fresh need from those who, having gone before, have already tasted life and Shakspere, and can give some little help to further progress than their own, by telling the following generation what they have found. Suppose that this cry had been raised last century, after good Dr. Johnson had ceased to produce to the eyes of men the facts about his own incapacity which he presumed to be criticisms of Shakspere, where would our aids be now to the understanding of the dramatist? Our own conviction is, when we reflect with how much labour we have deepened our knowledge of him, and thereby found in him *the best* -- for the best lies not on the surface for the careless reader -- our own conviction is, that not half has been done that ought to be done to help young people at least to understand the master mind of their country. Few among them can ever give the attention or work to it that we have given; but much may be done with judicious aid. And a profound knowledge of their greatest writer would do more than almost anything else to bind together as Englishmen, in a true and unselfish way, the hearts of the coming generations; for his works are our country in a convex magic mirror.

When a man finds that every time he reads a book not only does some obscurity melt away, but deeper depths, which he had not before seen, dawn upon him, he is not likely to think that the time for ceasing to write about the book has come. And certainly in Shakspere, as in all true artistic work, as in nature herself, the depths are not to be revealed utterly; while every new generation needs a new aid towards discovering itself and its own thoughts in these forms of the past. And of all that read about Shakspere there are few whom more than one or two utterances have reached. The speech or the writing must go forth to find the soil for the growth of its kernel of truth. We shall, therefore, with the full consciousness that perhaps more has been already said and written about Shakspere than about any other writer, yet venture to add to the mass by a few general remarks.

And first we would remind our readers of the marvel of the combination in Shakspere of such a high degree of two faculties, one of which is generally altogether inferior to the other: the faculties of reception and production. Rarely do we find that great receptive power, brought into operation either by reading or by observation, is combined with originality of thought. Some hungers are quite satisfied by taking in what others have thought and felt and done. By the assimilation of this food many minds grow and prosper; but other minds feed far more upon what rises from their own depths; in the answers they are compelled to provide to the questions that come unsought; in the theories they cannot help constructing for the inclusion in one whole of the various facts around them, which seem at first sight to strive with each other like the atoms of a chaos; in the examination of those impulses of hidden origin which at one time indicate a height of being far above the thinker's present condition, at another a gulf of evil into which he may possibly fall. But in Shakspere the two powers of beholding and originating meet like the rejoining halves of a sphere. A man who thinks his own thoughts much, will often walk through London streets and see nothing. In the man who observes only, every passing object mirrors itself in its prominent peculiarities, having a kind of harmony with all the rest, but arouses no magician from the inner chamber to charm and chain its image to his purpose. In Shakspere, on the contrary, every outer form of humanity and nature spoke to that ever-moving, self-vindicating -- we had almost said, and in a sense it would be true, self-generating -- humanity within him. The sound of any action without him, struck in him just the chord which, in motion in him, would have produced a similar action. When anything was done, he felt as if he were doing it -- perception and origination conjoining in one consciousness.

But to this gift was united the gift of utterance, or representation. Many a man both receives and generates who, somehow, cannot represent. Nothing is more disappointing sometimes than our first experience of the artistic attempts of a man who has roused our expectations by a social display of familiarity with, and command over, the subjects of conversation. Have we not sometimes found that when such a one sought to give vital or artistic form to these thoughts, so that they might not be born and die in the same moment upon his lips, but might *exist*, a poor, weak, faded *simulacrum* alone was the result? Now Shakspere was a great talker, who enraptured the listeners, and was himself so rapt in his speech that he could scarcely come to a close; but when he was alone with his art, then and then only did he rise to the height of his great argument, and all the talk was but as the fallen mortar and stony chips lying about the walls of the great temple of his drama.

But, along with all this wealth of artistic speech, an artistic virtue of an opposite nature becomes remarkable: his reticence. How often might he not say fine things, particularly poetic things, when he does not, because it would not suit the character or the time! How many delicate points are there not in his plays which we only discover after many readings, because he will not put a single tone of success into the flow of natural utterance, to draw our attention to the triumph of the author, and jar with the all-important reality of his production! Wherever an author obtrudes his own self-importance, an unreality is the consequence, of a nature similar to that which we feel in the old moral plays, when historical and allegorical personages, such as *Julius Caesar* and *Charity*, for instance, are introduced at the same time on the same stage, acting in the same story. Shakspere never points to any stroke of his own wit or art. We may find it or not: there it is, and no matter if no one see it!

Much has been disputed about the degree of consciousness of his own art possessed by Shakspere: whether he did it by a grand yet blind impulse, or whether he knew what he wanted to do, and knowingly used the means to arrive at that end. Now we cannot here enter upon the question; but we would recommend any of our readers who are interested in it not to attempt to make up their minds upon it before considering a passage in another of his poems, which may throw some light on the subject for them. It is the description of a painting, contained in "The Rape of Lucrece," towards the end of the poem. Its very minuteness involves the expression of principles, and reveals that, in relation to an art not his own, he could hold principles of execution, and indicate perfection of finish, which, to say the least, must proceed from a general capacity for art, and therefore might find an equally conscious operation in his own peculiar province of it. For our own part, we think that his results are a perfect combination of the results of consciousness and unconsciousness; consciousness where the arrangements of the play, outside the region of inspiration, required the care of the wakeful intellect; unconsciousness where the subject itself bore him aloft on the wings of its own creative delight.

There is another manifestation of his power which will astonish those who consider it. It is this: that, while he was able to go down to the simple and grand realities of human nature, which are all tragic; and while, therefore, he must rejoice most in such contemplations of human nature as find fit outlet in a "Hamlet," a "Lear," a "Timon," or an "Othello," the tragedies of Doubt, Ingratitude, and Love, he can yet, when he chooses, float on the very surface of human nature, as in "Love's Labour's Lost," "The Merry Wives of Windsor," "The Comedy of Errors," "The Taming of the Shrew;" or he can descend half way as it were, and there remain suspended in the characters and feelings of ordinary nice people, who, interesting enough to meet in society, have neither received that development, nor are placed in those circumstances, which admit of the highest and simplest poetic treatment. In these he will bring out the ordinary noble or the ordinary vicious. Of this nature are most of his comedies, in which he gives an ideal representation of common social life, and steers perfectly clear of what in such relations and surroundings would be *heroics*. Look how steadily he keeps the noble-minded youth *Orlando* in this middle region; and look how the best comes out at last in the wayward and *recalcitrant* and *bizarre*, but honest and true natures of *Beatrice* and *Benedick*; and this without any untruth to the nature of comedy, although the circumstances border on the tragic. When he wants to give the deeper affairs of the heart, he throws the whole at once out of the social circle with its multiform restraints. As in "Hamlet" the stage on which the whole is acted is really the heart of *Hamlet*, so he makes his visible stage as it were, slope off into the misty infinite, with a grey, starless heaven overhead, and Hades open beneath his feet. Hence young people brought up in the country understand the tragedies far sooner than they can comprehend the comedies. It needs acquaintance with society and social ways to clear up the latter.

The remarks we have made on "Hamlet" by way of illustration, lead us to point out how Shakspere prepares, in some of his plays, a stage suitable for all the representation. In "A Midsummer Night's Dream" the place which gives tone to the whole is a midnight wood in the first flush and youthful delight of summer. In "As You Like it" it is a daylight wood in spring, full of morning freshness, with a cold wind now and then blowing through the half-clothed boughs. In "The Tempest" it is a solitary island, circled by the mysterious-horizon, over which what may come who can tell? -- a place where the magician may work his will, and have all nature at the beck of his superior knowledge.

The only writer who would have had a chance of rivalling Shakspere in his own walk, if he had been born in the same period of English history, is Chaucer. He has the same gift of individualizing the general, and idealizing the portrait. But the best of the dramatic writers of Shakspere's time, in their desire of dramatic individualization, forget the modifying multiformity belonging to individual humanity. In their anxiety to present a *character*, they take, as it were, a human mould, label it with a certain peculiarity, and then fill in speeches and forms according to the label. Thus the indications of character, of peculiarity, so predominate, the whole is so much of one colour, that the result resembles one of those allegorical personifications in which, as much as possible, everything human is eliminated except what belongs to the peculiarity, the personification. How different is it with Shakspere's representations! He knows that no human being ever was like that. He makes his most peculiar characters speak very much like other people; and it is only over the whole that their peculiarities manifest themselves with indubitable plainness. The one apparent exception is *Jaques*, in "As You Like it." But there we must remember that Shakspere is representing a man who so chooses to represent himself. He is a man *in his humour*, or his own peculiar and chosen affectation. *Jaques* is the writer of his own part; for with him "all the world's a stage, and all the men and women," himself first, "merely players." We have his own presentation of himself, not, first of all, as he is, but as he chooses to be taken. Of course his real self does come out in it, for no man can seem altogether other than he is; and besides, the *Duke*, who sees quite through him, rebukes him in the manner already referred to; but it is his affectation that gives him the unnatural peculiarity of his modes and speeches. He wishes them to be such.

There is, then, for every one of Shakspere's characters the firm ground of humanity, upon which the weeds, as well as the flowers, glorious or fantastic, as the case may be, show themselves. His more heroic persons are the most profoundly human. Nor are his villains unhuman, although inhuman enough. Compared with Marlowe's Jew, *Shylock* is a terrible *man* beside a dreary *monster*, and, as far as logic and the *lex talionis* go, has the best of the argument. It is the strength of human nature itself that makes crime strong. Wickedness could have no power of itself: it lives by the perverted powers of good. And so great is Shakspere's sympathy with *Shylock* even, in the hard and unjust doom that overtakes him, that he dismisses him with some of the spare sympathies of the more tender-hearted of his spectators. Nowhere is the justice of genius more plain than in Shakspere's utter freedom from party-spirit, even with regard to his own creations. Each character shall set itself forth from its own point of view, and only in the choice and scope of the whole shall the judgment of the poet be beheld. He never allows his opinion to come out to the damaging of the individual's own self-presentation. He knows well that for the worst something can be said, and that a feeling of justice and his own right will be strong in the mind of a man who is yet swayed by perfect selfishness. Therefore the false man is not discoverable in his speech, not merely because the villain will talk as like a true man as he may, but because seldom is the villainy clear to the villain's own mind. It is impossible for us to determine whether, in their fierce bandying of the lie, *Bolingbroke* or *Norfolk* spoke the truth. Doubtless each believed the other to be the villain that he called him. And Shakspere has no desire or need to act the historian in the decision of that question. He leaves his reader in full sympathy with the perplexity of *Richard*; as puzzled, in fact, as if he had been present at the interrupted combat.

If every writer could write up to his own best, we should have far less to marvel at in Shakspere. It is in great measure the wealth of Shakspere's suggestions, giving him abundance of the best to choose from, that lifts him so high above those who, having felt the inspiration of a good idea, are forced to go on writing, constructing, carpentering, with dreary handicraft, before the exhausted faculty has recovered sufficiently to generate another. And then comes in the unerring choice of the best of those suggestions. Yet if any one wishes to see what variety of the same kind of thoughts he could produce, let him examine the treatment of the same business in different plays; as, for instance, the way in which instigation to a crime is managed in "Macbeth," where *Macbeth* tempts the two murderers to kill *Banquo*; in "King John," when *the King* tempts *Hubert* to kill *Arthur*; in "The Tempest," when *Antonio* tempts *Sebastian* to kill *Alonzo*; in "As You Like it," when *Oliver* instigates *Charles* to kill *Orlando*; and in "Hamlet," where *Claudius* urges *Laertes* to the murder of *Hamlet*.

He shows no anxiety about being original. When a man is full of his work he forgets himself. In his desire to produce a good play he lays hold upon any material that offers itself. He will even take a bad play and make a good one of it. One of the most remarkable discoveries to the student of Shakspere is the hide-bound poverty of some of the stories, which, informed by his life-power; become forms of strength, richness, and grace. He does what the *Spirit* in "Comus" says the music he heard might do, --

> *"create a soul*
>
> *Under the ribs of death;"*

and then death is straightway "clothed upon." And nowhere is the refining operation of his genius more evident than in the purification of these stories. Characters and incidents which would have been honey and nuts to Beaumont and Fletcher are, notwithstanding their dramatic recommendations, entirely remodelled by him. The fair *Ophelia* is, in the old tale, a common woman, and *Hamlet's* mistress; while the policy of the *Lady of Belmont*, who in the old story occupies the place for which he invented the lovely *Portia*, upon which policy the whole story turns, is such that it is as unfit to set forth in our pages as it was unfit for Shakspere's purposes of art. His noble art refuses to work upon base matter. He sees at once the capabilities of a tale, but he will not use it except he may do with it what he pleases.

If we might here offer some assistance to the young student who wants to help himself, we would suggest that to follow, in a measure, Plutarch's fashion of comparison, will be the most helpful guide to the understanding of the poet. Let the reader take any two characters, and putting them side by side, look first for differences, and then for resemblances between them, with the causes of each; or let him make a wider attempt, and setting two plays one over against the other, compare or contrast them, and see what will be the result. Let him, for instance, take the two characters *Hamlet* and *Brutus*, and compare their beginnings and endings, the resemblances in their characters, the differences in their conduct, the likeness and unlikeness of what was required of them, the circumstances in which action was demanded of each, the helps or hindrances each had to the working out of the problem of his life, the way in which each encounters the supernatural, or any other question that may suggest itself in reading either of the plays, ending off with the main lesson taught in each; and he will be astonished to find, if he has not already discovered it, what a rich mine of intellectual and spiritual wealth is laid open to his delighted eyes.

Perhaps not the least valuable end to be so gained is, that the young Englishman, who wants to be delivered from any temptation to think himself the centre around which the universe revolves, will be aided in his endeavours after honourable humility by looking up to the man who towers, like Saul, head and shoulders above his brethren, and seeing that he is humble, may learn to leave it to the pismire to be angry, to the earwig to be conceited, and to the spider to insist on his own importance.

But to return to the main course of our observations. The dramas of Shakspere are so natural, that this, the greatest praise that can be given them, is the ground of one of the difficulties felt by the young student in estimating them. The very simplicity of Shakspere's art seems to throw him out of any known groove of judgment. When he hears one say, "*Look at this, and admire*," he feels inclined to rejoin, "Why, he only says in the simplest way what the thing must have been. It is as plain as daylight." Yes, to the reader; and because Shakspere wrote it. But there were a thousand wrong ways of doing it: Shakspere took the one right way. It is he who has made it plain in art, whatever it was before in nature; and most likely the very simplicity of it in nature was scarcely observed before he saw it and represented it. And is it not the glory of art to attain this simplicity? for simplicity is the end of all -- all manners, all morals, all religion. To say that the thing could not have been done otherwise, is just to say that you forget the art in beholding its object, that you forget the mirror because you see nature reflected in the mirror. Any one can see the moon in Lord Rosse's telescope; but who made the reflector?[56] And let the student try to express anything in prose or in verse, in painting or in modelling, just as it is. No man knows till he has made many attempts, how hard to reach is this simplicity of art. And the greater the success, the fewer are the signs of the labour expended. Simplicity is art's perfection.

But so natural are all his plays, and the great tragedies to which we would now refer in particular, amongst the rest, that it may appear to some, at first sight, that Shakspere could not have constructed them after any moral plan, could have had no lesson of his own to teach in them, seeing they bear no marks of individual intent, in that they depart

---

[56] William Parsons, the 3rd earl of Rosse, (1807-1841) was an Irish peer and an astronomer who built the largest reflecting telescope in the 19th century, which was known as "Leviathan."

nowhere from, nature, the construction of the play itself going straight on like a history. The directness of his plays springs in part from the fact that it is humanity and not circumstance that Shakspere respects. Circumstance he uses only for the setting forth of humanity; and for the plot of circumstance, so much in favour with Ben Jonson, and others of his contemporaries, he cares nothing.[57] As to their looking too natural to have any design in them, we are not of those who believe that it is unlike nature to have a design and a result. If the proof of a high aim is to be what the critics used to call *poetic justice*, a kind of justice that one would gladly find more of in grocers' and linen-drapers' shops, but can as well spare from a poem, then we must say that he has not always a high end: the wicked man is not tortured, nor is the good man smothered in bank-notes and rose -- leaves. Even when he shows the outward ruin and death that comes upon Macbeth at last, it is only as an unavoidable little consequence, following in the wake of the mighty vengeance of nature, even of God, that Macbeth cannot say *Amen*; that Macbeth can sleep no more; that Macbeth is "cabined cribbed, confined, bound in to saucy doubts and fears;" that his very brain is a charnel-house, whence arise the ghosts of his own murders, till he envies the very dead the rest to which his hand has sent them. That immediate and eternal vengeance upon crime, and that inner reward of well-doing, never fail in nature or in Shakspere, appear as such a matter of course that they hardly look like design either in nature or in the mirror which he holds up to her. The secret is that, in the ideal, habit and design are one.

Most authors seem anxious to round off and finish everything in full sight. Most of Shakspere's tragedies compel our thoughts to follow their *persons* across the bourn. They need, as Jean Paul says, a piece of the next world painted in to complete the picture, And this is surely nature: but it need not therefore be no design.[58] What could be done with Hamlet, but send him into a region where he has some chance of finding his difficulties solved; where he will know that his reverence

---

[57] Benjamin Jonson (1572-1637) was an English playwright known for his satirical work.

[58] Jean Paul (1763-1825) was the penn name for Johann Paul Friedrich Richter, a German Romantic writer. Much of Paul's work incorporated the significance of the unseen world. "Jean Paul," *New World Encyclopedia*, accessed August 19, 2021, https://www.newworldencyclopedia.org/entry/Jean_Paul.

for God, which was the sole stay left him in the flood of human worthlessness, has not been in vain; that the skies are not "a foul and pestilent congregation of vapours;" that there are noble women, though his mother was false and Ophelia weak; and that there are noble men, although his uncle and Laertes were villains and his old companions traitors? If Hamlet is not to die, the whole of the play must perish under the accusation that the hero of it is left at last with only a superadded misery, a fresh demand for action, namely, to rule a worthless people, as they seem to him, when action has for him become impossible; that he has to live on, forsaken even of death, which will not come though the cup of misery is at the brim.

But a high end may be gained in this world, and the vision into the world beyond so justified, as in King Lear. The passionate, impulsive, unreasoning old king certainly must have given his wicked daughters occasion enough of making the charges to which their avarice urged them. He had learned very little by his life of kingship. He was but a boy with grey hair. He had had no inner experiences. And so all the development of manhood and age has to be crowded into the few remaining weeks of his life. His own folly and blindness supply the occasion. And before the few weeks are gone, he has passed through all the stages of a fever of indignation and wrath, ending in a madness from which love redeems him; he has learned that a king is nothing if the man is nothing; that a king ought to care for those who cannot help themselves; that love has not its origin or grounds in favours flowing from royal resource and munificence, and yet that love is the one thing worth living for, which gained, it is time to die. And now that he has the experience that life can give, has become a child in simplicity of heart and judgment, he cannot lose his daughter again; who, likewise, has learned the one thing she needed, as far as her father was concerned, a little more excusing tenderness. In the same play it cannot be by chance that at its commencement Gloucester speaks with the utmost carelessness and *off-hand* wit about the parentage of his natural son Edmund, but finds at last that this son is his ruin.

Edgar, the true son, says to Edmund, after having righteously dealt him his death-wound, --

The gods are just, and of our pleasant vices

Make instruments to scourge us:

> *The dark and vicious place where thee he got*
>
> *Cost him his eyes.*[59]

To which the dying and convicted villain replies, --

> *Thou hast spoken right; 'tis true:*
>
> *The wheel is come full circle; I am here.*[60]

Could anything be put more plainly than the moral lesson in this?

It would be easy to produce examples of fine design from his comedies as well; as for instance, from "Much Ado about Nothing:" the two who are made to fall in love with each other, by being each severally assured of possessing the love of the other, Beatrice and Benedick, are shown beforehand to have a strong inclination towards each other, manifested in their continual squabbling after a good-humoured fashion; but not all this is sufficient to make them heartily in love, until they find out the nobility of each other's character in their behaviour about the calumniated Hero; and the author takes care they shall not be married without a previous acquaintance with the trick that has been played upon them. Indeed we think the remark, that Shakspere never leaves any of his characters the same at the end of a play as he took them up at the beginning, will be found to be true. They are better or worse, wiser or more irretrievably foolish. The historical plays would illustrate the remark as well as any.

But of all the terrible plays we are inclined to think "Timon" the most terrible, and to doubt whether justice has been done to the finish and completeness of it. At the same time we are inclined to think that it was printed (first in the first folio, 1623, seven years after Shakspere's death) from a copy, corrected by the author, but not *written fair*, and containing consequent mistakes. The same account might belong to others of the plays, but more evidently perhaps belongs to the "Timon." The idea of making the generous spendthrift, whose old idolaters had forsaken him because the idol had no more to give, into the high-priest of the Temple of Mammon, dispensing the gold which he hated and despised, that it might be a curse to the race which he had

---

[59] "King Lear," Act 5, scene 3, lines 166-169.

[60] Ibid., lines 170-171.

learned to hate and despise as well; and the way in which Shakspere discloses the depths of Timon's wound, by bringing him into comparison with one who hates men by profession and humour -- are as powerful as anything to be found even in Shakspere.

We are very willing to believe that "Julius Caesar" was one of his latest plays; for certainly it is the play in which he has represented a hero in the high and true sense. *Brutus* is this hero, of course; a hero because he will do what he sees to be right, independently of personal feeling or personal advantage. Nor does his attempt fail from any overweening or blindness, in himself. Had he known that the various papers thrown in his way, were the concoctions of *Cassius*, he would not have made the mistake of supposing that the Romans longed for freedom, and therefore would be ready to defend it. As it was, he attempted to liberate a people which did not feel its slavery. He failed for others, but not for himself; for his truth was such that everybody was true to him. Unlike Jaques with his seven acts of the burlesque of human life, Brutus says at the last, --

> *Countrymen,*
>
> *My heart doth joy, that yet, in all my life,*
>
> *I found no man but he was true to me.*[61]

Of course all this is in Plutarch. But it is easy to see with what relish Shakspere takes it up, setting forth all the aids in himself and in others which Brutus had to being a hero, and thus making the representation as credible as possible.

We must heartily confess that no amount of genius alone will make a man a good man; that genius only shows the right way -- drives no man to walk in it. But there is surely some moral scent in us to let us know whether a man only cares for good from an artistic point of view, or whether he admires and loves good. This admiration and love cannot be *prominently* set forth by any dramatist true to his art; but it must come out over the whole. His predilections must show themselves in the scope of his artistic life, in the things and subjects he chooses, and the way in which he represents them. Notwithstanding

---

[61] "Julius Caesar," Act 5, scene 5, lines 33-35.

Uncle Toby and Maria, who will venture to say that Sterne was noble or virtuous, when he looks over the whole that he has written? But in Shakspere there is no suspicion of a cloven foot. Everywhere he is on the side of virtue and of truth. Many small arguments, with great cumulative force, might be adduced to this effect.

For ourselves we cannot easily believe that the calmness of his art could be so unvarying except he exercised it with a good conscience; that he could have kept looking out upon the world around him with the untroubled regard necessary for seeing all things as they are, except there had been peace in his house at home; that he could have known all men as he did, and failed to know himself. We can understand the co-existence of any degree of partial or excited genius with evil ways, but we cannot understand the existence of such calm and universal genius, wrought out in his works, except in association with all that is noblest in human nature. Nor is it other than on the side of the argument for his rectitude that he never forces rectitude upon the attention of others. The strong impression left upon our minds is, that however Shakspere may have strayed in the early portion of his life in London, he was not only an upright and noble man for the main part, but a repentant man, and a man whose life was influenced by the truths of Christianity.

Much is now said about a memorial to Shakspere. The best and only true memorial is no doubt that described in Milton's poem on this very subject: the living and ever-changing monument of human admiration, expressed in the faces and forms of those absorbed in the reading of his works.[62] But if the external monument might be such as to foster the constant reproduction of the inward monument of love and admiration, then, indeed, it might be well to raise one; and with this object in view let us venture to propose one mode which we think would favour the attainment of it.

Let a Gothic hall of the fourteenth century be built; such a hall as would be more in the imagination of Shakspere than any of the architecture of his own time. Let all the copies that can be procured of every early edition of his works, singly or collectively, be stored in this hall. Let a copy of every other edition ever printed be procured and deposited. Let every book or treatise that can be found, good, bad, or

---

[62] MacDonald is referring to John Milton's poem "On Shakespeare" (1630).

indifferent, written about Shakspere or any of his works, be likewise collected for the Shakspere library. Let a special place be allotted to the shameless corruptions of his plays that have been produced as improvements upon them, some of which, to the disgrace of England, still partially occupy the stage instead of what Shakspere wrote. Let one department contain every work of whatever sort that tends to direct elucidation of his meaning, chiefly those of the dramatic writers who preceded him and closely followed him. Let the windows be filled with stained glass, representing the popular sports of his own time and the times of his English histories. Let a small museum be attached, containing all procurable antiquities that are referred to in his plays, along with first editions, if possible, of the best books that came out in his time, and were probably read by him. Let the whole thus as much as possible represent his time. Let a marble statue in the midst do the best that English art can accomplish for the representation of the vanished man; and let copies, if not the originals, of the several portraits be safely shrined for the occasional beholding of the multitude. Let the perpetuity of care necessary for this monument be secured by endowment; and let it be for the use of the public, by means of a reading-room fitted for the comfort of all who choose to avail themselves of these facilities for a true acquaintance with our greatest artist. Let there likewise be a simple and moderately-sized theatre attached, not for regular, but occasional use; to be employed for the representation of Shakspere's plays *only*, and allowed free of expense for amateur or other representations of them for charitable purposes. But within a certain cycle of -- if, indeed, it would be too much to expect that out of the London play-goers a sufficient number would be found to justify the representation of all the plays of Shakspere once in the season -- let the whole of Shakspere's plays be acted in the best manner possible to the managers for the time being.

The very existence of such a theatre would be a noble protest of the highest kind against the sort of play, chiefly translated and adapted from the French, which infests our boards, the low tone of which, even where it is not decidedly immoral, does more harm than any amount of the rough, honest plain-spokenness of Shakspere, as judged by our more fastidious, if not always purer manners. The representation of such plays forms the real ground of objection to theatre-going. We believe that other objections, which may be equally urged against large assemblies of any sort, are not really grounded upon such an amount of objectionable fact as good people often suppose. At all events it is not against the drama itself, but its concomitants, its avoidable concomitants, that such objections are, or ought to be, felt and directed. The dramatic impulse, as well as all other impulses of our nature, are from the Maker.

A monument like this would help to change a blind enthusiasm and a *dilettante*-talk into knowledge, reverence, and study; and surely this would be the true way to honour the memory of the man who appeals to posterity by no mighty deeds of worldly prowess, but has left behind him food for heart, brain, and conscience, on which the generations will feed till the end of time. It would be the one true and natural mode of perpetuating his fame in kind; helping him to do more of that for which he was born, and because of which we humbly desire to do him honour, as the years flow farther away from the time when, at the age of fifty-two, he left the world a richer legacy of the results of intellectual labour than any other labourer in literature has ever done. It would be to raise a monument to his mind more than to his person.

But to honour Shakspere in the best way we must not gaze upon some grand memorial of his fame, we must not talk largely of his wonderful doings, we must not even behold the representation of his works on the stage, invaluable aid as that is to the right understanding of what he has written; but we must, by close, silent, patient study, enter into an understanding with the spirit of the departed poet-sage, and thus let his own words be the necromantic spell that raises the dead, and brings us into communion with that man who knew what was in men more than any other mere man ever did. Well was it for Shakspere that he was humble; else on what a desolate pinnacle of companionless solitude must he have stood! Where was he to find his peers? To most thoughtful minds it is a terrible fancy to suppose that there were no greater human being than themselves. From the terror of such a *truth* Shakspere's love for men preserved him. He did not think about himself so much as he thought about them. Had he been a self-student alone, or chiefly, could he ever have written those dramas? We close with the repetition of this truth: that the love of our kind is the one key to the knowledge of humanity and of ourselves. And have we not sacred authority for concluding that he who loves his brother is the more able and the more likely to love Him who made him and his brother also, and then told them that love is the fulfilling of the law?

The Art of Shakspere, as Revealed by Himself

Who taught you this?
I learn'd it out of women's faces.

Winter's Tale, Act ii. scene 1.

One occasionally hears the remark, that the commentators upon Shakspere find far more in Shakspere than Shakspere ever intended to express. Taking this assertion as it stands, it may be freely granted, not only of Shakspere, but of every writer of genius. But if it be intended by it, that nothing can *exist* in any work of art beyond what the writer was conscious of while in the act of producing it, so much of its scope is false.

No artist can have such a claim to the high title of *creator*, as that he invents for himself the forms, by means of which he produces his new result; and all the forms of man and nature which he modifies and combines to make a new region in his world of art, have their own original life and meaning. The laws likewise of their various combinations are natural laws, harmonious with each other. While, therefore, the artist employs many or few of their original aspects for his immediate purpose, he does not and cannot thereby deprive them of the many more which are essential to their vitality, and the vitality likewise of his presentation of them, although they form only the background from which his peculiar use of them stands out. The objects presented must therefore fall, to the eye of the observant reader, into many different combinations and harmonies of operation and result, which are indubitably there, whether the writer saw them or not. These latent combinations and relations will be numerous and true, in proportion to the scope and the truth of the representation; and the greater the number of meanings, harmonious with each other, which any work of art presents, the greater claim it has to be considered a work of genius. It must, therefore, be granted, and that joyfully, that there may be meanings in Shakspere's writings which Shakspere himself did not see, and to which therefore his art, as art, does not point.

But the probability, notwithstanding, must surely be allowed as well, that, in great artists, the amount of conscious art will bear some proportion to the amount of unconscious truth: the visible volcanic light will bear a true relation to the hidden fire of the globe; so that it will not seem likely that, in such a writer as Shakspere, we should find many indications of present and operative *art*, of which he was himself unaware. Some truths may be revealed through him, which he himself knew only potentially; but it is not likely that marks of work, bearing upon the results of the play, should be fortuitous, or that the work thus indicated should be unconscious work. A stroke of the mallet may be more effective than the sculptor had hoped; but it was intended. In the drama it is easier to discover individual marks of the chisel, than in the marble whence all signs of such are removed: in the drama the lines themselves fall into the general finish, without necessary obliteration as lines: Still, the reader cannot help being fearful, lest, not as regards truth only, but as regards art as well, he be sometimes clothing the idol of his intellect with the weavings of his fancy. My conviction is, that it is the very consummateness of Shakspere's art, that exposes his work to the doubt that springs from loving anxiety for his honour; the dramatist, like the sculptor, avoiding every avoidable hint of the process, in order to render the result a vital whole. But, fortunately, we are not left to argue entirely from probabilities. He has himself given us a peep into his studio -- let me call it *workshop*, as more comprehensive.

It is not, of course, in the shape of *literary* criticism, that we should expect to meet such a revelation; for to use art even consciously, and to regard it as an object of contemplation, or to theorize about it, are two very different mental operations. The productive and critical faculties are rarely found in equal combination; and even where they are, they cannot operate equally in regard to the same object. There is a perfect satisfaction in producing, which does not demand a re-presentation to the critical faculty. In other words, the criticism which a great writer brings to bear upon his own work, is from within, regarding it upon the hidden side, namely, in relation to his own idea; whereas criticism, commonly understood, has reference to the side turned to the public gaze. Neither could we expect one so prolific as Shakspere to find time for the criticism of the works of other men, except in such moments of relaxation as those in which the friends at the Mermaid Tavern sat silent beneath the flow of his wisdom and humour, or made the street ring with the overflow of their own enjoyment.[1]

But if the artist proceed to speculate upon the nature or productions of another art than his own, we may then expect the principles upon which he operates in his own, to take outward and visible form -- a form modified by the difference of the art to which he now applies them. In one of Shakspere's poems, we have the description of an imagined production of a sister-art -- that of Painting -- a description so brilliant that the light reflected from the poet-picture illumines the art of the Poet himself, revealing the principles which he held with regard to representative art generally, and suggesting many thoughts with regard to detail and harmony, finish, pregnancy, and scope. This description is found in "The Rape of Lucrece." Apology will hardly be necessary for making a long quotation, seeing that, besides the convenience it will afford of easy reference to the ground of my argument, one of the greatest helps which even the artist can give to us, is to isolate peculiar beauties, and so compel us to perceive them.

Lucrece has sent a messenger to beg the immediate presence of her husband. Awaiting his return, and worn out with weeping, she looks about for some variation of her misery.

1.

At last she calls to mind where hangs a piece

  Of skilful painting, made for Priam's Troy;

Before the which is drawn the power of Greece,

  For Helen's rape the city to destroy,

  Threatening cloud -- kissing Ilion with annoy;

Which the conceited painter drew so proud,

  As heaven, it seemed, to kiss the turrets, bowed.

---

[1] The Mermaid Tavern was located east of St. Paul's Cathedral in London and was the meeting place for poets and writers. "Mermaid Tavern.," accessed August 19, 2021, http://www.luminarium.org/encyclopedia/mermaid.htm.

2.

A thousand lamentable objects there,

    In scorn of Nature, Art gave lifeless life:

Many a dry drop seemed a weeping tear,

    Shed for the slaughtered husband by the wife;

    The red blood reeked, to show the painter's strife.

And dying eyes gleamed forth their ashy lights,

Like dying coals burnt out in tedious nights.

3.

There might you see the labouring pioneer

    Begrimed with sweat, and smeared all with dust;

And, from the towers of Troy there would appear

    The very eyes of men through loopholes thrust,

    Gazing upon the Greeks with little lust:

Such sweet observance in this work was had,

That one might see those far -- off eyes look sad.

4.

In great commanders, grace and majesty

    You might behold, triumphing in their faces;

In youth, quick bearing and dexterity;

    And here and there the painter interlaces

    Pale cowards, marching on with trembling paces,

Which heartless peasants did so well resemble,

That one would swear he saw them quake and tremble.

5.

In Ajax and Ulysses, O what art

    Of physiognomy might one behold!

The face of either ciphered either's heart;

    Their face their manners most expressly told:

In Ajax' eyes blunt rage and rigour rolled;
But the mild glance that sly Ulysses lent
Showed deep regard, and smiling government.

6.

There pleading might you see grave Nestor stand,
   As 'twere encouraging the Greeks to fight;
Making such sober action with his hand,
    That it beguiled attention, charmed the sight;
    In speech, it seemed his beard, all silver -- white,
Wagged up and down, and from his lips did fly
Thin winding breath, which purled up to the sky.

7.

About him were a press of gaping faces,
   Which seemed to swallow up his sound advice;
All jointly listening, but with several graces,
    As if some mermaid did their ears entice;
    Some high, some low, the painter was so nice.
The scalps of many, almost hid behind,
To jump up higher seemed, to mock the mind.

8.

Here one man's hand leaned on another's head,
   His nose being shadowed by his neighbour's ear;
Here one, being thronged, bears back, all bollen and red;
    Another, smothered, seems to pelt and swear;
    And in their rage such signs of rage they bear,
As, but for loss of Nestor's golden words,
It seemed they would debate with angry swords.

9.

For much imaginary work was there;
   Conceit deceitful, so compact, so kind,
 That for Achilles' image stood his spear,
   Griped in an armed hand; himself behind
   Was left unseen, save to the eye of mind:
A hand, a foot, a face, a leg, a head,
Stood for the whole to be imagined.

10.

And, from the walls of strong -- besieged Troy,
   When their brave hope, bold Hector, marched to field,
Stood many Trojan mothers, sharing joy
   To see their youthful sons bright weapons wield,
   And to their hope they such odd action yield;
That through their light joy seemed to appear,
Like bright things stained, a kind of heavy fear.

11.

And from the strond of Dardan, where they fought,
   To Simois' reedy banks, the red blood ran;
Whose waves to imitate the battle sought,
   With swelling ridges; and their ranks began
   To break upon the galled shore, and then
Retire again, till, meeting greater ranks,
They join, and shoot their foam at Simois' banks.

The oftener I read these verses, amongst the very earliest compositions of Shakspere, I am the more impressed with the carefulness with which he represents the *work* of the -- "shows the strife of the painter." The most natural thought to follow in sequence is: How like his own art!

The scope and variety of the whole picture, in which mass is effected by the accumulation of individuality; in which, on the one hand, Troy stands as the impersonation of the aim and object of the whole; and on the other, the Simois flows in foaming rivalry of the strife of men, -- the pictorial form of that sympathy of nature with human effort and passion, which he so often introduces in his plays, -- is like nothing else so much as one of the works of his own art. But to take a portion as a more condensed representation of his art in combining all varieties into one harmonious whole: his genius is like the oratory of Nestor as described by its effects in the seventh and eighth stanzas. Every variety of attitude and countenance and action is harmonized by the influence which is at once the occasion of debate, and the charm which restrains by the fear of its own loss: the eloquence and the listening form the one bond of the unruly mass. So the dramatic genius that harmonizes his play, is visible only in its effects; so ethereal in its own essence that it refuses to be submitted to the analysis of the ruder intellect, it is like the words of Nestor, for which in the picture there stands but "thin winding breath which purled up to the sky." Take, for an instance of this, the reconciling power by which, in the mysterious midnight of the summer-wood, he brings together in one harmony the graceful passions of childish elves, and the fierce passions of men and women, with the ludicrous reflection of those passions in the little convex mirror of the artisan's drama; while the mischievous Puck revels in things that fall out preposterously, and the Elf-Queen is in love with ass-headed Bottom, from the hollows of whose long hairy ears -- strange bouquet-holders -- bloom and breathe the musk-roses, the characteristic odour-founts of the play; and the philosophy of the unbelieving Theseus, with the candour of Hippolyta, lifts the whole into relation with the realities of human life. Or take, as another instance, the pretended madman Edgar, the court-fool, and the rugged old king going grandly mad, sheltered in one hut, and lapped in the roar of a thunderstorm.

My object, then, in respect to this poem, is to produce, from many instances, a few examples of the metamorphosis of such excellences as he describes in the picture, into the corresponding forms of the drama; in the hope that it will not then be necessary to urge the probability that the presence of those artistic virtues in his own practice, upon which he expatiates in his representation of another man's art, were accompanied by the corresponding consciousness -- that, namely, of the artist as differing from that of the critic, its objects being regarded from the concave side of the hammered relief. If this probability be granted, I would, from it, advance to a higher and far more important -- how unlikely it is that if the writer was conscious of such fitnesses, he should be unconscious of those grand embodiments of truth, which are indubitably present in his plays, whether he knew it or not. This portion of my argument will be strengthened by an instance to show that Shakspere was himself quite at home in the contemplation of such truths.

Let me adduce, then, some of those corresponding embodiments in words instead of in forms; in which colours yield to tones, lines to phrases. I will begin with the lowest kind, in which the art has to do with matters so small, that it is difficult to believe that *unconscious* art could have any relation to them. They can hardly have proceeded directly from the great inspiration of the whole. Their very minuteness is an argument for their presence to the poet's consciousness; while belonging, as they do, only to the *construction* of the play, no such independent existence can be accorded to them, as to *truths*, which, being in themselves realities, *are* there, whether Shakspere saw them or not. If he did not intend them, the most that can be said for them is, that such is the naturalness of Shakspere's representations, that there is room in his plays, as in life, for those wonderful coincidences which are reducible to no law.

Perhaps every one of the examples I adduce will be found open to dispute. This is a kind in which direct proof can have no share; nor should I have dared thus to combine them in argument, but for the ninth stanza of those quoted above, to which I beg my readers to revert. Its *imaginary work* -- work hinted at, and then left to the imagination of the reader. Of course, in dramatic representation, such work must exist on a great scale; but the minute particularization of the "conceit deceitful" in the rest of the stanza, will surely justify us in thinking it possible that Shakspere intended many, if not all, of the *little* fitnesses which a careful reader discovers in his plays. That such are not oftener discovered comes from this: that, like life itself, he so blends into vital beauty, that there are no salient points. To use a homely simile: he is not like the barn-door fowl, that always runs out cackling when she has laid an egg; and often when she has not. In the tone of an ordinary drama, you may know when something is coming; and the tone itself declares -- *I have done it.* But Shakspere will not spoil his art to show his art. It is there, and does its part: that is enough. If you can discover it, good and well; if not, pass on, and take what you can find. He can afford not to be fathomed for every little pearl that lies at the bottom of his ocean. If I succeed in showing that such art may exist where it is not readily discovered, this may give some additional probability to its existence in places where it is harder to isolate and define.

To produce a few instances, then:

In "Much Ado about Nothing," seeing the very nature of the play is expressed in its name, is it not likely that Shakspere named the two constables, Dogberry (*a poisonous berry*) and Verjuice (*the juice of crab -- apples*); those names having absolutely nothing to do with the stupid innocuousness of their characters, and so corresponding to their way of turning things upside down, and saying the very opposite of what they mean?

In the same play we find Margaret objecting to her mistress's wearing a certain rebato (*a large plaited ruff*), on the morning of her wedding: may not this be intended to relate to the fact that Margaret had dressed in her mistress's clothes the night before? She might have rumpled or soiled it, and so feared discovery.

In "King Henry IV.," Part I., we find, in the last scene, that the Prince kills Hotspur. This is not recorded in history: the conqueror of Percy is unknown. Had it been a fact, history would certainly have recorded it; and the silence of history in regard to a deed of such mark, is equivalent to its contradiction. But Shakspere requires, for his play's sake, to identify the slayer of Hotspur with his rival the Prince. Yet Shakspere will not contradict history, even in its silence. What is he to do? He will account for history *not knowing* the fact -- Falstaff claiming the honour, the Prince says to him:

"For my part, if a lie may do thee grace,

I'll gild it with the happiest terms I have;"

revealing thus the magnificence of his own character, in his readiness, for the sake of his friend, to part with his chief renown. But the Historic Muse could not believe that fat Jack Falstaff had killed Hotspur, and therefore she would not record the claim.

In the second part of the same play, act i. scene 2, we find Falstaff toweringly indignant with Mr. Dombledon, the silk mercer, that he will stand upon security with a gentleman for a short cloak and slops of satin. In the first scene of the second act, the hostess mentions that Sir John is going to dine with Master Smooth, the silkman. Foiled with Mr. Dombledon, he has already made himself so agreeable to Master Smooth, that he is "indited to dinner" with him. This is, by the bye, as to the action of the play; but as to the character of Sir John, is it not

"Conceit deceitful, so compact,

so kind"—kinned—natural?

The *conceit deceitful* in the painting, is the imagination that means more than its says. So the words of the speakers in the play, stand for more than the speakers mean. They are *Shakspere's* in their relation to his whole. To Achilles, his spear is but his spear: to the painter and his company, the spear of Achilles stands for Achilles himself.

Coleridge remarks upon *James Gurney*, in "King John:" "How individual and comical he is with the four words allowed to his dramatic life!" These words are those with which he answers the Bastard's request to leave the room. He has been lingering with all the inquisitiveness and privilege of an old servant; when Faulconbridge says: "James Gurney, wilt thou give us leave a while?" with strained politeness. With marked condescension to the request of the second son, whom he has known and served from infancy, James Gurney replies: "Good leave, good Philip;" giving occasion to Faulconbridge to show his ambition, and scorn of his present standing, in the contempt with which he treats even the Christian name he is so soon to exchange with his surname for *Sir Richard* and *Plantagenet; Philip* being the name for a sparrow in those days, when ladies made pets of them. Surely in these words of the serving-man, we have an outcome of the same art by which

"A hand, a foot, a face, a leg, a head,

Stood for the whole to be imagined."

In the "Winter's Tale," act iv. scene 3, Perdita, dressed with unwonted gaiety at the festival of the sheep -- shearing, is astonished at finding herself talking in full strains of poetic verse. She says, half-ashamed:

"Methinks I play as I have seen them do

In Whitsun pastorals: sure, this robe of mine

Does change my disposition!"

She does not mean this seriously. But the robe has more to do with it than she thinks. Her passion for Florizel is the warmth that sets the springs of her thoughts free, and they flow with the grace belonging to a princess-nature; but it is the robe that opens the door of her speech, and, by elevating her consciousness of herself, betrays her into what is only natural to her, but seems to her, on reflection, inconsistent with her low birth and poor education. This instance, however, involves far higher elements than any of the examples I have given before, and naturally leads to a much more important class of illustrations.

In "Macbeth," act ii. scene 4, why is the old man, who has nothing to do with the conduct of the play, introduced? -- That, in conversation with Rosse, he may, as an old man, bear testimony to the exceptionally terrific nature of that storm, which, we find -- from the words of Banquo:

"There's husbandry in heaven:

Their candles are all out,"—

had begun to gather, before supper was over in the castle. This storm is the sympathetic horror of Nature at the breaking open of the Lord's anointed temple -- horror in which the animal creation partakes, for the horses of Duncan, "the minions of their race," and therefore the most sensitive of their sensitive race, tear each other to pieces in the wildness of their horror. Consider along with this a foregoing portion of the second scene in the same act. Macbeth, having joined his wife after the murder, says:

'Who lies i' the second chamber?

'Lady M. Donalbain.

'There are two lodged together.'

These two, Macbeth says, woke each other -- the one laughing, the other crying *murder*. Then they said their prayers and went to sleep again. -- I used to think that the natural companion of Donalbain would be Malcolm, his brother; and that the two brothers woke in horror from the proximity of their father's murderer who was just passing the door. A friend objected to this, that, had they been together, Malcolm, being the elder, would have been mentioned rather than Donalbain. Accept this objection, and we find a yet more delicate significance: the *presence* operated differently on the two, one bursting out in a laugh, the other crying *murder*; but both were in terror when they awoke, and dared not sleep till they had said their prayers. His sons, his horses, the elements themselves, are shaken by one unconscious sympathy with the murdered king.

Associate with this the end of the third scene of the fourth act of "Julius Caesar;" where we find that the attendants of Brutus all cry out in their sleep, as the ghost of Caesar leaves their master's tent. This outcry is not given in Plutarch.

To return to "Macbeth:" Why is the doctor of medicine introduced in the scene at the English court? He has nothing to do with the progress of the play itself, any more than the old man already alluded to. -- He is introduced for a precisely similar reason. -- As a doctor, he is the best testimony that could be adduced to the fact, that the English King Edward the Confessor, is a fountain of health to his people, gifted for his goodness with the sacred privilege of curing *The King's Evil*, by the touch of his holy hands. The English King himself is thus introduced, for the sake of contrast with the Scotch King, who is a raging bear amongst his subjects.

In the "Winter's Tale," to which he gives the name because of the altogether extraordinary character of the occurrences (referring to it in the play itself, in the words: "*a sad tale's best for winter: I have one of sprites and goblins*") Antigonus has a remarkable dream or vision, in which Hermione appears to him, and commands the exposure of her child in a place to all appearance the most unsuitable and dangerous. Convinced of the reality of the vision, Antigonus obeys; and the whole marvellous result depends upon this obedience. Therefore the vision must be intended for a genuine one. But how could it be such, if Hermione was not dead, as, from her appearance to him, Antigonus firmly believed she was? I should feel this to be an objection to the art of the play, but for the following answer: -- At the time she appeared to him, she was still lying in that deathlike swoon, into which she fell when the news of the loss of her son reached her as she stood before the judgment-seat of her husband, at a time when she ought not to have been out of her chamber.

Note likewise, in the first scene of the second act of the same play, the changefulness of Hermione's mood with regard to her boy, as indicative of her condition at the time. If we do not regard this fact, we shall think the words introduced only for the sake of filling up the business of the play.

In "Twelfth Night," both ladies make the first advances in love. Is it not worthy of notice that one of them has lost her brother, and that the other believes she has lost hers? In this respect, they may be placed with Phoebe, in "As You Like It," who, having suddenly lost her love by the discovery that its object was a woman, immediately and heartily accepts the devotion of her rejected lover, Silvius. Along with these may be classed Romeo, who, rejected and, as he believes, inconsolable, falls in love with Juliet the moment he sees her. That his love for Rosaline, however, was but a kind of *calf-love* compared with his love for Juliet, may be found indicated in the differing tones of his speech under the differing conditions. Compare what he says in his conversation with Benvolio, in the first scene of the first act, with any of his many speeches afterwards, and, while *conceit* will be found prominent enough in both, the one will be found to be ruled by the fancy, the other by the imagination.

In this same play, there is another similar point which I should like to notice. In Arthur Brook's story, from which Shakspere took his, there is no mention of any communication from Lady Capulet to Juliet of their intention of marrying her to Count Paris. Why does Shakspere insert this? -- to explain her falling in love with Romeo so suddenly. Her mother has set her mind moving in that direction. She has never seen Paris. She is looking about her, wondering which may be he, and whether she shall be able to like him, when she meets the love-filled eyes of Romeo fixed upon her, and is at once overcome. What a significant speech is that given to Paulina in the "Winter's Tale," act v.

scene 1: "How? Not women?" Paulina is a thorough partisan, siding with women against men, and strengthened in this by the treatment her mistress has received from her husband. One has just said to her, that, if Perdita would begin a sect, she might "make proselytes of who she bid but follow." "How? Not women?" Paulina rejoins. Having received assurance that "women will love her," she has no more to say.

I had the following explanation of a line in "Twelfth Night" from a stranger I met in an old book-shop: -- Malvolio, having built his castle in the air, proceeds to inhabit it. Describing his own behaviour in a supposed case, he says (act ii. scene 5): "I frown the while; and perchance, wind up my watch, or play with my some rich jewel" -- A dash ought to come after *my*. Malvolio was about to say *chain*; but remembering that his chain was the badge of his office of steward, and therefore of his servitude, he alters the word to "*some rich jewel*" uttered with pretended carelessness.

In "Hamlet," act iii. scene 1, did not Shakspere intend the passionate soliloquy of Ophelia -- a soliloquy which no maiden knowing that she was overheard would have uttered, -- coupled with the words of her father:

"How now, Ophelia?

You need not tell us what lord Hamlet said,

We heard it all;" --

to indicate that, weak as Ophelia was, she was not false enough to be accomplice in any plot for betraying Hamlet to her father and the King? They had remained behind the arras, and had not gone out as she must have supposed.

Next, let me request my reader to refer once more to the poem; and having considered the physiognomy of Ajax and Ulysses, as described in the fifth stanza, to turn then to the play of "Troilus and Cressida," and there contemplate that description as metamorphosed into the higher form of revelation in speech. Then, if he will associate the general principles in that stanza with the third, especially the last two lines, I will apply this to the character of Lady Macbeth.

Of course, Shakspere does not mean that one regarding that portion of the picture alone, could see the eyes looking sad; but that the *sweet observance* of the whole so roused the imagination that it supplied what distance had concealed, keeping the far-off likewise in sweet observance with the whole: the rest pointed that way. -- In a manner something like this are we conducted to a right understanding of the character of Lady Macbeth. First put together these her utterances:

"You do unbend your noble strength, to think
So brainsickly of things."

"Get some water,
And wash this filthy witness from your hands."

"The sleeping and the dead
Are but as pictures."

"A little water clears us of this deed."

"When all's done,
You look but on a stool."

"You lack the season of all natures, sleep."—

Had these passages stood in the play unmodified by others, we might have judged from them that Shakspere intended to represent Lady Macbeth as an utter materialist, believing in nothing beyond the immediate communications of the senses. But when we find them associated with such passages as these –

"Memory, the warder of the brain,
Shall be a fume, and the receipt of reason
A limbeck only;"

"Had he not resembled

My father as he slept, I had done't;

"These deeds must not be thought

After these ways; so, it will make us mad;" --

then we find that our former theory will not do, for here are deeper and broader foundations to build upon. We discover that Lady Macbeth was an unbeliever *morally*, and so found it necessary to keep down all imagination, which is the upheaving of that inward world whose very being she would have annihilated. Yet out of this world arose at last the phantom of her slain self, and possessing her sleeping frame, sent it out to wander in the night, and rub its distressed and blood-stained hands in vain. For, as in this same "Rape of Lucrece,"

"the soul's fair temple is defaced;

To whose weak ruins muster troops of cares,

To ask the spotted princess how she fares."

But when so many lines of delineation meet, and run into, and correct one another, assuming such a natural and vital form, that there is no *making of a point* anywhere; and the woman is shown after no theory, but according to the natural laws of human declension, we feel that the only way to account for the perfection of the representation is to say that, given a shadow, Shakspere had the power to place himself so, that that shadow became his own -- was the correct representation as shadow, of his form coming between it and the sunlight. And this is the highest dramatic gift that a man can possess. But we feel at the same time, that this is, in the main, not so much art as inspiration. There would be, in all probability, a great mingling of conscious art with the inspiration; but the lines of the former being lost in the general glow of the latter, we may be left where we were as to any certainty about the artistic consciousness of Shakspere. I will now therefore attempt to give a few plainer instances of such *sweet observance* in his own work as he would have admired in a painting.

First, then, I would request my reader to think how comparatively seldom Shakspere uses poetry in his plays. The whole play is a poem in the highest sense; but truth forbids him to make it the rule for his characters to speak poetically. Their speech is poetic in relation to the whole and the end, not in relation to the speaker, or in the immediate utterance. And even although their speech is immediately poetic, in this sense, that every character is idealized; yet it is idealized *after its kind*; and poetry certainly would not be the ideal speech of most of the characters. This granted, let us look at the exceptions: we shall find that such passages not only glow with poetic loveliness and fervour, but are very jewels of *sweet observance*, whose setting allows them their force as lawful, and their prominence as natural. I will mention a few of such.

In "Julius Caesar," act i. scene 3, we are inclined to think the way *Casca* speaks, quite inconsistent with the "sour fashion" which *Cassius* very justly attributes to him; till we remember that he is speaking in the midst of an almost supernatural thunder-storm: the hidden electricity of the man's nature comes out in poetic forms and words, in response to the wild outburst of the overcharged heavens and earth.

Shakspere invariably makes the dying speak poetically, and generally prophetically, recognizing the identity of the poetic and prophetic moods, in their highest development, and the justice that gives them the same name. Even *Sir John*, poor ruined gentleman, *babbles of green fields*. Every one knows that the passage is disputed: I believe that if this be not the restoration of the original reading, Shakspere himself would justify it, and wish that he had so written it.

Romeo and *Juliet* talk poetry as a matter of course.

In "King John," act v. scenes 4 and 5, see how differently the dying *Melun* and the living and victorious *Lewis* regard the same sunset:

Melun.

. . . . . this night, whose black contagious breath

Already smokes about the burning crest

Of the old, feeble, and day -- wearied sun.

Lewis.

The sun in heaven, methought, was loath to set;

But stayed, and made the western welkin blush,

When the English measured backward their own ground.

The exquisite duet between *Lorenzo* and *Jessica*, in the opening of the fifth act of "The Merchant of Venice," finds for its subject the circumstances that produce the mood -- the lovely night and the crescent moon -- which first make them talk poetry, then call for music, and next speculate upon its nature.

Let us turn now to some instances of sweet observance in other kinds.

There is observance, more true than sweet, in the character of *Jacques*, in "As You Like It:" the fault-finder in age was the fault-doer in youth and manhood. *Jacques* patronizing the fool, is one of the rarest shows of self-ignorance.

In the same play, when *Rosalind* hears that *Orlando* is in the wood, she cries out, "Alas the day! what shall I do with my doublet and hose?" And when *Orlando* asks her, "Where dwell you, pretty youth?" she answers, tripping in her rôle, "Here in the skirts of the forest, like fringe upon a petticoat."

In the second part of "King Henry IV.," act iv. scene 3, *Falstaff* says of *Prince John*: "Good faith, this same young sober -- blooded boy doth not love me; nor a man cannot make him laugh; -- but that's no marvel: he drinks no wine." This is the *Prince John* who betrays the insurgents afterwards by the falsest of quibbles, and gains his revenge through their good faith.

In "King Henry IV.," act i. scene 2, *Poins* does not say *Falstaff* is a coward like the other two; but only -- "If he fight longer than he sees reason, I'll forswear arms." Associate this with *Falstaff's* soliloquy about *honour* in the same play, act v. scene 1, and the true character of his courage or cowardice -- for it may bear either name -- comes out.

Is there not conscious art in representing the hospitable face of the castle of *Macbeth*, bearing on it a homely welcome in the multitude of the nests of *the temple-haunting martlet* (Psalm lxxxiv. 3), just as *Lady Macbeth*, the fiend-soul of the house, steps from the door, like the speech of the building, with her falsely smiled welcome? Is there not *observance* in it?

But the production of such instances might be endless, as the work of Shakspere is infinite. I confine myself to two more, taken from "The Merchant of Venice."

Shakspere requires a character capable of the magnificent devotion of friendship which the old story attributes to *Antonio*. He therefore introduces us to a man sober even to sadness, thoughtful even to melancholy. The first words of the play unveil this characteristic. He holds "the world but as the world," --

"A stage where every man must play a part,

And mine a sad one."

The cause of this sadness we are left to conjecture. *Antonio* himself professes not to know. But such a disposition, even if it be not occasioned by any definite event or object, will generally associate itself with one; and when *Antonio* is accused of being in love, he repels the accusation with only a sad "Fie! fie!" This, and his whole character, seem to me to point to an old but ever cherished grief.

Into the original story upon which this play is founded, Shakspere has, among other variations, introduced the story of *Jessica* and *Lorenzo*, apparently altogether of his own invention. What was his object in doing so? Surely there were characters and interests enough already! -- It seems to me that Shakspere doubted whether the Jew would have actually proceeded to carry out his fell design against *Antonio*, upon the original ground of his hatred, without the further incitement to revenge afforded by another passion, second only to his love of gold -- his affection for his daughter; for in the Jew having reference to his own property, it had risen to a passion. Shakspere therefore invents her, that he may send a dog of a Christian to steal her, and, yet worse, to tempt her to steal her father's stones and ducats. I suspect Shakspere sends the old villain off the stage at the last with more of the pity of the audience than any of the other dramatists of the time would have ventured to rouse, had they been capable of doing so. I suspect he is the only human Jew of the English drama up to that time.

119

I have now arrived at the last and most important stage of my argument. It is this: If Shakspere was so well aware of the artistic relations of the parts of his drama, is it likely that the grand meanings involved in the whole were unperceived by him, and conveyed to us without any intention on his part -- had their origin only in the fact that he dealt with human nature so truly, that his representations must involve whatever lessons human life itself involves?

Is there no intention, for instance, in placing *Prospero*, who forsook the duties of his dukedom for the study of magic, in a desert island, with just three subjects; one, a monster below humanity; the second, a creature etherealized beyond it; and the third a complete embodiment of human perfection? Is it not that he may learn how to rule, and, having learned, return, by the aid of his magic wisely directed, to the home and duties from which exclusive devotion to that magic had driven him?

In "Julius Caesar," the death of *Brutus*, while following as the consequence of his murder of *Caesar*, is yet as much distinguished in character from that death, as the character of *Brutus* is different from that of *Caesar. Caesar's* last words were *Et tu Brute? Brutus,* when resolved to lay violent hands on himself, takes leave of his friends with these words:

"Countrymen,

My heart doth joy, that yet, in all my life,

I found no man, but he was true to me."

Here Shakspere did not invent. He found both speeches in Plutarch. But how unerring his choice!

Is the final catastrophe in "Hamlet" such, because Shakspere could do no better? -- It is: he could do no better than the best. Where but in the regions beyond could such questionings as *Hamlet's* be put to rest? It would have been a fine thing indeed for the most nobly perplexed of thinkers to be left -- his love in the grave; the memory of his father a torment, of his mother a blot; with innocent blood on his innocent hands, and but half understood by his best friend -- to ascend in desolate dreariness the contemptible height of the degraded throne, and shine the first in a drunken court!

Before bringing forward my last instance, I will direct the attention of my readers to a passage, in another play, in which the lesson of the play I am about to speak of, is *directly* taught: the first speech in the second act of "As You Like It," might be made a text for the exposition of the whole play of "King Lear."

The banished duke is seeking to bring his courtiers to regard their exile as a part of their moral training. I am aware that I point the passage differently, while I revert to the old text.

> "Are not these woods
>
> More free from peril than the envious court?
>
> Here feel we not the penalty of Adam—
>
> The season's difference, as the icy fang,
>
> And churlish chiding of the winter's wind?
>
> Which, when it bites and blows upon my body,
>
> Even till I shrink with cold, I smile and say—
>
> This is no flattery; these are counsellors
>
> That feelingly persuade me what I am.
>
> Sweet are the uses of adversity."

The line *Here feel we not the penalty of Adam?* has given rise to much perplexity. The expounders of Shakspere do not believe he can mean that the uses of adversity are really sweet. But the duke sees that *the penalty* of Adam is what makes the *woods more free from peril than the envious court;* that this penalty is in fact the best blessing, for it *feelingly persuades* man *what* he is; and to know what we are, to have no false judgments of ourselves, he considers so sweet, that to be thus taught, the *churlish chiding of the winter's wind* is well endured.

Now let us turn to *Lear*. We find in him an old man with a large heart, hungry for love, and yet not knowing what love is; an old man as ignorant as a child in all matters of high import; with a temper so unsubdued, and therefore so unkingly, that he storms because his dinner is not ready by the clock of his hunger; a child, in short, in everything but his grey hairs and wrinkled face, but his failing, instead of growing, strength. If a life end so, let the success of that life be otherwise what it may, it is a wretched and unworthy end. But let *Lear* be blown by the winds and beaten by the rains of heaven, till he pities "poor naked wretches;" till he feels that he has "ta'en too little care of" such; till pomp no longer conceals from him what "a poor, bare, forked animal" he is; and the old king has risen higher in the real social scale -- the scale of that country to which he is bound -- far higher than he stood while he still held his kingdom undivided to his thankless daughters. Then let him learn at last that "love is the only good in the world;" let him find his *Cordelia*, and plot with her how they will in their dungeon *singing like birds i' the cage*, and, dwelling in the secret place of peace, look abroad on the world like *God's spies*; and then let the generous great old heart swell till it breaks at last -- not with rage and hate and vengeance, but with love; and all is well: it is time the man should go to overtake his daughter; henceforth to dwell with her in the home of the true, the eternal, the unchangeable. All his suffering came from his own fault; but from the suffering has sprung another crop, not of evil but of good; the seeds of which had lain unfruitful in the soil, but were brought within the blessed influences of the air of heaven by the sharp tortures of the ploughshare of ill.

THE ELDER HAMLET

'Tis bitter cold,
And I am sick at heart.

The ghost in "Hamlet" is as faithfully treated as any character in the play. Next to Hamlet himself, he is to me the most interesting person of the drama. The rumour of his appearance is wrapped in the larger rumour of war. Loud preparations for uncertain attack fill the ears of "the subject of the land." The state is troubled. The new king has hardly compassed his election before his marriage with his brother's widow swathes the court in the dust -- cloud of shame, which the merriment of its forced revelry can do little to dispel. A feeling is in the moral air to which the words of Francisco, the only words of significance he utters, give the key: "'Tis bitter cold, and I am sick at heart." Into the frosty air, the pallid moonlight, the drunken shouts of Claudius and his court, the bellowing of the cannon from the rampart for the enlargement of the insane clamour that it may beat the drum of its own disgrace at the portals of heaven, glides the silent prisoner of hell, no longer a king of the day walking about his halls, "the observed of all observers," but a thrall of the night, wandering between the bell and the cock, like a jailer on each side of him. A poet tells the tale of the king who lost his garments and ceased to be a king: here is the king who has lost his body, and in the eyes of his court has ceased to be a man. Is the cold of the earth's night pleasant to him after the purging fire? What crimes had the honest ghost committed in his days of nature? He calls them foul crimes! Could such be his? Only who can tell how a ghost, with his doubled experience, may think of this thing or that? The ghost and the fire may between them distinctly recognize that as a foul crime which the man and the court regarded as a weakness at worst, and indeed in a king laudable.

Alas, poor ghost! Around the house he flits, shifting and shadowy, over the ground he once paced in ringing armour -- armed still, but his very armour a shadow! It cannot keep out the arrow of the cock's cry, and the heart that pierces is no shadow. Where now is the loaded axe with which, in angry dispute, he smote the ice at his feet that cracked to the blow? Where is the arm that heaved the axe? Wasting in the marble maw of the sepulchre, and the arm he carries now -- I know not what it can do, but it cannot slay his murderer. For that he seeks his son's. Doubtless his new ethereal form has its capacities and privileges. It can shift its garb at will; can appear in mail or night-gown, unaided of armourer or tailor; can pass through Hades-gates or chamber-door with equal ease; can work in the ground like mole or pioneer, and let its voice be heard from the cellarage. But there is one to whom it cannot appear, one whom the ghost can see, but to whom he cannot show himself. She has built a doorless, windowless wall between them, and sees the husband of her youth no more. Outside her heart -- that is the night in which he wanders, while the palace-windows are flaring, and the low wind throbs to the wassail shouts: within, his murderer sits by the wife of his bosom, and in the orchard the spilt poison is yet gnawing at the roots of the daisies.

Twice has the ghost grown out of the night upon the eyes of the sentinels. With solemn march, slow and stately, three times each night, has he walked by them; they, jellied with fear, have uttered no challenge. They seek Horatio, who the third night speaks to him as a scholar can. To the first challenge he makes no answer, but stalks away; to the second,

> It lifted up its head, and did address
> Itself to motion, like as it would speak;

but the gaoler cock calls him, and the kingly shape

> started like a guilty thing
> Upon a fearful summons;

and then

> shrunk in haste away,
> And vanished from our sight.

Ah, that summons! at which majesty welks and shrivels, the king and soldier starts and cowers, and, armour and all, withers from the air!

But why has he not spoken before? why not now ere the cock could claim him? He cannot trust the men. His court has forsaken his memory -- crowds with as eager discontent about the mildewed ear as ever about his wholesome brother, and how should he trust mere sentinels? There is but one who will heed his tale. A word to any other would but defeat his intent. Out of the multitude of courtiers and subjects, in all the land of Denmark, there is but one whom he can trust -- his student -- son. Him he has not yet found -- the condition of a ghost involving strange difficulties.

Or did the horror of the men at the sight of him wound and repel him? Does the sense of regal dignity, not yet exhausted for all the fasting in fires, unite with that of grievous humiliation to make him shun their speech?

But Horatio -- why does the ghost not answer him ere the time of the cock is come? Does he fold the cloak of indignation around him because his son's friend has addressed him as an intruder on the night, an usurper of the form that is his own? The companions of the speaker take note that he is offended and stalks away.

Much has the kingly ghost to endure in his attempt to re-open relations with the world he has left: when he has overcome his wrath and returns, that moment Horatio again insults him, calling him an illusion. But this time he will bear it, and opens his mouth to speak. It is too late; the cock is awake, and he must go. Then alas for the buried majesty of Denmark! with upheaved halberts they strike at the shadow, and would stop it if they might -- usage so grossly unfitting that they are instantly ashamed of it themselves, recognizing the offence in the majesty of the offended. But he is already gone. The proud, angry king has found himself but a thing of nothing to his body-guard -- for he has lost the body which was their guard. Still, not even yet has he learned how little it lies in the power of an honest ghost to gain credit for himself or his tale! His very privileges are against him.

All this time his son is consuming his heart in the knowledge of a mother capable of so soon and so utterly forgetting such a husband, and in pity and sorrow for the dead father who has had such a wife. He is thirty years of age, an obedient, honourable son -- a man of thought, of faith, of aspiration. Him now the ghost seeks, his heart burning like a coal with the sense of unendurable wrong. He is seeking the one drop that can fall cooling on that heart -- the sympathy, the answering rage and grief of his boy. But when at length he finds him, the generous, loving father has to see that son tremble like an aspen-leaf in his doubtful presence. He has exposed himself to the shame of eyes and the indignities of dullness, that he may pour the pent torrent of his wrongs into his ears, but his disfranchisement from the flesh tells against him even with his son: the young Hamlet is doubtful of the identity of the apparition with his father. After all the burning words of the phantom, the spirit he has seen may yet be a devil; the devil has power to assume a pleasing shape, and is perhaps taking advantage of his melancholy to damn him.

Armed in the complete steel of a suit well known to the eyes of the sentinels, visionary none the less, with useless truncheon in hand, resuming the memory of old martial habits, but with quiet countenance, more in sorrow than in anger, troubled -- not now with the thought of the hell-day to which he must sleepless return, but with that unceasing ache at the heart, which ever, as often as he is released into the cooling air of the upper world, draws him back to the region of his wrongs -- where having fallen asleep in his orchard, in sacred security and old custom, suddenly, by cruel assault, he was flung into Hades, where horror upon horror awaited him -- worst horror of all, the knowledge of his wife! -- armed he comes, in shadowy armour but how real sorrow! Still it is not pity he seeks from his son: he needs it not -- he can endure. There is no weakness in the ghost. It is but to the imperfect human sense that he is shadowy. To himself he knows his doom his deliverance; that the hell in which he finds himself shall endure but until it has burnt up the hell he has found within him -- until the evil he was and is capable of shall have dropped from him into the lake of fire; he nerves himself to bear. And the cry of revenge that comes from the sorrowful lips is the cry of a king and a Dane rather than of a wronged man. It is for public justice and not individual vengeance he calls. He cannot endure that the royal bed of Denmark should be a couch for luxury and damned incest. To stay this he would bring the murderer to justice. There is a worse wrong, for which he seeks no revenge: it involves his wife; and there comes in love, and love knows no amends but amendment, seeks only the repentance tenfold more needful to the wronger than the wronged. It is not alone the father's care for the human nature of his son that warns him to take no measures against his mother; it is the husband's tenderness also for her who once lay in his bosom. The murdered brother, the dethroned king, the dishonoured husband, the tormented sinner, is yet a gentle ghost. Has suffering already begun to make him, like Prometheus, wise?

But to measure the gentleness, the forgiveness, the tenderness of the ghost, we must well understand his wrongs. The murder is plain; but there is that which went before and is worse, yet is not so plain to every eye that reads the story. There is that without which the murder had never been, and which, therefore, is a cause of all the wrong. For listen to what the ghost reveals when at length he has withdrawn his son that he may speak with him alone, and Hamlet has forestalled the disclosure of the murderer:

"Ay, that incestuous, that adulterate beast,

With witchcraft of his wit, with traitorous gifts,

(O wicked wit and gifts that have the power

So to seduce!) won to his shameful lust

The will of my most seeming virtuous queen:

Oh, Hamlet, what a falling off was there!

From me, whose love was of that dignity

That it went hand in hand even with the vow

I made to her in marriage, and to decline

Upon a wretch, whose natural gifts were poor

To those of mine!

But virtue—as it never will be moved

Though lewdness court it in a shape of heaven,

So lust, though to a radiant angel linked,

Will sate itself in a celestial bed,

And prey on garbage."

Reading this passage, can any one doubt that the ghost charges his late wife with adultery, as the root of all his woes? It is true that, obedient to the ghost's injunctions, as well as his own filial instincts,

Hamlet accuses his mother of no more than was patent to all the world; but unless we suppose the ghost misinformed or mistaken, we must accept this charge. And had Gertrude not yielded to the witchcraft of Claudius' wit, Claudius would never have murdered Hamlet. Through her his life was dishonoured, and his death violent and premature: unhuzled, disappointed, unaneled, he woke to the air -- not of his orchard -- blossoms, but of a prison -- house, the lightest word of whose terrors would freeze the blood of the listener. What few men can say, he could -- that his love to his wife had kept even step with the vow he made to her in marriage; and his son says of him --

"so loving to my mother

That he might not beteem the winds of heaven

Visit her face too roughly;"

and this was her return! Yet is it thus he charges his son concerning her:

"But howsoever thou pursu'st this act,

Taint not thy mind, nor let thy soul contrive

Against thy mother aught; leave her to heaven,

And to those thorns that in her bosom lodge,

To prick and sting her."

And may we not suppose it to be for her sake in part that the ghost insists, with fourfold repetition, upon a sword -- sworn oath to silence from Horatio and Marcellus?

Only once again does he show himself -- not now in armour upon the walls, but in his gown and in his wife's closet.

Ever since his first appearance, that is, all the time filling the interval between the first and second acts, we may presume him to have haunted the palace unseen, waiting what his son would do. But the task has been more difficult than either had supposed. The ambassadors have gone to Norway and returned; but Hamlet has done nothing. Probably he has had no opportunity; certainly he has had no clear vision of duty. But now all through the second and third acts, together occupying, it must be remembered, only one day, something seems imminent. The play has been acted, and Hamlet has gained some assurance, yet the one chance presented of killing the king -- at his prayers -- he has refused. He is now in his mother's closet, whose eyes he has turned into her very soul. There, and then, the ghost once more appears -- come, he says, to whet his son's almost blunted purpose. But, as I have said, he does not know all the disadvantages of one who, having forsaken the world, has yet business therein to which he would persuade; he does not know how hard it is for a man to give credence to a ghost; how thoroughly he is justified in delay, and the demand for more perfect proof. He does not know what good reasons his son has had for uncertainty, or how much natural and righteous doubt has had to do with what he takes for the blunting of his purpose. Neither does he know how much more tender his son's conscience is than his own, or how necessary it is to him to be sure before he acts. As little perhaps does he understand how hateful to Hamlet is the task laid upon him -- the killing of one wretched villain in the midst of a corrupt and contemptible court, one of a world of whose women his mother may be the type!

Whatever the main object of the ghost's appearance, he has spoken but a few words concerning the matter between him and Hamlet, when he turns abruptly from it to plead with his son for his wife. The ghost sees and mistakes the terror of her looks; imagines that, either from some feeling of his presence, or from the power of Hamlet's words, her conscience is thoroughly roused, and that her vision, her conception of the facts, is now more than she can bear. She and her fighting soul are at odds. She is a kingdom divided against itself. He fears the consequences. He would not have her go mad. He would not have her die yet. Even while ready to start at the summons of that hell to which she has sold him, he forgets his vengeance on her seducer in his desire to comfort her. He dares not, if he could, manifest himself to her: what word of consolation could she hear from his lips? Is not the thought of him her one despair? He turns to his son for help: he cannot console his wife; his son must take his place. Alas! even now he thinks better of her than she deserves; for it is only the fancy of her son's madness that is terrifying her: he gazes on the apparition of which she sees nothing, and from his looks she anticipates an ungovernable outbreak.

"But look; amazement on thy mother sits!

Oh; step between her and her fighting soul

Conceit in weakest bodies strongest works.

Speak to her, Hamlet."

The call to his son to soothe his wicked mother is the ghost's last utterance. For a few moments, sadly regardful of the two, he stands -- while his son seeks in vain to reveal to his mother the presence of his father -- a few moments of piteous action, all but ruining the remnant of his son's sorely-harassed self-possession -- his whole concern his wife's distress, and neither his own doom nor his son's duty; then, as if lost in despair at the impassable gulf betwixt them, revealed by her utter incapacity for even the imagination of his proximity, he turns away, and steals out at the portal. Or perhaps he has heard the black cock crow, and is wanted beneath: his turn has come.

Will the fires ever cleanse *her*? Will his love ever lift him above the pain of its loss? Will eternity ever be bliss, ever be endurable to poor *King Hamlet*?

Alas! even the memory of the poor ghost is insulted. Night after night on the stage his effigy appears -- cadaverous, sepulchral -- no longer as Shakspere must have represented him, aerial, shadowy, gracious, the thin corporeal husk of an eternal -- shall I say ineffaceable? -- sorrow! It is no hollow monotone that can rightly upbear such words as his, but a sound mingled of distance and wind in the pine-tops, of agony and love, of horror and hope and loss and judgment -- a voice of endless and sweetest inflection, yet with a shuddering echo in it as from the caves of memory, on whose walls, are written the eternal blazon that must not be to ears of flesh and blood. The spirit that can assume form at will must surely be able to bend that form to completest and most delicate expression, and the part of the ghost in the play offers work worthy of the highest artist. The would-be actor takes from it vitality and motion, endowing it instead with the rigidity of death, as if the soul had resumed its cast-off garment, the stiffened and mouldy corpse -- whose frozen deadness it could ill model to the utterance of its lively will!

ON POLISH

By Polish I mean a certain well -- known and immediately recognizable condition of surface.[1] But I must request my reader to consider well what this condition really is. For the definition of it appears to us to be, that condition of surface which allows the inner structure of the material to manifest itself. Polish is, as it were, a translucent skin, in which the life of the inorganic comes to the surface, as in the animal skin the animal life. Once clothed in this, the inner glories of the marble rock, of the jasper, of the porphyry, leave the darkness behind, and glow into the day. From the heart of the agate the mossy landscape comes dreaming out. From the depth of the green chrysolite looks up the eye of its gold. The "goings on of life" hidden for ages under the rough bark of the patient forest-trees, are brought to light; the rings of lovely shadow which the creature went on making in the dark, as the oyster its opaline laminations, and its tree-earls of beautiful knots, where a beneficent disease has broken the geometrical perfection of its structure, gloom out in their infinite variousness.

Nor are the revelations of polish confined to things having variety in their internal construction; they operate equally in things of homogeneous structure. It is the polished ebony or jet which gives the true blank, the material darkness. It is the polished steel that shines keen and remorseless and cold, like that human justice whose symbol it is. And in the polished diamond the distinctive purity is most evident; while from it, I presume, will the light absorbed from the sun gleam forth on the dark most plentifully.

But the mere fact that the end of polish is revelation, can hardly be worth setting forth except for some ulterior object, some further revelation in the fact itself. -- I wish to show that in the symbolic use of the word the same truth is involved, or, if not involved, at least suggested. But let me first make another remark on the preceding definition of the word.

---

[1] 1865.

There is no denying that the first notion suggested by the word polish is that of smoothness, which will indeed be the sole idea associated with it before we begin to contemplate the matter. But when we consider what things are chosen to be "clothed upon" with this smoothness, then we find that the smoothness is scarcely desired for its own sake, and remember besides that in many materials and situations it is elaborately avoided. We find that here it is sought because of its faculty of enabling other things to show themselves -- to come to the surface.

I proceed then to examine how far my pregnant interpretation of the word will apply to its figurative use in two cases -- *Polish of Style*, and *Polish of Manners*. The two might be treated together, seeing that *Style* may be called the manners of intellectual utterance, and *Manners* the style of social utterance; but it is more convenient to treat them separately.

I will begin with the Polish of Style.

It will be seen at once that if the notion of polish be limited to that of smoothness, there can be little to say on the matter, and nothing worthy of being said. For mere smoothness is no more a desirable quality in a style than it is in a country or a countenance; and its pursuit will result at length in the gain of the monotonous and the loss of the melodious and harmonious. But it is only upon worthless material that polish can be *mere* smoothness; and where the material is not valuable, polish can be nothing but smoothness. No amount of polish in a style can render the production of value, except there be in it embodied thought thereby revealed; and the labour of the polish is lost. Let us then take the fuller meaning of polish, and see how it will apply to style.

If it applies, then Polish of Style will imply the approximately complete revelation of the thought. It will be the removal of everything that can interfere between the thought of the speaker and the mind of the hearer. True polish in marble or in speech reveals inlying realities, and, in the latter at least, mere smoothness, either of sound or of meaning, is not worthy of the name. The most polished style will be that which most immediately and most truly flashes the meaning embodied in the utterance upon the mind of the listener or reader.

"Will you then," I imagine a reader objecting, "admit of no ornament in style?"

"Assuredly," I answer, "I would admit of no ornament whatever."

But let me explain what I mean by ornament. I mean anything stuck in or on, like a spangle, because it is pretty in itself, although it reveals nothing. Not one such ornament can belong to a polished style. It is paint, not polish. And if this is not what my questioner means by *ornament*, my answer must then be read according to the differences in his definition of the word. What I have said has not the least application to the natural forms of beauty which thought assumes in speech. Between such beauty and such ornament there lies the same difference as between the overflow of life in the hair, and the dressing of that loveliest of utterances in grease and gold.

For, when I say that polish is the removal of everything that comes between thought and thinking, it must not be supposed that in my idea thought is only of the intellect, and therefore that all forms but bare intellectual forms are of the nature of ornament. As well might one say that the only essential portion of the human form is the bones. And every human thought is in a sense a human being, has as necessarily its muscles of motion, its skin of beauty, its blood of feeling, as its skeleton of logic. For complete utterance, music itself in its right proportions, sometimes clear and strong, as in rhymed harmonies, sometimes veiled and dim, as in the prose compositions of the masters of speech, is as necessary as correctness of logic, and common sense in construction. I should have said *conveyance* rather than utterance; for there may be utterance such as to relieve the mind of the speaker with more or less of fancied communication, while the conveyance of thought may be little or none; as in the speaking with tongues of the infant Church, to which the lovely babblement of our children has probably more than a figurative resemblance, relieving their own minds, but, the interpreter not yet at his post, neither instructing nor misleading any one. But as the object of grown-up speech must in the main be the conveyance of thought, and not the mere utterance, everything in the style of that speech which interposes between the mental eyes and the thought embodied in the speech, must be polished away, that the indwelling life may manifest itself.

What, then (for now we must come to the practical), is the kind of thing to be polished away in order that the hidden may be revealed?

All words that can be dismissed without loss; for all such more or less obscure the meaning upon which they gather. The first step towards the polishing of most styles is to strike out -- polish off -- the useless words and phrases. It is wonderful with how many fewer words most things could be said that are said; while the degree of certainty and rapidity with which an idea is conveyed would generally be found to be in an inverse ratio to the number of words employed.

All ornaments so called -- the nose and lip jewels of style -- the tattooing of the speech; all similes that, although true, give no additional insight into the meaning; everything that is only pretty and not beautiful; all mere sparkle as of jewels that lose their own beauty by being set in the grandeur of statues or the dignity of monumental stone, must be ruthlessly polished away.

All utterances which, however they may add to the amount of thought, distract the mind, and confuse its observation of the main idea, the essence or life of the book or paper, must be diligently refused. In the manuscript of *Comus* there exists, cancelled but legible, a passage of which I have the best authority for saying that it would have made the poetic fame of any writer.[2] But the grand old self-denier struck it out of the opening speech because that would be more polished without it -- because the *Attendant Spirit* would say more immediately and exclusively, and therefore more completely, what he had to say, without it. -- All this applies much more widely and deeply in the region of art; but I am at present dealing with the surface of style, not with the round of result.

I have one instance at hand, however, belonging to this region, than which I could scarcely produce a more apt illustration of my thesis. One of the greatest of living painters, walking with a friend through the late Exhibition of Art -- Treasures at Manchester, came upon Albert Dürer's *Melancholia*.[3] [4] After looking at it for a moment, he

---

[2] *Comus* is a masque (a festival or entertainment where participants wear masks) first presented by John Milton in 1634 and published anonymously in 1637. Milton contrasts the masked showy revelry and bravado with true private virtue.

"Comus," *Encyclopedia Britannica*, accessed July 30, 2021, https://www.britannica.com/topic/Comus.

[3] "The Art Treasures of Great Britain" was an art exhibition held in Manchester, England from May 5, 1857 to October 17, 1857. Displaying over 16,000 works of art, it is the largest exhibition ever held in the United Kingdom. "'The Art Treasures of Great Britain,' Perhaps the Largest Art Exhibition Ever Held : History of Information," History of Information, accessed July 30, 2021, https://www.historyofinformation.com/detail.php?id=3612.

[4] Albrecht Dürer (1471-1528) was a German Renaissance artist. Melencolia is an engraving completed in 1514 of a winged female representing melancholy.

told his friend that now for the first time he understood it, and proceeded to set forth what he saw in it. It was a very early impression, and the delicacy of the lines was so much the greater. He had never seen such a perfect impression before, and had never perceived the intent and scope of the engraving. The mere removal of accidental thickness and furriness in the lines of the drawing enabled him to see into the meaning of that wonderful production. The polish brought it to the surface. Or, what amounts to the same thing for my argument, the dulling of the surface had concealed it even from his experienced eyes.

In fine, and more generally, all cause whatever of obscurity must be polished away. There may lie in the matter itself a darkness of colour and texture which no amount of polishing can render clear or even vivid; the thoughts themselves may be hard to think, and difficulty must not be confounded with obscurity. The former belongs to the thoughts themselves; the latter to the mode of their embodiment. All cause of obscurity in this must, I say, be removed. Such may lie even in the region of grammar, or in the mere arrangement of a sentence. And while, as I have said, no ornament is to be allowed, so all roughnesses, which irritate the mental ear, and so far incapacitate it for receiving a true impression of the meaning from the words, must be carefully reduced. For the true music of a sentence, belonging as it does to the essence of the thought itself, is the herald which goes before to prepare the mind for the following thought, calming the surface of the intellect to a mirror-like reflection of the image about to fall upon it. But syllables that hang heavy on the tongue and grate harsh upon the ear are the trumpet of discord rousing to unconscious opposition and conscious rejection.

And now the consideration of the Polish of Manners will lead us to some yet more important reflections. Here again I must admit that the ordinary use of the phrase is analogous to that of the preceding; but its relations lead us deep into realities. For as diamond alone can polish diamond, so men alone can polish men; and hence it is that it was first by living in a city ([Greek: polis], *polis*) that men --

"rubbed each other's angles down,"

and became *polished*. And while a certain amount of ease with regard to ourselves and of consideration with regard to others is everywhere

135

necessary to a man's passing as a gentleman -- all unevenness of behaviour resulting either from shyness or self-consciousness (in the shape of awkwardness), or from overweening or selfishness (in the shape of rudeness), having to be polished away -- true human polish must go further than this. Its respects are not confined to the manners of the ball-room or the dinner-table, of the club or the exchange, but wherever a man may rejoice with them that rejoice or weep with them that weep, he must remain one and the same, as polished to the tiller of the soil as to the leader of the fashion.

But how will the figure of material polish aid us any further? How can it be said that Polish of Manners is a revelation of that which is within, a calling up to the surface of the hidden loveliness of the material? For do we not know that courtesy may cover contempt; that smiles themselves may hide hate; that one who will place you at his right hand when in want of your inferior aid, may scarce acknowledge your presence when his necessity has gone by? And how then can polished manners be a revelation of what is within? Are they not the result of putting on rather than of taking off? Are they not paint and varnish rather than polish?

I must yield the answer to each of these questions; protesting, however, that with such polish I have nothing to do; for these manners are confessedly false. But even where least able to mislead, they are, with corresponding courtesy, accepted as outward signs of an inward grace. Hence even such, by the nature of their falsehood, support my position. For in what forms are the colours of the paint laid upon the surface of the material? Is it not in as near imitations of the real right human feelings about oneself and others as the necessarily imperfect knowledge of such an artist can produce? He will not encounter the labour of polishing, for he does not believe in the divine depths of his own nature: he paints, and calls the varnish polish.

"But why talk of polish with reference to such a character, seeing that no amount of polishing can bring to the surface what is not there? No polishing of sandstone will reveal the mottling of marble. For it is sandstone, crumbling and gritty -- not noble in any way."

Is it so then? Can such be the real nature of the man? And can polish reach nothing deeper in him than such? May not this selfishness be polished away, revealing true colour and harmony beneath? Was not the man made in the image of God? Or, if you say that man lost that image, did not a new process of creation begin from the point of that loss, a process of re-creation in him in whom all shall be made alive, which, although so far from being completed yet, can never be checked? If we cut away deep enough at the rough block of our nature, shall we not arrive at some likeness of that true man who, the apostle says, dwells in us -- the hope of glory? He informs us -- that is, forms us from within.

Dr. Donne (who knew less than any other writer in the English language what Polish of Style means) recognizes this divine polishing to the full. He says in a poem called "The Cross:" --

As perchance carvers do not faces make,

But that away, which hid them there, do take,

Let Crosses so take what hid Christ in thee,

And be his Image, or not his, but He.[5]

This is no doubt a higher figure than that of *polish*, but it is of the same kind, revealing the same truth. It recognizes the fact that the divine nature lies at the root of the human nature, and that the polish which lets that spiritual nature shine out in the simplicity of heavenly childhood, is the true Polish of Manners of which all merely social refinements are a poor imitation. -- Whence Coleridge says that nothing but religion can make a man a gentleman.[6] -- And when these harmonies of our nature come to the surface, we shall be indeed "lively stones," fit for building into the great temple of the universe, and echoing the music of creation. Dr. Donne recognizes, besides, the notable fact that *crosses* or afflictions are the polishing powers by means

---

[5] John Donne (1572-1631), "The Cross" in *The Poems of John Donne*. 1896.

[6] Samuel Taylor Coleridge, *Letters of Samuel Taylor Coleridge*, ed. Ernest Hartley Coleridge, vol. 1, 2 vols. (London, UK: William Heinemann, 1895) and Samuel Taylor Coleridge, *Biographia Literaria* (New York, NY: Leavitt, Lord & Co., 1834). Coleridge writes a number of times on what true virtue is and how a gentleman should act. At the end of chapter 16 in Coleridge's *Biographia Literaria* (1817), he also discusses excellence and true polish of manner. In Letter II addressed "To a lady," he again speaks of the manners that make up a "perfect gentleman." Coleridge also had a mult-letter exchange with his friend Robert Southey on what being a "true gentleman" meant. Number 32, July 6, 1794, Number 33, July 15, 1794. It seems MacDonald's comment is a succinct summation of Coleridge's thoughts on the matter.

of which the beautiful realities of human nature are brought to the surface. One can tell at once by the peculiar loveliness of certain persons that they have suffered.

But, to look for a moment less profoundly into the matter, have we not known those whose best never could get to the surface just from the lack of polish? -- persons who, if they could only reveal the kindness of their nature, would make men believe in human nature, but in whom some roughness of awkwardness or of shyness prevents the true self from appearing? Even the dread of seeming to claim a good deed or to patronize a fellow-man will sometimes spoil the last touch of tenderness which would have been the final polish of the act of giving, and would have revealed infinite depths of human devotion. For let the truth out, and it will be seen to be true.

Simplicity is the end of all Polish, as of all Art, Culture, Morals, Religion, and Life. The Lord our God is one Lord, and we and our brothers and sisters are one Humanity, one Body of the Head.

Now to the practical: what are we to do for the polish of our manners?

Just what I have said we must do for the polish of our style. Take off; do not put on. Polish away this rudeness, that awkwardness. Correct everything self-assertive, which includes nine tenths of all vulgarity. Imitate no one's behaviour; that is to paint. Do not think about yourself; that is to varnish. Put what is wrong right, and what is in you will show itself in harmonious behaviour.

But no one can go far in this track without discovering that true polish reaches much deeper; that the outward exists but for the sake of the inward; and that the manners, as they depend on the morals, must be forgotten in the morals of which they are but the revelation. Look at the high-shouldered, ungainly child in the corner: his mother tells him to go to his book, and he wants to go to his play. Regard the swollen lips, the skin tightened over the nose, the distortion of his shape, the angularity of his whole appearance. Yet he is not an awkward child by nature. Look at him again the moment after he has given in and kissed his mother. His shoulders have dropped to their place; his limbs are free from the fetters that bound them; his motions are graceful, and the one blends harmoniously with the other. He is no longer thinking of himself. He has given up his own way. The true childhood comes to the surface, and you see what the boy is meant to be always. Look at the jerkiness of the conceited man. Look at the quiet *fluency* of motion in the modest man. Look how anger itself which forgets self, which is unhating and righteous, will elevate the carriage and ennoble the movements.

But how far can the same rule of *omission* or *rejection* be applied with safety to this deeper character -- the manners of the spirit?

It seems to me that in morals too the main thing is to avoid doing wrong; for then the active spirit of life in us will drive us on to the right. But on such a momentous question I would not be dogmatic. Only as far as regards the feelings I would say: it is of no use to try to make ourselves feel thus or thus. Let us fight with our wrong feelings; let us polish away the rough ugly distortions of feeling. Then the real and the good will come of themselves. Or rather, to keep to my figure, they will then show themselves of themselves as the natural home -- produce, the indwelling facts of our deepest -- that is, our divine nature.

Here I find that I am sinking through my subject into another and deeper -- a truth, namely, which should, however, be the foundation of all our building, the background of all our representations: that Life is at work in us -- the sacred Spirit of God travailing in us. That Spirit has gained one end of his labour -- at which he can begin to do yet more for us -- when he has brought us to beg for the help which he has been giving us all the time.

I have been regarding infinite things through the medium of one limited figure, knowing that figures with all their suggestions and relations could not reveal them utterly. But so far as they go, these thoughts raised by the word Polish and its figurative uses appear to me to be most true.

BROWNING'S "CHRISTMAS EVE"

Goethe says:—

"Poems are painted window panes.[1]

If one looks from the square into the church,

Dusk and dimness are his gains --

Sir Philistine is left in the lurch!

The sight, so seen, may well enrage him,

Nor anything henceforth assuage him.

"But come just inside what conceals;

Cross the holy threshold quite --

All at once 'tis rainbow-bright,

Device and story flash to light,

A gracious splendour truth reveals.

This to God's children is full measure,

It edifies and gives you pleasure!"

This is true concerning every form in which truth is embodied, whether it be sight or sound, geometric diagram or scientific formula. Unintelligible, it may be dismal enough, regarded from the outside;

---

[1] Johann Wolfgang von Goethe, "Songs" in Goethe's Works, illustrated by the best German artists, 5 vols. (Philadelphia: G. Barrie, 1885). Vol. 1. Accessed July 28, 2021.

https://oll.libertyfund.org/title/boyesen-goethe-s-works-vol-1-poems#lf0841-01_head_385

Goethe (1749-1832) was a German poet, statesman, and social commentator. MacDonald translates this line as "Poems;" however, the majority of English translations translate this line and title the poem as "Songs."

prismatic in its revelation of truth from within. Such is the world itself, as beheld by the speculative eye; a thing of disorder, obscurity, and sadness: only the child-like heart, to which the door into the divine idea is thrown open, can understand somewhat the secret of the Almighty. In human things it is particularly true of art, in which the fundamental idea seems to be the revelation of the true through the beautiful. But of all the arts it is most applicable to poetry; for the others have more that is beautiful on the outside; can give pleasure to the senses by the form of the marble, the hues of the painting, or the sweet sounds of the music, although the heart may never perceive the meaning that lies within. But poetry, except its rhythmic melody, and its scattered gleams of material imagery, for which few care that love it not for its own sake, has no attraction on the outside to entice the passer to enter and partake of its truth. It is inwards that its colours shine, within that its forms move, and the sound of its holy organ cannot be heard from without.

Now, if one has been able to reach the heart of a poem, answering to Goethe's parabolic description; or even to discover a loop-hole, through which, from an opposite point, the glories of its stained windows are visible; it is well that he should seek to make others partakers in his pleasure and profit. Some who might not find out for themselves, would yet be evermore grateful to him who led them to the point of vision. Surely if a man would help his fellow-men, he can do so far more effectually by exhibiting truth than exposing error, by unveiling beauty than by a critical dissection of deformity. From the very nature of the things it must be so. Let the true and good destroy their opposites. It is only by the good and beautiful that the evil and ugly are known. It is the light that makes manifest.

The poem "Christmas Eve," by Robert Browning, with the accompanying poem "Easter Day," seems not to have attracted much notice from the readers of poetry, although highly prized by a few. This is, perhaps, to be attributed, in a great measure, to what many would call a considerable degree of obscurity. But obscurity is the appearance which to a first glance may be presented either by profundity or carelessness of thought. To some, obscurity itself is attractive, from the hope that worthiness is the cause of it. To apply a test similar to that by which Pascal tries the Koran and the Scriptures: what is the character of those portions, the meaning of which is plain?[2] Are they wise or foolish? If the former, the presumption is that the obscurity of other parts is caused not by opacity, but profundity. But some will object, notwithstanding, that a writer ought to make himself plain to his readers; nay, that if he has a clear idea himself, he must be able to express that idea clearly. But for communion of thought, two minds, not one, are necessary. The fault may lie in him that receives or in him that gives, or it may be in neither. For how can the result of much thought, the idea which for mouths has been shaping itself in the mind of one man, be at once received by another mind to which it comes a stranger and unexpected? The reader has no right to complain of so caused obscurity. Nor is that form of expression, which is most easily understood at first sight, necessarily the best. It will not, therefore, continue to move; nor will it gather force and influence with more intimate acquaintance. Here Goethe's little parable, as he calls it, is peculiarly applicable. But, indeed, if after all a writer is obscure, the man who has spent most labour in seeking to enter into his thoughts, will be the least likely to complain of his obscurity; and they who have the least difficulty in understanding a writer, are frequently those who understand him the least.

To those to whom the religion of Christ has been the law of liberty; who by that door have entered into the universe of God, and have begun to feel a growing delight in all the manifestations of God, it is cause of much joy to find that, whatever may be the position taken by men of science, or by those in whom the intellect predominates, with regard to the Christian religion, men of genius, at least, in virtue of what is child-like in their nature, are, in the present time, plainly manifesting deep devotion to Christ. There are exceptions, certainly; but even in those, there are symptoms of feelings which, one can hardly help thinking, tend towards him, and will one day flame forth in conscious worship. A mind that recognizes any of the multitudinous meanings of the revelation of God, in the world of sounds, and forms, and colours, cannot be blind to the higher manifestation of God in common humanity; nor to him in whom is hid the key to the whole, the First-born of the creation of God, in whose heart lies, as yet but

---

2 Blaise Pascal (1623-1662) was a French philosopher, theologian, and mathematician. He is known for his development of modern probability theory, his work in physics, and "Pascal's Wager" in theology.

partially developed, the kingdom of heaven, which is the redemption of the earth. The mind that delights in that which is lofty and great, which feels there is something higher than self, will undoubtedly be drawn towards Christ; and they, who at first looked on him as a great prophet, came at length to perceive that he was the radiation of the Father's glory, the likeness of his unseen being.

A description of the poem may, perhaps, both induce to the reading of it, and contribute to its easier comprehension while being perused. On a stormy Christmas Eve, the poet, or rather the seer (for the whole must be regarded as a poetic vision), is compelled to take refuge in the "lath and plaster entry" of a little chapel, belonging to a congregation of Calvinistic Methodists, who are at the time assembling for worship. Wonderful in its reality is the description of various of the flock that pass him as they enter the chapel, from

"the many-tattered

Little old-faced, peaking sister-turned-mother

Of the sickly babe she tried to smother

Somehow up, with its spotted face,

From the cold, on her breast, the one warm place:"

to the "shoemaker's lad;" whom he follows, determined not to endure the inquisition of their looks any longer, into the chapel. The humour of the whole scene within is excellent. The stifling closeness, both of the atmosphere and of the sermon, the wonderful content of the audience, the "old fat woman," who

"purred with pleasure,

And thumb round thumb went twirling faster,

While she, to his periods keeping measure,

Maternally devoured the pastor;"

are represented by a few rapid touches that bring certain points of the reality almost unpleasantly near. At length, unable to endure it longer, he rushes out into the air. Objection may, probably, be made to the mingling of the humorous, even the ridiculous, with the serious; at least, in a work of art like this, where they must be brought into such close proximity. But are not these things as closely connected in the world as they can be in any representation of it? Surely there are few who have never had occasion to attempt to reconcile the thought of the two in their own minds. Nor can there be anything human that is not, in some connexion or other, admissible into art. The widest idea of art must comprehend all things. A work of this kind must, like God's world, in which he sends rain on the just and on the unjust, be taken as a whole and in regard to its design. The requisition is, that everything introduced have a relation to the adjacent parts and to the whole suitable to the design. Here the thing is real, is true, is human; a thing to be thought about. It has its place amongst other phenomena, with which, however apparently incongruous, it is yet vitally connected within.

A coolness and delight visit us, on turning over the page and commencing to read the description of sky, and moon, and clouds, which greet him outside the chapel. It is as a vision of the vision-bearing world itself, in one of its fine, though not, at first, one of its rarest moods. And here a short digression to notice like feelings in unlike dresses, one thought differently expressed will, perhaps, be pardoned. The moon is prevented from shining out by the "blocks" of cloud "built up in the west:" --

"And the empty other half of the sky

Seemed in its silence as if it knew

What, any moment, might look through

A chance-gap in that fortress massy."

Old Henry Vaughan says of the "Dawning:" --

"The whole Creation shakes off night,

And for thy shadow looks the Light;

Stars now vanish without number,

Sleepie Planets set and slumber,

The pursie Clouds disband and scatter,

145

All expect some sudden matter."

Calmness settles down on his mind. He walks on, thinking of the scene he had left, and the sermon he had heard. In the latter he sees the good and the bad intimately mingled; and is convinced that the chief benefit derived from it is a reproducing of former impressions. The thought crosses him, in how many places and how many different forms the same thing takes place, "a convincing" of the "convinced;" and he rejoices in the contrast which his church presents to these; for in the church of Nature his love to God, assurance of God's love to him, and confidence in the design of God regarding him, commenced. While exulting in God and the knowledge of Him to be attained hereafter, he is favoured with a sight of a glorious moon-rainbow, which elevates his worship to ecstasy. During which --

"All at once I looked up with terror --

He was there.

He himself with His human air,

On the narrow pathway, just before:

I saw the back of Him, no more --

He had left the chapel, then, as I.

I forgot all about the sky.

No face: only the sight

Of a sweepy garment, vast and white,

With a hem that I could recognize.

I felt terror, no surprise:

My mind filled with the cataract,

At one bound, of the mighty fact.

I remembered, He did say

Doubtless, that, to this world's end,

Where two or three should meet and pray,

He would be in the midst, their friend:

Certainly He was there with them.

And my pulses leaped for joy

Of the golden thought without alloy,

That I saw His very vesture's hem.

Then rushed the blood back, cold and clear,

With a fresh enhancing shiver of fear."

Praying for forgiveness wherein he has sinned, and prostrate in adoration before the form of Christ, he is "caught up in the whirl and drift" of his vesture, and carried along with him over the earth.

Stopping at length at the entrance of St. Peter's in Rome, he remains outside, while the form disappears within. He is able, however, to see all that goes on, in the crowded, hushed interior. It is high mass. He has been carried at once from the little chapel to the opposite aesthetic pole. From the entry, where --

"The flame of the single tallow candle

In the cracked square lanthorn I stood under

Shot its blue lip at me,"

to —

"This miraculous dome of God --

This colonnade

With arms wide open to embrace

The entry of the human race

To the breast of . . . what is it, yon building,

Ablaze in front, all paint and gilding,

With marble for brick, and stones of price

For garniture of the edifice?"

to "those fountains" —

"Growing up eternally

Each to a musical water-tree,

Whose blossoms drop, a glittering boon,

Before my eyes, in the light of the moon,

To the granite lavers underneath;"

from the singing of the chapel to the organ self-restrained, that "holds his breath and grovels latent," while expecting the elevation of the Host. Christ is within; he is left without. Reflecting on the matter, he thinks his Lord would not require him to go in, though he himself entered, because there was a way to reach him there. By-and-by, however, his heart awakes and declares that Love goes beyond error with them, and if the Intellect be kept down, yet Love is the oppressor; so next time he resolves to enter and praise along with them. The passage commencing, "Oh, love of those first Christian days!" describing Love's victory over Intellect, is very fine.

Again he is caught up and carried along as before. This time halt is made at the door of a college in a German town, in which the class -- room of one of the professors is open for lecture this Christmas Eve. It is, intellectually considered, the opposite pole to both the Methodist chapel and the Roman Basilica. The poet enters, fearful of losing the society of "any that call themselves his friends." He describes the assembled company, and the entrance of "the hawk-nosed, high-cheek-boned professor," of part of whose Christmas Eve's discourse he proceeds to give the substance. The professor takes it for granted that "plainly no such life was liveable," and goes on to inquire what explanation of the phenomena of the life of Christ it were best to adopt. Not that it mattered much, "so the idea be left the same." Taking the popular story, for convenience sake, and separating all extraneous matter from it, he found that Christ was simply a good man, with an honest, true heart; whose disciples thought him divine; and whose doctrine, though quite mistaken by those who received and published it, "had yet a meaning quite as respectable." Here the poet takes advantage of a pause to leave him; reflecting that though the air may be poisoned by the sects, yet here "the critic leaves no air to poison."

His meditations and arguments following, are among the most valuable passages in the book. The professor, notwithstanding the idea of Christ has by him been exhausted of all that is peculiar to it, yet recommends him to the veneration and worship of his hearers, "rather than all who went before him, and all who ever followed after." But why? says the poet. For his intellect,

> "Which tells me simply what was told
>
> (If mere morality, bereft
>
> Of the God in Christ, be all that's left)
>
> Elsewhere by voices manifold?"

with which must be combined the fact that this intellect of his did not save him from making the "important stumble," of saying that he and God were one. "But his followers misunderstood him," says the objector. Perhaps so; but "the stumbling -- block, his speech, who laid it?" Well then, is it on the score of his goodness that he should rule his race?

> "You pledge
>
> Your fealty to such rule? What, all --
>
> From Heavenly John and Attic Paul,
>
> And that brave weather-battered Peter,
>
> Whose stout faith only stood completer
>
> For buffets, sinning to be pardoned,
>
> As the more his hands hauled nets, they hardened—
>
> All, down to you, the man of men,
>
> Professing here at Göttingen,
>
> Compose Christ's flock! So, you and I
>
> Are sheep of a good man! And why?"

Did Christ *invent* goodness? or did he only demonstrate that of which the common conscience was judge?

149

"I would decree

Worship for such mere demonstration

And simple work of nomenclature,

Only the day I praised, not Nature,

But Harvey, for the circulation."

The worst man, says the poet, *knows* more than the best man *does*. God in Christ appeared to men to help them to *do*, to awaken the life within them.

"Morality to the uttermost,

Supreme in Christ as we all confess,

Why need we prove would avail no jot

To make Him God, if God he were not?

What is the point where Himself lays stress?

Does the precept run, 'Believe in good,

In justice, truth, now understood

For the first time?' -- or, 'Believe in ME,

Who lived and died, yet essentially

Am Lord of life'? Whoever can take

The same to his heart, and for mere love's sake

Conceive of the love, -- that man obtains

A new truth; no conviction gains

Of an old one only, made intense

By a fresh appeal to his faded sense."

In this lies the most direct practical argument with regard to what is commonly called the Divinity of Christ. Here is a man whom those that magnify him the least confess to be a good man, the best of men. He *says*, "I and the Father are one." Will an earnest heart, knowing this, be likely to draw back, or will it draw nearer to behold the great sight?

Will not such a heart feel: "A good man like this would not have said so, were it not so. In all probability the great truth of God lies behind this veil." The reality of Christ's nature is not to be proved by argument. He must be beheld. The manifestation of Him must "gravitate inwards" on the soul. It is by looking that one can know. As a mathematical theorem is to be proved only by the demonstration of that theorem itself, not by talking *about* it; so Christ must prove himself to the human soul through being beheld. The only proof of Christ's divinity is his humanity. Because his humanity is not comprehended, his divinity is doubted; and while the former is uncomprehended, an assent to the latter is of little avail. For a man to theorize theologically in any form, while he has not so apprehended Christ, or to neglect the gazing on him for the attempt to substantiate to himself any form of belief respecting him, is to bring on himself, in a matter of divine import, such errors as the expounders of nature in old time brought on themselves, when they speculated on what a thing must be, instead of observing what it was; this *must be* having for its foundation not self-evident truth, but notions whose chief strength lay in their preconception. There are thoughts and feelings that cannot be called up in the mind by any power of will or force of imagination; which, being spiritual, must arise in the soul when in its highest spiritual condition; when the mind, indeed, like a smooth lake, reflects only heavenly images. A steadfast regarding of Him will produce this calm, and His will be the heavenly form reflected from the mental depth.

But to return to the poem. The fact that Christ remains inside, leads the poet to reflect, in the spirit of Him who found all the good in men he could, neglecting no point of contact which presented itself, whether there was anything at this lecture with which he could sympathize; and he finds that the heart of the professor does something to rescue him from the error of his brain. In his brain, even, "if Love's dead there, it has left a ghost." For when the natural deduction from his argument would be that our faith

"Be swept forthwith to its natural dust-hole, --

He bids us, when we least expect it,

Take back our faith -- if it be not just whole,

Yet a pearl indeed, as his tests affect it,

151

Which fact pays the damage done rewardingly,

So, prize we our dust and ashes accordingly!"

Love as well as learning being necessary to the understanding of the New Testament, it is to the poet matter of regret that "loveless learning" should leave its proper work, and make such havoc in that which belongs not to it. But while he sits "talking with his mind," his mood begins to degenerate from sympathy with that which is good to indifference towards all forms, and he feels inclined to rest quietly in the enjoyment of his own religious confidence, and trouble himself in no wise about the faith of his neighbours; for doubtless all are partakers of the central light, though variously refracted by the varied translucency of the mental prism . . .

"'Twas the horrible storm began afresh!

The black night caught me in his mesh,

Whirled me up, and flung me prone!

I was left on the college-step alone.

I looked, and far there, ever fleeting

Far, far away, the receding gesture,

And looming of the lessening vesture,

Swept forward from my stupid hand,

While I watched my foolish heart expand

In the lazy glow of benevolence

O'er the various modes of man's belief.

I sprang up with fear's vehemence.

-- Needs must there be one way, our chief

Best way of worship: let me strive

To find it, and when found, contrive

My fellows also take their share.

This constitutes my earthly care:

God's is above it and distinct!"

The symbolism in the former part of this extract is grand. As soon as he ceases to look practically on the phenomena with which he is surrounded, he is enveloped in storm and darkness, and sees only in the far distance the disappearing skirt of his Lord's garment. God's care is over all, he goes on to say; I must do *my part*. If I look speculatively on the world, there is nothing but dimness and mystery. If I look practically on it,

> No mere mote's-breadth, but teems immense
> With witnessings of Providence.

And whether the world which I seek to help censures or praises me -- that is nothing to me. My life -- how is it with me?

> "Soul of mine, hadst thou caught and held
>
> By the hem of the vesture . . .
>
> And I caught
>
> At the flying robe, and, unrepelled,
>
> Was lapped again in its folds full-fraught
>
> With warmth and wonder and delight,
>
> God's mercy being infinite.
>
> And scarce had the words escaped my tongue,
>
> When, at a passionate bound, I sprung
>
> Out of the wandering world of rain,
>
> Into the little chapel again."

Had he dreamed? how then could he report of the sermon and the preacher? of which and of whom he proceeds to give a very external account. But correcting himself --

> "Ha! Is God mocked, as He asks?
>
> Shall I take on me to change his tasks,
>
> And dare, despatched to a river-head
>
> For a simple draught of the element,

Neglect the thing for which He sent,

And return with another thing instead!

Saying . . . 'Because the water found

Welling up from underground,

Is mingled with the taints of earth,

While Thou, I know, dost laugh at dearth,

And couldest, at a word, convulse

The world with the leap of its river-pulse, --

Therefore I turned from the oozings muddy,

And bring thee a chalice I found, instead.

See the brave veins in the breccia ruddy!

One would suppose that the marble bled.

What matters the water? A hope I have nursed,

That the waterless cup will quench my thirst.'

 -- Better have knelt at the poorest stream

That trickles in pain from the straitest rift!

For the less or the more is all God's gift,

Who blocks up or breaks wide the granite seam.

And here, is there water or not, to drink?"

He comes to the conclusion, that the best for him is that mode of worship which partakes the least of human forms, and brings him nearest to the spiritual; and, while expressing good wishes for the Pope and the professor --

"Meantime, in the still recurring fear

Lest myself, at unawares, be found,

While attacking the choice of my neighbours round,

Without my own made -- I choose here!"

He therefore joins heartily in the hymn which is sung by the congregation of the little chapel at the close of their worship. And this concludes the poem.

What is the central point from which this poem can be regarded? It does not seem to be very hard to find. Novalis has said: "Die Philosophie ist eigentlich Heimweh, ein Trieb überall zu Hause zu sein." (Philosophy is really home-sickness, an impulse to be at home everywhere.)[3] The life of a man here, if life it be, and not the vain image of what might be a life, is a continual attempt to find his place, his centre of recipiency, and active agency. He wants to know where he is, and where he ought to be and can be; for, rightly considered, the position a man ought to occupy is the only one he truly *can* occupy. It is a climbing and striving to reach that point of vision where the multiplex crossings and apparent intertwistings of the lines of fact and feeling and duty shall manifest themselves as a regular and symmetrical design. A contradiction, or a thing unrelated, is foreign and painful to him, even as the rocky particle in the gelatinous substance of the oyster; and, like the latter, he can only rid himself of it by encasing it in the pearl-like enclosure of faith; believing that hidden there lies the necessity for a higher theory of the universe than has yet been generated in his soul. The quest for this home-centre, in the man who has faith, is calm and ceaseless; in the man whose faith is weak, it is stormy and intermittent. Unhappy is that man, of necessity, whose perceptions are keener than his faith is strong. Everywhere Nature herself is putting strange questions to him; the human world is full of dismay and confusion; his own conscience is bewildered by contradictory appearances; all which may well happen to the man whose eye is not yet single, whose heart is not yet pure. He is not at home; his soul is astray amid people of a strange speech and a stammering tongue. But the faithful man is led onward; in the stillness that his confidence produces arise the bright images of truth; and visions of God, which are only beheld in solitary places, are granted to his soul.

---

[3] Georg Philipp Friedrich Freiherr von Hardenberg (1772-1801) was a German poet and philosopher who published under the pen name "Novalis."

"O struggling with the darkness all the night,

And visited all night by troops of stars!"

What is true of the whole, is true of its parts. In all the relations
of life, in all the parts of the great whole of existence, the true man is
ever seeking his home. This poem seems to show us such a quest.
"Here I am in the midst of many who belong to the same family. They
differ in education, in habits, in forms of thought; but they are called
by the same name. What position with regard to them am I to assume?
I am a Christian; how am I to live in relation to Christians?" Such seems
to be something like the poet's thought. What central position can he
gain, which, while it answers best the necessities of his own soul with
regard to God, will enable him to feel himself connected with the
whole Christian world, and to sympathize with all; so that he may not
be alone, but one of the whole. Certainly the position necessary for
both requirements is one and the same. He that is isolated from his
brethren, loses one of the greatest helps to draw near to God. Now, in
this time, which is so peculiarly transitional, this is a question of no
little import for all who, while they gladly forsake old, or rather *modern*,
theories, for what is to them a more full development of Christianity
as well as a return to the fountain-head, yet seek to be saved from the
danger of losing sympathy with those who are content with what they
are compelled to abandon. Seeing much in the common modes of
thought and belief that is inconsistent with Christianity, and even
opposed to it, they yet cannot but see likewise in many of them a power
of spiritual good; which, though not dependent on the peculiar mode,
is yet enveloped, if not embodied, in that mode.

"Ask, else, these ruins of humanity,

This flesh worn out to rags and tatters,

This soul at struggle with insanity,

Who thence take comfort, can I doubt,

Which an empire gained, were a loss without."

The love of God is the soul of Christianity. Christ is the body of
that truth. The love of God is the creating and redeeming, the forming
and satisfying power of the universe. The love of God is that which

kills evil and glorifies goodness. It is the safety of the great whole. It is the home-atmosphere of all life. Well does the poet of the "Christmas Eve" say: --

"The loving worm within its clod,

Were diviner than a loveless God

Amid his worlds, I will dare to say."

Surely then, inasmuch as man is made in the image of God nothing less than a love in the image of God's love, all-embracing, quietly excusing, heartily commending, can constitute the blessedness of man; a love not insensible to that which is foreign to it, but overcoming it with good. Where man loves in his kind, even as God loves in His kind, then man is saved, then he has reached the unseen and eternal. But if, besides the necessity to love that lies in a man, there be likewise in the man whom he ought to love something in common with him, then the law of love has increased force. If that point of sympathy lies at the centre of the being of each, and if these centres are brought into contact, then the circles of their being will be, if not coincident, yet concentric. We must wait patiently for the completion of God's great harmony, and meantime love everywhere and as we can.

But the great lesson which this poem teaches, and which is taught more directly in the "Easter Day" (forming part of the same volume), is that the business of a man's life is to be a Christian. A man has to do with God first; in Him only can he find the unity and harmony he seeks. To be one with Him is to be at the centre of things. If one acknowledges that God has revealed himself in Christ; that God has recognized man as his family, by appearing among them in their form; surely that very acknowledgment carries with it the admission that man's chief concern is with this revelation. What does God say and mean, teach and manifest, herein? If this world is God's making, and he is present in all nature; if he rules all things and is present in all history; if the soul of man is in his image, with all its circles of thought and multiplicity of forms; and if for man it be not enough to be rooted in God, but he must likewise lay hold on God; then surely no question, in whatever direction, can be truly answered, save by him who stands at the side of Christ. The doings of God cannot be understood, save by him who has the mind of Christ, which is the mind of God. All things must be strange to one who sympathizes not with the thought of the Maker, who understands not the design of the Artist. Where is he to begin? What light has he by which to classify? How will he bring order out of this apparent confusion, when the order is higher than his thought; when the confusion to him is *caused* by the order's being greater than he can comprehend? Because he stands outside and not within, he sees an entangled maze of forces, where there is in truth an intertwining dance of harmony. There is for no one any solution of the world's mystery, or of any part of its mystery, except he be able to say with our poet:—

"I have looked to Thee from the beginning,

Straight up to Thee through all the world,

Which, like an idle scroll, lay furled

To nothingness on either side:

And since the time Thou wast descried,

Spite of the weak heart, so have I

Lived ever, and so fain would die,

Living and dying, Thee before!"

Christianity is not the ornament, or even complement, of life; it is its necessity; it is life itself glorified into God's ideal.

Dr. Chalmers, from considering the minuteness of the directions given to Moses for the making of the tabernacle, was led to think that he himself was wrong in attending too little to the "*petite morale*" of dress.[4] Will this be excuse enough for occupying a few sentences with the rhyming of this poem? Certainly the rhymes of a poem form no small part of its artistic existence. Probably there is a deeper meaning in this part of the poetic art than has yet been made clear to poet's mind. In this poem the rhymes have their share in its humorous charm. The writer's power of using double and triple rhymes is remarkable,

---

[4] Thomas Chalmers, D.D. (1780-1847), *He Supreme Importance of a Right Moral to a Right Economical State of the Community* (Glasgow: William Collins, 1832).

and the effect is often pleasing, even where they are used in the more solemn parts of the poem. Take the lines:—

"No! love which, on earth, amid all the shows of it,

Has ever been seen the sole good of life in it,

The love, ever growing there, spite of the strife in it,

Shall arise, made perfect, from death's repose of it."

A poem is a thing not for the understanding or heart only, but likewise for the ear; or, rather, for the understanding and heart through the ear. The best poem is best set forth when best read. If, then, there be rhymes which, when read aloud, do, by their composition of words, prevent the understanding from laying hold on the separate words, while the ear lays hold on the rhymes, the perfection of the art must here be lost sight of, notwithstanding the completeness which the rhyming manifests on close examination. For instance, in *"equipt yours,"* *"Scriptures;"* *"Manchester,"* *"haunches stir;"* or *"affirm any,"* *"Germany;"* where two words rhyme with one word. But there are very few of them that are objectionable on account of this difficulty and necessity of rapid analysis.

One of the most wonderful things in the poem is, that so much of argument is expressed in a species of verse, which one might be inclined, at first sight, to think the least fitted for embodying it. But, in fact, the same amount of argument in any other kind of verse would, in all likelihood, have been intolerably dull as a work of art. Here the verse is full of life and vigour, flagging never. Where, in several parts, the exact meaning is difficult to reach, this results chiefly from the dramatic rapidity and condensation of the thoughts. The argumentative power is indeed wonderful; the arguments themselves powerful in their simplicity, and embodied in words of admirable force. The poem is full of pathos and humour; full of beauty and grandeur, earnestness and truth.

Essays on Some of the Forms of Literature

Schoppe, the satiric chorus of Jean Paul's romance of *Titan*, makes his appearance at a certain masked ball, carrying in front of him a glass case, in which the ball is remasked, repeated, and again reflected in a mirror behind, by a set of puppets, ludicrously aping the apery of the courtiers, whose whole life and outward manifestation was but a body-mask mechanically moved with the semblance of real life and action.[1] The court simulates reality.[2] The masks are a multiform mockery at their own unreality, and as such are regarded by Schoppe, who takes them off with the utmost ridicule in his masked puppet-show, which, with its reflection in the mirror, is again indefinitely multiplied in the many-sided reflector of Schoppe's, or of Richter's, or of the reader's own imagination. The successive retreating and beholding in this scene is suggested to the reviewer by the fact that the last of these essays by Mr. Lynch is devoted in part to reviews. So that the reviews review books, -- Mr. Lynch reviews the reviews, and the present Reviewer finds himself (somewhat presumptuously, it may be) attempting to review Mr. Lynch. In this, however, his office must be very different from that of Schoppe (for there is a deeper and more real correspondence between the position of the showman and the reviewer than that outward resemblance which first caused the one to suggest the other). The latter's office, in the present instance, was, by mockery, to destroy the false, the very involution of the satire adding to the strength of the ridicule. His glass case was simply a review uttered by shapes and wires instead of words and handwriting. And the work of the true critic must sometimes be to condemn, and, as far as his strength can reach, utterly to destroy the false, -- scorching and

---

[1] Jean Paul (1763-1825) was a German Romantic writer. Schoppe is a character in Jean Paul's novel *Titan* published in four volumes from 1800 to 1803.

[2] "Essays on some of the Forms of Literature." By T.T. Lynch, Author of "Theophilus Trinal." Longmans.

withering its seeming beauty, till it is reduced to its essence and original groundwork of dust and ashes. It is only, however, when it wears the form of beauty which is the garment of truth, and so, like the Erl-maidens, has power to bewitch, that it is worth the notice and attack of the critic.[3] Many forms of error, perhaps most, are better left alone to die of their own weakness, for the galvanic battery of criticism only helps to perpetuate their ghastly life. The highest work of the critic, however, must surely be to direct attention to the true, in whatever form it may have found utterance. But on this let us hear Mr. Lynch himself in the last of these four lectures which were delivered by him at the Royal Institution, Manchester, and are now before us in the form of a book: --

> The kritikos, the discerner, if he is ever saying to us, This is not gold; and never, This is; is either very humbly useful, or very perverse, or very unfortunate.[4] This is not gold, he says. Thank you, we reply, we perceived as much. And this is not, he adds. True, we answer, but we see gold grains glittering out of its rude, dark mass. Well, at least, this is not, he proceeds. Perverse man! we retort, are you seeking what is not gold? We are inquiring for what is, and unfortunate indeed are we if, born into a world of Nature, and of Spirit once so rich, we are born but to find that it has spent or has lost all its wealth. Unhappy man would he be, who, walking his garden, should scent only the earthy savour of leaves dead or dying, never perceiving, and that

---

[3] The Erl-King was a figure from Danish folklore who was a malevolent spirit or king of the fairies. This reference to the Erl-maidens most likely refers to those mentioned in a ballad by Johann Gottfried Herder title "The Erl-King's Daughter" (1778) where the Erl-maidens, like sirens, try to tempt the hero to his doom. The Erl-King was also the subject of a work by Goethe published in 1782. Both are based on an older Scandinavian tale known sometimes as "Sir Olof and the Elves."

Then youths, if through the wood you ride,

 When night repose is bringing,

Turn from the Erl-King's mound aside,

 Though songs through the air be ringing.

Danger will ever him betide,

 Who heeds the Erl-maidens singing!

- From "The Erl-King's Daughter" by Herder

[4] "Kritikos" is Greek meaning "to judge, or discern."

afar off, the heavenly odour of roses fresh to-day from the Maker's hands. The discerning by spiritual aroma may lead to discernment by the eye, and to that careful scrutiny, and thence greater knowledge, of which the eye is instrument and minister.

And again: --

The critic criticized, if dealt with in the worst fashion of his own class, must be pronounced a mere monster, "seeking whom he may devour;" and, therefore, to be hunted and slain as speedily as possible, and stuffed for the museum, where he may be regarded with due horror, but in safety.[5] But if dealt with after the best fashion of his class, a very honourable and beneficent office is assigned him, and he is warned only -- though zealously -- against its perversions. A judicial chair in the kingdom of human thought, filled by a man of true integrity, comprehensiveness, and delicacy of spirit, is a seat of terror and praise, whose powers are at once most fostering to whatever is good, most repressive of whatever is evil . . . The critic, in his office of censurer, has need so much to controvert, expose, and punish, because of the abundance of literary faults; and as there is a right and a wrong side in warfare, so there will be in criticism. And as when soldiers are numerous, there will be not a few who are only tolerable, if even that, so of critics. But then the critic is more than the censurer; and in his higher and happier aspect appears before us and serves us, as the discoverer, the vindicator, and the eulogist of excellence.

But resisting the temptation to quote further from Mr. Lynch's book on this matter of Criticism, which seemed the natural point of contact by which the Reviewer could lay hold on the book, he would pass on with the remark that his duty in the present instance is of the nobler and better sort -- nobler and better, that is, with regard to the object, for duty in the man remains ever the same -- namely, the exposition of excellence, and not of its opposite. Mr. Lynch is a man of true insight and large heart, who has already done good in the world, and will do more; although, possibly, he belongs rather to the last class

---

[5] From 1 Peter 5:8 KJV "Be sober and watch; because your adversary the devil, as a roaring lion, walketh about, seeking whom he may devour."

of writers described by himself, in the extract I am about to give from this same essay, than to any of the preceding: --

> Some of the best books are written avowedly, or with evident consciousness of the fact, for the select public that is constituted by minds of the deeper class, or minds the more advanced of their time. Such books may have but a restricted circulation and limited esteem in their own day, and may afterwards extend both their fame and the circle of their readers. Others of the best books, written with a pathos and a power that may be universally felt, appeal at once to the common humanity of the world, and get a response marvellously strong and immediate. An ordinary human eye and heart, whose glances are true, whose pulses healthy, will fit us to say of much that we read -- This is good, that is poor. But only the educated eye and the experienced heart will fit us to judge of what relates to matters veiled from ordinary observation, and belonging to the profounder region of human thought and emotion. Powers, however, that the few only possess, may be required to paint what everybody can see, so that everybody shall say, How beautiful! how like! And powers adequate to do this in the finest manner will be often adequate to do much more -- may produce, indeed, books or pictures, whose singular merit only the few shall perceive, and the many for awhile deny, and books or pictures which, while they give an immediate and pure pleasure to the common eye, shall give a far fuller and finer pleasure to that eye that is the organ of a deeper and more cultivated soul. There are, too, men of *peculiar* powers, rare and fine, who can never hope to please the large public, at least of their own age, but whose writings are a heart's ease and heart's joy to the select few, and serve such as a cup of heavenly comfort for the earth's journey, and a lamp of heavenly light for the shadows of the way.

One other extract from the general remarks on Books in this essay, and we will turn to another: --

> In all our estimation of the various qualities of books, if it be true that our reading assists our life, it is true also that our life assists our reading. If we let our spirit talk to us in undistracted moments -- if we commune with friendly, serious Nature, face to face, often -- if we pursue

honourable aims in a steady progress -- if we learn how a man's best work falls below his thought, yet how still his failure prompts a tenderer love of his thought -- if we live in sincere, frank relations with some few friends, joying in their joy, hearing the tale and sharing the pain of their grief, and in frequent interchange of honest, household sensibility -- if we look about us on character, marking distinctly what we can see, and feeling the prompting of a hundred questions concerning what is out of our ken: -- if we live thus, we shall be good readers and critics of books, and improving ones.

The second and third of these essays are on Biography and Fiction respectively and principally; treating, however, of collateral subjects as well. Deep is the relation between the life shadowed forth in a biography, and the life in a man's brain which he shadows forth in a fiction -- when that fiction is of the highest order, and written in love, is beheld even by the writer himself with reverence. Delightful, surely, it must be; yes, awful too, to read to-day the embodiment of a man's noblest thought, to follow the hero of his creation through his temptations, contests, and victories, in a world which likewise is --

"All made out of the carver's brain;"[6]

and to-morrow to read the biography of this same writer. What of his own ideal has he realized? Where can the life-fountain be detected within him which found issue to the world's light and air, in this ideal self? Shall God's fiction, which is man's reality, fall short of man's fiction? Shall a man be less than what he can conceive and utter? Surely it will not, cannot end thus. If a man live at all in harmony with the great laws of being -- if he will permit the working out of God's idea in him, he must one day arrive at something greater than what now he can project and behold. Yet, in biography, we do not so often find traces of those struggles depicted in the loftier fiction. One reason may be that the contest is often entirely within, and so a man may have won his spiritual freedom without any outward token directly significant of the victory; except, if he be an artist, such expression as it finds in

------

[6] Samuel Taylor Coleridge, "Christabel," 1816.

165

fiction, whether the fiction be in marble, or in sweet harmonies, or in ink. Nor can we determine the true significance of any living act; for being ourselves within the compass of the life-mystery, we cannot hold it at arm's length from us and look at its lines of configuration. Nor of a life can we in any measure determine the success by what we behold of it. It is to us at best but a truncated spire, whose want of completion may be the greater because of the breadth of its base, and its slow taper, indicating the lofty height to which it is intended to aspire. The idea of our own life is more than we can embrace. It is not ours, but God's, and fades away into the infinite. Our comprehension is finite; we ourselves infinite. We can only trust in God and do the truth; then, and then only, is our life safe, and sure both of continuance and development.

But the reviewer perhaps too often merely steals his author's text and writes upon it; or, like a man who lies in bed thinking about a dream till its folds enwrap him and he sinks into the midst of its visions, he forgets his position of beholding, and passes from observation into spontaneous utterance. What says our author about "biography, autobiography, and history?" This lecture has pleased the reviewer most of the four. Reading it in a lonely place, under a tree, with wide fields and slopes around, it produced on his mind the two effects which perhaps Mr. Lynch would most wish it should produce -- namely, first, a longing to lead a more true and noble life; and, secondly, a desire to read more biography. Nor can he but hope that it must produce the same effect on every earnest reader, on every one whose own biography would not be altogether a blank in what regards the individual will and spiritual aim.

> In meditative hours, when we blend despair of ourself with complaint of the world, the biography of a man successful in this great business of living is as the visit of an angel sent to strengthen us. Give the soldier his sword, the farmer his plough, the carpenter his hammer and nails, the manufacturer his machines, the merchant his stores, and the scholar his books; these are but implements; the man is more than his work or tools. How far has he fulfilled the law of his being, and attained its desire? Is his life a whole; the days as threads and as touches; the life, the well-woven garment, the well-painted picture? Which of two sacrifices has he offered -- the one so acceptable to the powers of dark worlds, the other so acceptable to powers of bright

ones -- that of soul to body, or that of body to soul? Has he slain what was holiest in him to obtain gifts from Fashion or Mammon? Or has he, in days so arduous, so assiduous, that they are like a noble army of martyrs, made burnt-offering of what was secondary, throwing into the flames the salt of true moral energy and the incense of cordial affections? We want the work to show us by its parts, its mass, its form, the qualities of the man, and to see that the man is perfected through his work as well as the work finished by his effort.

Perhaps the highest moral height which a man can reach, and at the same time the most difficult of attainment, is the willingness to be *nothing* relatively, so that he attain that positive excellence which the original conditions of his being render not merely possible, but imperative. It is nothing to a man to be greater or less than another -- to be esteemed or otherwise by the public or private world in which he moves. Does he, or does he not, behold, and love, and live, the unchangeable, the essential, the divine? This he can only do according as God hath made him. He can behold and understand God in the least degree, as well as in the greatest, only by the godlike within him; and he that loves thus the good and great, has no room, no thought, no necessity for comparison and difference. The truth satisfies him. He lives in its absoluteness. God makes the glow-worm as well as the star; the light in both is divine. If mine be an earth-star to gladden the wayside, I must cultivate humbly and rejoicingly its green earth-glow, and not seek to blanch it to the whiteness of the stars that lie in the fields of blue. For to deny God in my own being is to cease to behold him in any. God and man can meet only by the man's becoming that which God meant him to be. Then he enters into the house of life, which is greater than the house of fame. It is better to be a child in a green field than a knight of many orders in a state ceremonial.

One biography may help conjecture or satisfy reason concerning the story of a thousand unrecorded lives. And how few even of the deserving among the multitude can deserve, as "dear sons of memory," to be shrined in the public heart. Few of us die unwept, but most of us unwritten. We shall find a grave -- less certainly a tombstone -- and with much less likelihood a biographer. Those "bright particular" stars that at evening look towards us from afar, yet still are individual in the distance, are at

167

clearest times but about a thousand; but the milky lustre that runs through mid heaven is composed of a million million lights, which are not the less separate because seen undistinguishably. Absorbed, not lost, in the multitude of the unrecorded, our private dear ones make part in this mild, blissful shining of the "general assembly," the great congregation of the skies.[7] Thus the past is aglow with the unwritten, the nameless. The leaders, sons of fame, conspicuous in lustre, eminent in place; these are the few, whose great individuality burns with distinct, starry light through the dark of ages. Such stars, without the starry way, would not teach us the vastness of heaven; and the "way," without these, were not sufficient to gladden and glorify the night with pomp of Hierarchical Ascents of Domination.

There are many passages in this essay with which the reviewer would be glad to enrich his notice of the book, but limitation of space, and perhaps justice to the essay itself, which ought to be read in its own completeness, forbid. Mr. Lynch looks to the heart of the matter, and makes one put the question -- "Would not a biography written by Mr. Lynch himself be a valuable addition to this kind of literature?" His would not be an interesting account of outward events and relationships and progress, nor even a succession of revelations of inward conditions, but we should expect to find ourselves elevated by him to a point of view from which the life of the man would assume an artistic individuality, as it were an isolation of existence; for the supposed author could not choose for his regard any biography for which this would be impossible; or in which the reticulated nerves of purpose did not combine the whole, with more or less of success, into a true and remarkable unity. One passage more from this essay,—

> Biography, then, makes life known to us as more wealthy in character, and much more remarkable in its every-day stories, than we had deemed it. Another good it does us is this. It introduces us to some of our most agreeable and stimulative friendships. People may be more beneficially

---

[7] The writer of Hebrews refers to a "great cloud of witnesses" in Hebrews 12:1 who came before the writer and contemporaries who lived a life of faith. Daniel also refers to wise and righteous individuals as "lights" or "stars" in Daniel 12:3 (NKJV) Those who are wise shall shine like the brightness of the firmament, and those who turn many to righteousness like the stars forever and ever."

intimate with one they never saw than even with a neighbour or brother. Many a solitary, puzzled, incommunicative person, has found society provided, his riddle read, and his heart's secret, that longed and strove for utterance, outspoken for him in a biography. And both a love purer than any yet entertained may be originated, and a pure but ungratified love already existing, find an object, by the visit of a biography. In actual life you see your friend to-day, and will see him again to-morrow or next year; but in the dear book, you have your friend and all his experiences at once and ever. He is with you wholly, and may be with you at any time. He lives for you, and has already died for you, to give finish to the meaning, fulness, and sanctity, to the comfort of his days. He is mysteriously above as well as before you, by this fact, that he has died. Thus your intimate is your superior, your solace, but your support, too, and an example of the victory to which he calls you. His end, or her end, is our own in view, and the flagging spirit revives. We see the goal, and gird our loins anew for the race. Or, speaking of things minor, there is fresh prospect of the game, there is companionship in the hunt, and spirit for the winning. Such biography, too, is a mirror in which we see ourselves; and we see that we may trim or adorn, or that the plain signs of our deficient health or ill-ruled temper may set us to look for, and to use the means of improvement. But such a mirror is as a water one; in which first you may see your face, and which then becomes for you a bath to wash away the stains you see, and to offer its pure, cool stream as a restorative and cosmetic for your wrinkles and pallors. And what a pleasure there will be sometimes as we peruse a biography, in finding another who is so like ourself -- saying the same things, feeling the same dreads, and shames, and flutterings; hampered and harassed much as poor self is. Then, the escapes of such a friend give us hope of deliverance for ourself; and his better, or if not better, yet rewarded, patience, freshens our eye and sinews, and puts a staff into our hand. And certain seals of impossibility that we had put on this stone, and on that, beneath which our hopes lay buried, are by this biography, as by a visiting angel, effectually broken, and our hopes arise again. Our view of life becomes more complete because we see the whole of his, or of hers. We view life, too, in a more composed, tender way. Wavering faith, in its chosen determining principles, is confirmed. In quiet comparison of ourselves with one of our own class, or one who has made the mark for which we are striving, we are shamed to have done no better, and stirred to attempt former things again, or fresh ones in a stronger and more patient spirit.

It is, indeed, well with him who has found a friend whose spirit touches his own and illuminates it.

I missed him when the sun began to bend;

I found him not when I had lost his rim;

With many tears I went in search of him,

Climbing high mountains which did still ascend,

And gave me echoes when I called my friend;

Through cities vast and charnel-houses grim,

And high cathedrals where the light was dim;

Through books, and arts, and works without an end—

But found him not, the friend whom I had lost.

And yet I found him, as I found the lark,

A sound in fields I heard but could not mark;

I found him nearest when I missed him most,

I found him in my heart, a life in frost,

A light I knew not till my soul was dark.[8]

Next to possessing a true, wise, and victorious friend seated by your fireside, it is blessed to have the spirit of such a friend embodied -- for spirit can assume any embodiment -- on your bookshelves. But in the latter case the friendship is all on one side. For full friendship your friend must love you, and know that you love him. Surely these biographies are not merely spiritual links connecting us in the truest manner with past times and vanished minds, and thus producing strong

---

[8] George MacDonald, "Lost and Found."

half friendships. Are they not likewise links connecting us with a future, wherein these souls shall dawn upon ours, rising again from the death of the past into the life of our knowledge and love? Are not these biographies letters of introduction, forwarded, but not yet followed by him whom they introduce, for whose step we listen, and whose voice we long to hear; and whom we shall yet meet somewhere in the Infinite? Shall I not one day, "somewhere, somehow," clasp the large hand of Novalis, and, gazing on his face, compare his features with those of Saint John?

The essay on light literature must be left to the spontaneous appreciation of those who are already acquainted with this book, or who may be induced, by the representations here made, to become acquainted with it. Before proceeding to notice the first essay in the little volume, namely, that on Poetry, its subject suggests the fact of the publication of a second edition of the *Memorials of Theophilus Trinal*, by the same author, a portion of which consists of interspersed poems. These are of true poetic worth; and although in some cases wanting in rhythmic melody, yet in most of these cases they possess a wild and peculiar rhythm of their own. The reviewer knows of some whose hearts this book has made glad, and doubtless there are many such.

The essay on Poetry is itself poetic throughout in its expression. And how else shall Poetry be described than by Poetry? What form shall embrace and define the highest? Must it not be self-descriptive as self-existent? For what man is to this planet, what the eye is to man himself, Poetry is to Literature. Yet one can hardly help wishing that the poetic forms in this Essay were fewer and less minute, and the whole a little more scientific; though it is a question how far we have a right to ask for this. As you open it, however, the pages seem absolutely to sparkle, as if strewn with diamond sparks. It is no dull, metallic, surface lustre, but a shining from within, as well as from the superficies. Still one cannot deny that fancy is too prominent in Mr. Lynch's writings. It is true that his Fancy is the fairy attendant on his Imagination, which latter uses the former for her own higher ends; and that there is little or no *mere* fancy to be found in his books; for if you look below the surface-form you find a truth. But it were to be desired that the Truth clothed herself always in the living forms of Imagination, and thus walked forth amongst her worshippers, looking on them from living eyes, rather than that she should show herself through the windows of fancy. Sometimes there may be an offence against taste, as in page 20; sometimes an image may be expanded too much, and sometimes the very exuberance of imaginative fancy (if the combination be correct) may lead to an association of images that suggests incongruity. Still the essay is abundantly beautiful and true. The poetical quotations are not isolated, or exposed to view as specimens, but are worked into the web of the prose like the flowers in the damask, and do their part in the evolution of the continuous thought.

> If poetry, as light from the heart of God, is for our heart, that we may brighten and distinguish individual things; if it is to transfigure for us the round, dusk world as by an inner radiance; if it is to present human life and history as Rembrandt[9] pictures, in which darkness serves and glorifies light; if, like light, formless in its essence, all things shapen towards the perfection of their forms under its influence; if, entering as through crevices in single beams, it makes dimmest places cheerful and sacred with its golden touch: then must the heart of the Poet in which this true light shineth be as a hospice on the mountain pathways of the world, and his verse must be the lamp seen from far that burns to tell us where bread and shelter, drink, fire, and companionship, may be found; and he himself should have the mountaineer's hardiness and resolution. From the heart as source, to the heart in influence, Poetry comes. The inward, the upward, and the onward, whether we speak of an individual or a nation, may not be separated in our consideration. Deep and sacred imaginative meditations are needed for the true earthward as well as for the heavenward progress of men and peoples. And Poetry, whether old or new, streaming from the heart moved by the powerful spirit of love, has influence on the heart public and individual, and thence on the manners, laws, and institutions of nations. If Poesy visit the length and breadth of a country after years unfruitfully dull, coming like a showery fertilizing wind after drought, the corners and the valley-hidings are visited too, and these perhaps she now visits first, as these sometimes she has visited only. For miles and for miles, the public corn, the bread of the

---

[9] Rembrandt Harmenszoon van Rijn (1606-1669) was a Dutch painter in the Dutch Golden Age.

nation's life, is bettered; and in our own endeared spot, the roses, delight of our individual eye and sense, yield us more prosperingly their colour and their fragrance. For the universal sunshine which brightens a thousand cities, beautifies ten thousand homesteads, and rejoices ten times ten thousand hearts. And as rains in the mid season renew for awhile the faded greenness of spring; and trees in fervent summers, when their foliage has deepened or fully fixed its hue, bedeck themselves through the fervency with bright midsummer shoots; so, by Poetry are the youthful hues of the soul renewed, and truths that have long stood full-foliaged in our minds, are by its fine influences empowered to put forth fresh shoots. Thus age, which is a necessity for the body, may be warded off as a disease from the soul, and we may be like the old man in Chaucer, who had nothing hoary about him but his hairs—

Though I be hoor I fare as doth a tree

That blosmeth er the fruit ywoxen be,

The blosmy tree n' is neither drie ne ded:

I feel me nowhere hoor, but on my head.

Min herte and all my limmes ben as grene

As laurel through the yere is for to sene.[10]

Hear our author again as to the calling of the poet:—

To unite earthly love and celestial -- 'true to the kindred points of heaven and home;' to reconcile time and eternity; to draw presage of joy's victory from the delight of the secret honey dropping from the clefts of rocky sorrow; *to harmonize our instinctive longings for the definite and the infinite, in the ideal Perfect*; to read creation as a human book of the heart, both plain and mystical, and divinely written: such is the office fulfilled by best -- loved poets. Their ladder of celestial ascent must be fixed on its base, earth, if its top is to securely rest on heaven."

---

[10] Geoffrey Chaucer, "The Merchant's Tale" in *Canterbury Tales* (1400), lines 249-254.

Beautifully, too, does he describe the birth of Poetry; though one may doubt its correctness, at least if attributed to the highest kind of poetry.

> When words of felt truth were first spoken by the first pair, in love of their garden, their God, and one another, and these words were with joyful surprise felt to be in their form and glow answerable to the happy thought uttered; then Poetry sprang. And when the first Father and first Mother, settling their soul upon its thought, found that thought brighten; and when from it, as thus they mused, like branchlets from a branch, or flowerets from their bud, other thoughts came, ranging themselves by the exerted, yet painlessly exerted, power of the soul, in an order felt to be beautiful, and of a sound pleasant in utterance to ear and soul; being withal, through the sweetness of their impression on the heart, fixed for memory's frequentest recurrence; then was the world's first poem composed, and in the joyful flutter of a heart that had thus become a maker, the maker of a 'thing of beauty,' like in beauty even unto God's heaven, and trees, and flowers, the secret of Poesy shone tremulously forth.

Whether this be so or not, the highest poetic feeling of which we are now conscious springs not from the beholding of perfected beauty, but from the mute sympathy which the creation with all its children manifests with us in the groaning and travailing which looketh for the sonship.[11] Because of our need and aspiration, the snowdrop gives birth in our hearts to a loftier spiritual and poetic feeling, than the rose most complete in form, colour, and odour. The rose is of Paradise -- the snowdrop is of the striving, hoping, longing Earth. Perhaps our highest poetry is the expression of our aspirations in the sympathetic forms of visible nature. Nor is this merely a longing for a restored Paradise; for even in the ordinary history of men, no man or woman that has fallen can be restored to the position formerly occupied. Such must rise to a yet higher place, whence they can behold their former standing far beneath their feet. They must be restored by attaining

---

[11] This is referring to Romans 8:22-23 where Paul writes, "We know that the whole creation has been groaning in labor pains until now; 23 and not only the creation, but we ourselves, who have the first fruits of the Spirit, groan inwardly while we wait for adoption, the redemption of our bodies."

something better than they ever possessed before, or not at all. If the law be a weariness, we must escape it by being filled with the spirit, for not otherwise can we fulfil the law than by being above the law. There is for us no escape, save as the Poet counsels us:—

Is thy strait horizon dreary?

Is thy foolish fancy chill?

Change the feet that have grown weary,

For the wings that never will.

Burst the flesh and live the spirit;

Haunt the beautiful and far;

Thou hast all things to inherit,

And a soul for every star.[12]

But the Reviewer must hasten to take leave, though unwillingly, of this pleasing, earnest, and profitable book. Perhaps it could be wished that the writer helped his readers a little more into the channel of his thought; made it easier for them to see the direction in which he is leading them; called out to them, "Come up hither," before he said, "I will show you a thing." But the Reviewer says this with deference; and takes his leave with the hope that Mr. Lynch will be listened to for two good reasons: first, that he speaks the truth; last, that he has already suffered for the Truth's sake.

---

[12] George MacDonald. "In the Winter."

Essays on Some of the Forms of Literature

The History and Heroes of Medicine

In this volume, Dr. Russell has not merely aimed at the production of a book that might be serviceable to the Faculty, by which the history of its own art is not at all sufficiently studied, but has aspired to the far more difficult success of writing a history of medicine which shall be readable to all who care for true history -- that history, namely, in which not merely growth and change are represented, but the secret supplies and influences as well, which minister to the one and occasion the other.[1] If the difficulty has been greater (although with his evidently wide sympathies and keen insight into humanity we doubt if it has), the success is the more honourable; for a success it certainly is. The partially biographical plan on which he has constructed his work has no doubt aided in the accomplishment of this purpose; for it is much easier to present the subject in its human relations, when its history is given in connexion with the lives of those who were most immediately associated with it. But it would be a great mistake to conclude from this, that it is the less a history of the art itself; for no art or science has life in itself, apart from the minds which foresee, discover, and verify it. Whatever point in its progress it may have reached, it will there remain until a new man appears, whose new questions shall illicit new replies from nature -- replies which are the essential food of the science, by which it lives, grows, and makes itself a history.

Nor must our readers suppose that because the book is readable, it is therefore slight, either in material or construction. Much reading and research have provided the material, while real thought and argument have superintended the construction. Nor is it by any means without the adornment that a poetic temperament and a keen sense of humour can supply.

Naturally, the central life in the book is that of Lord Bacon, the man who brought out of his treasures things both new and old. Up to

---

[1] * By J. Rutherfurd Russell, M.D.

him the story gradually leads from the prehistoric times of Aesculapius, the pathway first becoming plainly visible in the life and labours of Hippocrates.[2] [3] His fine intellect and powers of acute observation afforded the material necessary for the making of a true physician. The Greek mind, partly, perhaps, from its artistic tendencies, seems to have been peculiarly impatient of incomplete forms, and therefore, to have much preferred the construction of a theory from the most shadowy material, to the patient experiment and investigation necessary for the procuring of the real substance; and Hippocrates, not knowing how to advance to a theory by rational experiment, and too honest to invent one, assumes the traditional theories, founded on the vaguest and most obtrusive generalizations. Those which his experience taught him to reject, were adopted and maintained by Galen and all who followed him for centuries, the chief instance of progress being only the substitution by the Arabians of some of the milder medicines now in use, for the terrible and often fatal drugs employed by the Greek and Roman physicians.[4] The fanciful classification of diseases into four kinds -- hot, cold, moist and dry, with the corresponding arbitrary classification of remedies to be administered by contraries, continued to be the only recognized theory of medicine for many centuries after the Christian era.

But Lord Bacon, amongst other branches of knowledge which he considers ill -- followed, makes especial mention of medicine, which he would submit to the same rules of observation and experiment laid down by him for the advancement of learning in general. With regard to it, as with regard to the discovery of all the higher laws of nature, he considers "that men have made too untimely a departure, and too

---

[2] George Bohigian, "The Caduceus vs. Staff of Aesculapius - One Snake or Two?," *Missouri Medicine* 116, no. 6 (2019): 476–477. In Greek mythology, Aesculapius was the god of medicine. Aesculapis's staff entwined with a snake is still the modern symbol of medicine.

[3] Ibid., Hippocrates of Kos (450-380 B.C.) was a physician who is considered the father of Western Medicine. The Hippocratic Oath for new physicians began with "I swear by Apollo the physician, and Asclepius . . ."

[4] "Galen: Greek Physician," *Encyclopedia Britannica*, accessed August 5, 2021, https://www.britannica.com/biography/Galen. Galen (129-216 AD) was a Greek physician who continued and expanded the Greek influence on medical theory and practice.

remote a recess from particulars."[5] Men have hurried to conclusions, and then argued from them as from facts. Therefore let us have no traditional theories, and make none for ourselves but such as are revealed in the form of laws to the patient investigator, who has "straightened and held fast Proteus, that he might be compelled to change his shapes," and so reveal his nature.[6] [7] Hence one of the aspects in which Lord Bacon was compelled to appear was that of a destroyer of what preceded. In this he resembled Cardan and Paracelsus who went before him, and who like him pulled down, but could not, like him, build up. He resembled them, however, in the possession of another element of character, namely, that poetic imagination which looks abroad into the regions of possibilities, and foresees or invents. But in the case of the charlatan, the vaguest suggestions of his mind in its favourite mood, is adopted as a theory all but proved, if not as a direct revelation to the favoured individual; while the true thinker seeks but an hypothesis corresponding in some measure to facts already discovered, in order that he may have the suggestion of new experiments and investigations in the course of his attempts to verify or disprove the hypothesis. Lord Bacon considered hypothesis invaluable in the discovery of truth, but he only used it as a board upon which to write his questions to nature; or, to use another figure, hypothesis with him is as the next stepping -- stone in the swollen river, which he supposes to be here or there, and so feels for with his staff. But it must be proved before it be regarded as a law, and greatly corroborated before it be even adopted as a theory. Cardan and Paracelsus were destroyers and mystics only; they destroyed on the earth that they might build in the air: Lord Bacon united both characters in the philosopher. He looked abroad into the regions of the unknown, whence all knowledge comes; he called wonder the seed of knowledge; but he would build nowhere but on the earth -- on the firm land of ascertained truth. That which kept him right was his practical humanity. It was for the sake of delivering men from the ills of life, by discovering the laws of the elements amidst which that life must be led, that he laboured and thought. This object kept him true, made him able

---

[5] Francis Bacon, *The Advancement of Learning*, II.VII.5

[6] Ibid., II.I.6.

[7]

to discover the very laws of discovery; brought him so far into *rapport* with the heart of nature herself, that, like a physical prophet, his seeing could outspeed his knowing, and behold a law -- dimly, it is true, but yet behold it -- long before his intellect, which had to build bridges and find straw to make the bricks, could dare to affirm its approach to the same conclusion. Truth to humanity made him true to fact; and truth to fact made him true in theory.

It was in this spirit of devotion to his kind that he said, "Therefore here is the deficience which I find, that physicians have not ... set down and delivered over certain experimental medicines for the cure of particular diseases."

Dr. Russell's true insight into the relation of Lord Bacon to the medical as well as to all science, has suggested the above remarks. What our author chiefly desires is, that the same principles which made medicine what it is, should be allowed to carry it yet further, and make it what it ought to be, and must become. As he goes on to show, through succeeding lives and theories, that just in proportion as these principles have been followed -- the principles of careful observation, hypothesis, and experiment -- have men made discoveries that have been helpful to their fellow -- men; while, on the other hand, the most elaborate theories of the most popular physicians, which have owed their birth to premature generalization and invention, have passed away, like the crackling of thorns under a pot. Belonging to the latter class of men, we have Stahl, Hoffman, Boerhaave, Cullen, and Brown; while to the former belong Harvey, Sydenham, Jenner, and Hahnemann.

After the last name, there is no need to say that our author is a homoeopath. Whatever may be our private opinion of the system, justice requires that we should say at least that books such as these are quite as open to refutation as to ridicule; for it is only a good argument that is worth refuting by a better. But we fear there are few books on this subject that treat of it with the calmness and fairness which would incline an honest homoeopath to put them into the hands of one of the opposite party as an exposition of his opinions. There is no excitement in these pages. They are the work of a man of liberal education, of refinement, and of truthfulness, with power to understand, and facility to express; one of whose main objects is to vindicate for homoeopathy, on the most rightful of all grounds -- those on which alone science can stand -- on the ground, that is, of laws discovered by observation and experiment -- the place not only of a fact in the history of medicine, but the right to be considered as one of the greatest advances towards the establishment of a science of curing. Certainly if he and the rest of its advocates should fail utterly in this, the heresy will yet have established for itself a memorial in history, as one of the most powerful illusions that have ever deceived both priests and people. But the chief advantage which the system will derive from Dr. Russell's book will spring, it seems to us, from his attempt -- a successful one it must be confessed—to prove *that homoeopathy is a development, and not a mere reaction*; that it has its roots far down in the history of science. The first mention of it in the book, however, is made for the purpose of disavowing the claim, advanced by many homoeopathists, to Hippocrates as one of their order. Not to mention the curious story about Galen and the patient ill from an overdose of theriacum, who was cured by another dose of the same substance, nor the ridicule of the doctrine of contraries by Paracelsus and Van Helmont, nor the fact that the *contraries* of Boerhaave, by his own explanation, merely signify whatever substances prove their contrariety to the disease by curing it -- to pass by these, we find one of the main objects of homoeopathy, the discovery of specifics, insisted upon by Lord Bacon in his words already quoted. Not that homoeopaths, while they depend upon specifics, believe that there is any such thing as a specific for a disease -- a disease being as various as the individuality of the human beings whom it may attack; but that an approximate specific may be found for every well-defined stage in every individual disease; a disease having its process of change, development, and decline, like a vegetable or animal life. Besides an equally strong desire for specifics, and a determined opposition to compound medicines, Boyle, who was born the year of Bacon's death, and inherited the mantle of the great philosopher, manifests a strong belief in the power of the infinitesimal dose. Neither Bacon nor Boyle, however, were medical men by profession. But Sydenham followed them, according to Dr. Russell, in their tendency towards specifics. It is almost needless to mention Jenner's victory over the small -- pox as, in the eyes of the homoeopaths, a grand step in the development of their system. It gives Dr. Russell an opportunity of showing in a strong instance that the best discoveries for delivering mankind from those ills even of which they are most sensible have been received with derision, with more than bare unbelief. This is one of his objects in the book, and while it is no proof whatever of the truth of homoepathy, it shows at least that the opposition manifested to it is no proof of its falsehood. This is enough; for it seeks to be tried on its own merits; and its foes are bound to accord it this when it is advocated in such an honest and dignified manner as in the book before us.

The need of man, in physics as well as in higher things, is the guide to truth. With evils of any sort we need no further acquaintance than may be gained in the endeavour to combat them. The discovery of what will cure diseases seems the only natural mode of rising by generalization to the discovery of the laws of cure and the nature of disease.

Those portions of the volume which discuss the influence of Christianity on the healing art, likewise those relating to the different feelings with which at different times in different countries physicians have been regarded, are especially interesting.

The only portion of the book we should be inclined to find fault with, as to the quality of the thought expended upon it, is the dissertation in the second chapter on the [Greek: psuchae] and [Greek: pneuma]. We doubt likewise whether the author gives the Archaeus of Van Helmont quite fair play; but these are questions so purely theoretical that they scarcely admit of discussion here. We rise from the perusal of the book, whatever may be our feelings with regard to the truth or falsehood of the system it advocates, with increased respect for the profession of medicine, with enlarged hope for its future, and with a strong feeling of the nobility conferred by the art upon every one of its practitioners who is aware of the dignity of his calling.

Wordsworth's Poetry

The history of the poetry of Wordsworth is a true reflex of the man himself.[1] [2] The life of Wordsworth was not outwardly eventful, but his inner life was full of conflict, discovery, and progress. His outward life seems to have been so ordered by Providence as to favour the development of the poetic life within. Educated in the country, and spending most of his life in the society of nature, he was not subjected to those violent external changes which have been the lot of some poets. Perfectly fitted as he was to cope with the world, and to fight his way to any desired position, he chose to retire from it, and in solitude to work out what appeared to him to be the true destiny of his life.

The very element in which the mind of Wordsworth lived and moved was a Christian pantheism. Allow me to explain the word. The poets of the Old Testament speak of everything as being the work of God's hand: -- We are the "work of his hand;" "The world was made by him." But in the New Testament there is a higher form used to express the relation in which we stand to him -- "We are his offspring;" not the work of his hand, but the children that came forth from his heart.[3] Our own poet Goldsmith, with the high instinct of genius, speaks of God as having "loved us into being."[4] Now I think this is

---

[1] Delivered extempore at Manchester.

[2] Williams Wordsworth (1770-1850) was an English Romantic poet.

[3] Isaiah 64:8, John 1:10, Acts 17:18

[4] Macdonald is referring to Oliver Goldsmith (1730-1774). This quote is from "The Citizen of the World: or, letters from a Chinese philosopher, residing in London, to his friends in the east"

Letter XLVI, pg 207. "I know but of two sects of philosophers in the world that have endeavoured to inculcate that fortitude is but an imaginary virtue; I mean the followers of Con|fucius, and those who profess the doctrines of Christ. All other sects teach pride under misfortunes; they alone teach humility. Night, says our Chinese philo|sopher, not more surely follows day, than groans and tears grow out of pain; when misfortunes, therefore, oppress, when tyrants threaten, it is our interest, it is our duty, to fly even to dissipation forsupport, to seek redress from friendship, to seek redress from that best of friends who loved us into being."

not only true with regard to man, but true likewise with regard to the world in which we live. This world is not merely a thing which God hath made, subjecting it to laws; but it is an expression of the thought, the feeling, the heart of God himself. And so it must be; because, if man be the child of God, would he not feel to be out of his element if he lived in a world which came, not from the heart of God, but only from his hand? This Christian pantheism, this belief that God is in everything, and showing himself in everything, has been much brought to the light by the poets of the past generation, and has its influence still, I hope, upon the poets of the present. We are not satisfied that the world should be a proof and varying indication of the intellect of God. That was how Paley viewed it.[5] He taught us to believe there is a God from the mechanism of the world. But, allowing all the argument to be quite correct, what does it prove? A mechanical God, and nothing more.

Let us go further; and, looking at beauty, believe that God is the first of artists; that he has put beauty into nature, knowing how it will affect us, and intending that it should so affect us; that he has embodied his own grand thoughts thus that we might see them and be glad. Then, let us go further still, and believe that whatever we feel in the highest moments of truth shining through beauty, whatever comes to our souls as a power of life, is meant to be seen and felt by us, and to be regarded not as the work of his hand, but as the flowing forth of his heart, the flowing forth of his love of us, making us blessed in the union of his heart and ours.

Now, Wordsworth is the high priest of nature thus regarded. He saw God present everywhere; not always immediately, in his own form, it is true; but whether he looked upon the awful mountain-peak, sky-encompassed with loveliness, or upon the face of a little child, which is as it were eyes in the face of nature -- in all things he felt the solemn presence of the Divine Spirit. By Keats this presence was recognized only as the spirit of beauty; to Wordsworth, God, as the Spirit of Truth, was manifested through the forms of the external world.[6]

---

[5] William Paley (1743-1805) was an English clergyman and philosopher. He is best known for the teleological argument using the watchmaker analogy.

[6] John Keats (1795-1821) was an English Romantic poet and a contemporary of Lord Byron and Percy Bysshe Shelley.

I have said that the life of Wordsworth was so ordered as to bring this out of him, in the forms of *his* art, to the ears of men. In childhood even his conscience was partly developed through the influences of nature upon him. He thus retrospectively describes this special influence of nature:—

One summer evening (led by her) I found
A little boat, tied to a willow tree,
Within a rocky cave, its usual home.
Straight I unloosed her chain, and stepping in,
Pushed from the shore. It was an act of stealth,
And troubled pleasure, nor without the voice
Of mountain echoes did my boat move on,
Leaving behind her still, on either side,
Small circles glittering idly in the moon,
Until they melted all into one track
Of sparkling light. But now, like one who rows
Proud of his skill, to reach a chosen point
With an unswerving line, I fixed my view
Upon the summit of a craggy ridge,
The horizon's utmost boundary; far above
Was nothing but the stars and the grey sky.
She was an elfin pinnace; lustily
I dipped my oars into the silent lake,
And, as I rose upon the stroke, my boat
Went heaving through the water like a swan;
When, from behind that craggy steep, till then
The horizon's bound, a huge peak, black and huge,
As if with voluntary power instinct,
Upreared its head. I struck and struck again,
And, growing still in stature, the grim shape

Towered up between me and the stars, and still

For so it seemed, with purpose of its own,

And measured motion like a living thing,

Strode after me. With trembling oars I turned,

And through the silent water stole my way

Back to the covert of the willow tree;

There in her mooring place I left my bark,

And through the meadows homeward went, in grave

And serious mood; but after I had seen

That spectacle, for many days, my brain

Worked with a dim and undetermined sense

Of unknown modes of being; o'er my thoughts

There hung a darkness, call it solitude,

Or blank desertion. No familiar shapes

Remained, no pleasant images of trees,

Of sea, or sky, no colours of green fields;

But huge and mighty forms, that do not live

Like living men, moved slowly through the mind

By day, and were a trouble to my dreams.

Here we see that a fresh impulse was given to his life even in boyhood, by the influence of nature. If we have had any similar experience, we shall be able to enter into this feeling of Wordsworth's; if not, the tale will be almost incredible.

One passage more I would refer to, as showing what Wordsworth felt with regard to nature, in his youth; and the growth that took place in him in consequence. Nature laid up in the storehouse of his mind and heart her most beautiful and grand forms, whence they might be brought, afterwards, to be put to the highest human service. I quote only a few lines from that poem, deservedly a favourite with all the lovers of Wordsworth, "Lines written above Tintern Abbey:"—

I cannot paint
What then I was. The sounding cataract

Haunted me like a passion; the tall rock,

The mountain, and the deep and gloomy wood,

Their colours and their forms, were then to me

An appetite; a feeling and a love,

That had no need of a remoter charm

By thought supplied, nor any interest

Unborrowed from the eye. -- That time is past,

And all its aching joys are now no more,

And all its dizzy raptures. Not for this

Faint I, nor mourn nor murmur; other gifts

Have followed; for such loss, I would believe,

Abundant recompense. For I have learned

To look on nature, not as in the hour

Of thoughtless youth; but hearing oftentimes

The still, sad music of humanity,

Nor harsh, nor grating, though of ample power

To chasten and subdue. And I have felt

A presence that disturbs me with the joy

Of elevated thoughts; a sense sublime

Of something far more deeply interfused,

Whose dwelling is the light of setting suns,

And the round ocean, and the living air

And the blue sky, and in the mind of man;

A motion and a spirit, that impels

All thinking things, all objects of all thought,

And rolls through all things.

In this little passage you see the growth of the influence of nature
on the mind of the poet. You observe, too, that nature passes into
poetry; that form is sublimed into speech. You see the result of the
conjunction of the mind of man, and the mind of God manifested in

His works; spirit coming to know the speech of spirit. The outflowing of spirit in nature is received by the poet, and he utters again, in his form, what God has already uttered in His. Wordsworth wished to give to man what he found in nature. It was to him a power of good, a world of teaching, a strength of life. He knew that nature was not his, and that his enjoyment of nature was given to him that he might give it to man. It was the birthright of man.

But what did Wordsworth find in nature? To begin with the lowest; he found amusement in nature. Right amusement is a part of teaching; it is the childish form of teaching, and if we can get this in nature, we get something that lies near the root of good. In proof that Wordsworth found this, I refer to a poem which you probably know well, "The Daisy." The poet sits playing with the flower, and listening to the suggestions that come to him of odd resemblances that this flower bears to other things. He likens the daisy to—

> A little cyclops, with one eye
>
> Staring to threaten and defy,
>
> That thought comes next—and instantly
>
>   The freak is over,
>
> The shape will vanish -- and behold
>
> A silver shield with boss of gold,
>
> That spreads itself, some faëry bold
>
>   In fight to cover!

Look at the last stanza, too, and you will see how close amusement may lie to deep and earnest thought:—

> Bright Flower! for by that name at last
>
> When all my reveries are past,
>
> I call thee, and to that cleave fast,
>
>   Sweet silent creature!
>
> That breath'st with me in sun and air,
>
> Do thou, as thou art wont, repair
>
> My heart with gladness, and a share

Of thy meek nature!

But Wordsworth found also joy in nature, which is a better thing than amusement, and consequently easier to be found. We can often have   joy   where   we   can   have   no   amusement,—

    I wandered lonely as a cloud

    That floats on high o'er vales and hills

    When all at once I saw a crowd,

     A host, of golden daffodils;

    Beside the lake, beneath the trees,

    Fluttering and dancing in the breeze.

    The waves beside them danced; but they

     Out -- did the sparkling waves in glee:

    A poet could not but be gay,

     In such a jocund company:

    I gazed -- and gazed -- but little thought

    What Health the show to me had brought.

    "For oft, when on my couch I lie

     In vacant or in pensive mood,

    They flash upon that inward eye

    Which is the bliss of solitude;

    And then my heart with pleasure fills,

    And dances with the daffodils."

This is the joy of the eye, as far as that can be separated from the joy of the whole nature; for his whole nature rejoiced in the joy of the eye; but it was simply joy; there was no further teaching, no attempt to go through this beauty and find the truth below it. We are not always to be in that hungry, restless condition, even after truth itself. If we keep our minds quiet and ready to receive truth, and *sometimes* are hungry for it, that is enough.

Going a step higher, you will find that he sometimes *draws* a lesson from nature, seeming almost to force a meaning from her. I do not object to this, if he does not make too much of it as *existing* in nature. It is rather finding a meaning in nature that he brought to it. The meaning exists, if not *there*. For illustration I refer to another poem. Observe that Wordsworth found the lesson because he looked for it, and *would* find it.

This Lawn, a carpet all alive

With shadows flung from leaves—to strive

   In dance, amid a press

Of sunshine, an apt emblem yields

Of Worldlings revelling in the fields

   Of strenuous idleness.

Yet, spite of all this eager strife,

This ceaseless play, the genuine life

   That serves the steadfast hours,

Is in the grass beneath, that grows

Unheeded, and the mute repose

   Of sweetly -- breathing flowers.

Whether he forced this lesson from nature, or not, it is a good lesson, teaching a great many things with regard to life and work.

Again, nature sometimes flashes a lesson on his mind; *gives* it to him -- and when nature gives, we cannot but receive. As in this sonnet composed during a storm,—

One who was suffering tumult in his soul

Yet failed to seek the sure relief of prayer,

Went forth; his course surrendering to the care

Of the fierce wind, while mid-day lightnings prowl

Insiduously, untimely thunders growl;

While trees, dim-seen, in frenzied numbers tear

The lingering remnant of their yellow hair,

And shivering wolves, surprised with darkness, howl

As if the sun were not. He raised his eye

Soul-smitten; for, that instant, did appear

Large space (mid dreadful clouds) of purest sky,

An azure disc-shield of Tranquillity;

Invisible, unlooked-for, minister

Of providential goodness ever nigh!

Observe that he was not looking for this; he had not thought of praying; he was in such distress that it had benumbed the out-goings of his spirit towards the source whence alone sure comfort comes. He went out into the storm; and the uproar in the outer world was in harmony with the tumult within his soul. Suddenly a clear space in the sky makes him feel -- he has no time to think about it -- that there is a shield of tranquillity spread over him. For was it not as it were an opening up into that region where there are no storms; the regions of peace, because the regions of love, and truth, and purity, -- the home of God himself?

There is yet a higher and more sustained influence exercised by nature, and that takes effect when she puts a man into that mood or condition in which thoughts come of themselves. That is perhaps the best thing that can be done for us, the best at least that nature can do. It is certainly higher than mere intellectual teaching. That nature did this for Wordsworth is very clear; and it is easily intelligible. If the world proceeded from the imagination of God, and man proceeded from the love of God, it is easy to believe that that which proceeded from the imagination of God should rouse the best thoughts in the mind of a being who proceeded from the love of God. This I think is the relation between man and the world. As an instance of what I mean, I refer to one of Wordsworth's finest poems, which he classes under the head of

"Evening Voluntaries." It was composed upon an evening of extraordinary splendour and beauty:—

"Had this effulgence disappeared
With flying haste, I might have sent,
Among the speechless clouds, a look
Of blank astonishment;
But 'tis endued with power to stay,
And sanctify one closing day,
That frail Mortality may see --
What is? -- ah no, but what can, be!
Time was when field and watery cove
With modulated echoes rang,
While choirs of fervent Angels sang
Their vespers in the grove;
Or, crowning, star-like, each some sovereign height,
Warbled, for heaven above and earth below,
Strains suitable to both. Such holy rite,
Methinks, if audibly repeated now
From hill or valley, could not move
Sublimer transport, purer love,
Than doth this silent spectacle -- the gleam --
The shadow -- and the peace supreme!

"No sound is uttered, -- but a deep
 And solemn harmony pervades
The hollow vale from steep to steep,
 And penetrates the glades.

"Wings at my shoulders seem to play;

But, rooted here, I stand and gaze

On those bright steps that heaven-ward raise

Their practicable way.

Come forth, ye drooping old men, look abroad,

And see to what fair countries ye are bound!

"Dread Power! whom peace and calmness serve

No less than Nature's threatening voice,

From THEE, if I would swerve,

Oh, let Thy grace remind me of the light

Full early lost, and fruitlessly deplored;

Which, at this moment, on my waking sight

Appears to shine, by miracle restored;

My soul, though yet confined to earth,

Rejoices in a second birth!"

Picture the scene for yourselves; and observe how it moves in him the sense of responsibility, and the prayer, that if he has in any matter wandered from the right road, if he has forgotten the simplicity of childhood in the toil of life, he may, from this time, remember the vow that he now records -- from this time to press on towards the things that are unseen, but which are manifested through the things that are seen. I refer you likewise to the poem "Resolution and Independence," commonly called "The Leech Gatherer;" also to that grandest ode that has ever been written, the "Ode on Immortality." You will find there, whatever you may think of his theory, in the latter, sufficient proof that nature was to him a divine teaching power. Do not suppose that I mean that man can do without more teaching than nature's, or that a man with only nature's teaching would have seen these things in nature. No, the soul must be tuned to such things. Wordsworth could not have found such things, had he not known something that was more definite and helpful to him; but this known, then nature was full of teaching. When we understand the Word of God, then we understand the works of God; when we know the nature of an artist, we know his pictures; when we have known and talked with the poet, we understand his poetry far better. To the man of God, all nature will be but changeful reflections of the face of God.

Loving man as Wordsworth did, he was most anxious to give him this teaching. How was he to do it? By poetry. Nature put into the crucible of a loving heart becomes poetry. We cannot explain poetry scientifically; because poetry is something beyond science. The poet may be man of science, and the man of science may be a poet; but poetry includes science, and the man who will advance science most, is the man who, other qualifications being equal, has most of the poetic faculty in him. Wordsworth defines poetry to be "the impassioned expression which is on the face of science." Science has to do with the construction of things. The casting of the granite ribs of the mighty earth, and all the thousand operations that result in the manifestations on its surface, this is the domain of science. But when there come the grass -- bearing meadows, the heaven -- reared hills, the great streams that go ever downward, the bubbling fountains that ever arise, the wind that wanders amongst the leaves, and the odours that are wafted upon its wings; when we have colour, and shape, and sound, then we have the material with which poetry has to do. Science has to do with the underwork. For what does this great central world exist, with its hidden winds and waters, its upheavings and its downsinkings, its strong frame of rock, and its heart of fire? What do they all exist for? Not for themselves surely, but for the sake of this out-spreading world of beauty, that floats up, as it were, to the surface of the shapeless region of force. Science has to do with the one, and poetry with the other: poetry is "the impassioned expression that is on the face of science." To illustrate it still further. You are walking in the woods, and you find the first primrose of the year. You feel almost as if you had found a child. You know in yourself that you have found a new beauty and a new joy, though you have seen it a thousand times before. It is a primrose. A little flower that looks at me, thinks itself into my heart, and gives me a pleasure distinct in itself, and which I feel as if I could not do without. The impassioned expression on the face of this little outspread flower is its childhood; it means trust, consciousness of protection, faith, and hope. Science, in the person of the botanist, comes after you, and pulls it to pieces to see its construction, and delights the intellect; but the science itself is dead, and kills what it touches. The flower exists not for it, but for the expression on its face, which is its poetry, -- that expression which you feel to mean a living thing; that expression which makes you feel that this flower is, as it were, just growing out of the heart of God. The intellect itself is but the scaffolding for the uprearing of the spiritual nature.

It will make all this yet plainer, if you can suppose a human form to be created without a soul in it. Divine science *has* put it together, but only for the sake of the outshining soul that shall cause it to live, and move, and have a being of its own in God. When you see the face lighted up with soul, when you recognize in it thought and feeling, joy and love, then you know that here is the end for which it was made. Thus you see the relation that poetry has to science; and you find that, to speak in an apparent paradox, the surface is the deepest after all; for, through the surface, for the sake of which all this building went on, we have, as it were, a window into the depths of truth. There is not a form that lives in the world, but is a window cloven through the blank darkness of nothingness, to let us look into the heart, and feeling, and nature of God. So the surface of things is the best and the deepest, provided it is not mere surface, but the impassioned expression, for the sake of which the science of God has thought and laboured.

Satisfied that this was the nature of poetry, and wanting to convey this to the minds of his fellow-men, "What vehicle," Wordsworth may be supposed to have asked himself, "shall I use? How shall I decide what form of words to employ? Where am I to find the right language for speaking such great things to men?" He saw that the poetry of the eighteenth century (he was born in 1770) was not like nature at all, but was an artificial thing, with no more originality in it than there would be in a picture a hundred times copied, the copyists never reverting to the original. You cannot look into this eighteenth century poetry, excepting, of course, a great proportion of the poetry of Cowper and Thompson, without being struck with the sort of agreement that nothing should be said naturally.[7] [8] A certain set form and mode was employed for saying things that ought never to have been said twice in the same way. Wordsworth resolved to go back to the root of the thing, to the natural simplicity of speech; he would have none of these stereotyped forms of expression. "Where shall I find," said he, "the language that will be simple and powerful?" And he came to the conclusion that the language of the common people was the only language suitable for his purpose. Your experience of the everyday language of the common people may be that it is not poetical. True, but not even a poet can speak poetically in his stupid moments. Wordsworth's idea was to take the language of the common people in their uncommon moods, in their high and, consequently, simple moods, when their minds are influenced by grief, hope, reverence, worship, love; for then he believed he could get just the language suitable for the poet. As far as that language will go, I think he was right, if I may venture to give an opinion in support of Wordsworth. Of course, there will occur necessities to the poet which would not be comprehended in the language of a man whose thoughts had never moved in the same directions, but the kind of language will be the right thing, and I have heard such amongst the common people myself -- language which they did not know to be poetic, but which fell upon my ear and heart as profoundly poetic both in its feeling and its form.

In attempting to carry out this theory, I am not prepared to say that Wordsworth never transgressed his own self-imposed laws. But he adhered to his theory to the last. A friend of the poet's told me that

---

[7] William Cowper (1731-1800) was a popular English poet and hymnwriter. He was friends with John Newton, who wrote "Amazing Grace" and wrote a number of anti-slavery poems. Cowper was the most quoted poet in the abolitionist movements in both Great Britain and the United States. "Cowper, Slave Narratives, And The Antebellum American Reading Public | Cowper & Newton Museum," October 13, 2016, accessed September 6, 2021,
https://cowperandnewtonmuseum.org.uk/journal/j6-article-turner/.

[8] It's not clear which eighteenth century poet to which MacDonald is referring. William Thompson (1712-1766) was an English poet and rector. His best known work is one titled "Sickness" (1746) which describes various diseases. Since the point of MacDonald statement that Cowper and Thompson are two poets who do say things naturally, William Thompson may be the best fit. The more well-known poet with a similar nama is James Thomson (1700-1748); however, the spelling is slightly different. Thomson's best known works are "Rule, Britannia!", "The Seasons," and "The Castle of Indolence." Thomson is memorialized at the Poets' Corner in Westminster Abbey.

Wordsworth had to him expressed his belief that he would be remembered longest, not by his sonnets, as his friend thought, but by his lyrical ballads, those for which he had been reviled and laughed at; the most by critics who could not understand him, and who were unworthy to read what he had written. As a proof of this let me read to you three verses, composing a poem that was especially marked for derision: --

She dwelt among the untrodden ways,

Beside the springs of Dove;

A maid whom there were none to praise,

And very few to love.

A violet by a mossy stone.

Half hidden from the eye;

Fair as a star, when only one

Is shining in the sky.

She lived unknown, and few could know

When Lucy ceased to be;

But she is in her grave, and Oh!

The difference to me.

The last line was especially chosen as the object of ridicule; but I think with most of us the feeling will be, that its very simplicity of expression is overflowing in suggestion, it throws us back upon our own experience; for, instead of trying to utter what he felt, he says in those simple and common words, "You who have known anything of the kind, will know what the difference to me is, and only you can know." "My intention and desire," he says in one of his essays, "are that the interest of the poem shall owe nothing to the circumstances; but that the circumstances shall be made interesting by the thing itself." In most novels, for instance, the attempt is made to interest us in worthless, commonplace people, whom, if we had our choice, we would far rather not meet at all, by surrounding them with peculiar and extraordinary circumstances; but this is a low source of interest. Wordsworth was determined to owe nothing to such an adventitious cause. For illustration allow me to read that well-known little ballad, "The Reverie of Poor Susan," and you will see how entirely it bears out what he lays down as his theory. The scene is in London:—

> At the corner of Wood-street, when daylight appears,
>
> Hangs a Thrush that sings loud, it has sung for three years;
>
> Poor Susan has passed by the spot, and has heard,
>
> In the silence of morning, the song of the Bird.
>
>
> 'Tis a note of enchantment: what ails her? She sees
>
> A mountain ascending, a vision of trees;
>
> Bright volumes of vapour through Lothbury glide,
>
> And a river flows on through the vale of Cheapside.
>
>
> Green pastures she views in the midst of the dale,
>
> Down which she so often has tripped with her pail;
>
> And a single small cottage, a nest like a dove's,
>
> The one only dwelling on earth that she loves.
>
>
> She looks, and her heart is in heaven: but they fade,
>
> The mist and the river, the hill and the shade:
>
> The stream will not flow, and the hill will not rise,
>
> And the colours have all passed away from her eyes!

Is any of the interest here owing to the circumstances? Is it not a very common incident? But has he not treated it so that it is not *commonplace* in the least? We recognize in this girl just the feelings we discover in ourselves, and acknowledge almost with tears her sisterhood to us all.

I have tried to make you feel something of what Wordsworth attempts to do, but I have not given you the best of his poems. Allow me to finish by reading the closing portion of the *Prelude*, the poem that was published after his death. It is addressed to Coleridge:—

Oh! yet a few short years of useful life,

And all will be complete, thy race be run,

Thy monument of glory will be raised;

Then, though (too weak to head the ways of truth)

This age fall back to old idolatry,

Though men return to servitude as fast

As the tide ebbs, to ignominy and shame

By nations sink together, we shall still

Find solace -- knowing what we have learnt to know --

Rich in true happiness, if allowed to be

Faithful alike in forwarding a day

Of firmer trust, joint labourers in the work

(Should Providence such grace to us vouchsafe)

Of their deliverance, surely yet to come.

Prophets of Nature, we to them will speak

A lasting inspiration, sanctified

By reason, blest by faith: what we have loved,

Others will love, and we will teach them how;

Instruct them how the mind of man becomes

A thousand times more beautiful than the earth

On which he dwells, above this frame of things

(Which, 'mid all revolution in the hopes

And fears of men, doth still remain unchanged)

In beauty exalted, as it is itself

Of quality and fabric more divine.

SHELLEY

Whatever opinion may be held with regard to the relative position occupied by Shelley as a poet, it will be granted by most of those who have studied his writings, that they are of such an individual and original kind, that he can neither be hidden in the shade, nor lost in the brightness, of any other poet. No idea of his works could be conveyed by instituting a comparison, for he does not sufficiently resemble any other among English writers to make such a comparison possible.

Percy Bysshe Shelley was born at Field Place, near Horsham, in the county of Sussex, on the 4th of August, 1792. He was the son of Timothy Shelley, Esq., and grandson of Sir Bysshe Shelley, the first baronet. His ancestors had long been large landed proprietors in Sussex.

As a child his habits were noticeable. He was especially fond of rambling by moonlight, of inventing wonderful tales, of occupying himself with strange, and sometimes dangerous, amusements. At the age of thirteen he went to Eton. In this little world, that determined opposition to whatever appeared to him an invasion of human rights and liberty, which was afterwards the animating principle of most of his writings, was first roused in the mind of Shelley. Were we not aware of far keener distress which he afterwards endured from yet greater injustice, we might suppose that the sufferings he had to bear from placing himself in opposition to the custom of the school, by refusing to fag, had made him morbidly sensitive on the point of liberty. At a time, however, when freedom of speech, as indicating freedom of thought, was especially obnoxious to established authorities; when no allowance could be made on the score of youth, still less on that of individual peculiarity, Shelley became a student at Oxford. He was then eighteen. Devoted to metaphysical speculation, and especially fond of logical discussion, he, in his first year, printed and distributed among the authorities and members of his college a pamphlet, if that can be called a pamphlet which consisted only of two pages, in which he opposed the usual arguments for the existence of a Deity; arguments which, perhaps, the most ardent believers have equally considered inconclusive. Whether Shelley wrote this pamphlet as an embodiment of his own opinions, or merely as a logical confutation of certain arguments, the mode of procedure adopted with him was certainly not one which necessarily resulted from the position of those to whose care the education of his opinions was entrusted. Without waiting to be assured that he was the author, and satisfying themselves with his refusal to answer when questioned as to the authorship, they handed him his sentence of expulsion, which had been already drawn up in due form.

About this time Shelley wrote, or commenced writing, *Queen Mab*, a poem which he never published, although he distributed copies among his friends. In after years he had such a low opinion of it in every respect, that he regretted having printed it at all; and when an edition of it was published without his consent, he applied to the Court of Chancery for an injunction to suppress it.

Shelley's opinions in politics and theology, which he appears to have been far more anxious to maintain than was consistent with the peace of the household, were peculiarly obnoxious to his father, a man as different from his son as it is possible to conceive; and his expulsion from Oxford was soon followed by exile from his home. He went to London, where, through his sisters, who were at school in the neighbourhood, he made the acquaintence of Harriet Westbrook, whom he eloped with and married, when he was nineteen and she sixteen years of age. It seems doubtful whether the attachment between them was more than the result of the reception accorded by the enthusiasm of the girl to the enthusiasm of the youth, manifesting itself in wild talk about human rights, and equally wild plans for their recovery and security. However this may be, the result was unfortunate. They wandered about England, Scotland, and Ireland, with frequent and sudden change of residence, for rather more than two years. During this time Shelley gained the friendship of some of the most eminent men of the age, of whom the one who exercised the most influence upon his character and future history was William Godwin, whose instructions and expostulations tended to reduce to solidity and form the vague and extravagant opinions and projects of the youthful reformer.[1] Shortly after the commencement of the third year of their

---

[1] William Godwin (1756-1836) was a philosopher and journalist. He is best known for "An Enquiry Concerning Political Justice" and "Things as They Are."

married life, an estrangement of feeling, which had been gradually widening between them, resulted in the final separation of the poet and his wife. We are not informed as to the causes of this estrangement, further than that it seems to have been owing, in a considerable degree, to the influence of an elder sister of Mrs. Shelley, who domineered over her, and whose presence became at last absolutely hateful to Shelley. His wife returned to her father's house; where, apparently about three years after, she committed suicide. There seems to have been no immediate connection between this act and any conduct of Shelley. One of his biographers informs us, that while they were living happily together, suicide was with Mrs. Shelley a favourite subject of speculation and conversation.

Shortly after his first wife's death, Shelley married the daughter of William Godwin. He had lived with her almost from the date of the separation, during which time they had twice visited Switzerland. In the following year (1817), it was decreed in Chancery that Shelley was not a proper person to take charge of his two children by his first wife, who had lived with her till her death. The bill was filed in Chancery by their grandfather, Mr. Westbrook. The effects of this proceeding upon Shelley may be easily imagined. Perhaps he never recovered from them, for they were not of a nature to pass away. During this year he resided at Marlow, and wrote *The Revolt of Islam*, besides portions of other poems; and the next year he left England, not to return. The state of his health, for he had appeared to be in a consumption for some time, and the fear lest his son, by his second wife, should be taken from him, combined to induce him to take refuge in Italy from both impending evils. At Lucca he began his *Prometheus*, and wrote *Julian and Maddalo*. He moved from place to place in Italy, as he had done in his own country. Their two children dying, they were for a time left childless; but the loss of these grieved Shelley less than that of his eldest two, who were taken from him by the hand of man. In 1819, Shelley finished his *Prometheus Unbound*, writing the greater part at Rome, and completing it at Florence. In this year also he wrote his tragedy, *The Cenci*, which attracted more attention during his lifetime than any other of his works. The *Ode to a Skylark* was written at Leghorn in the spring of 1820; and in August of the same year, the *Witch of Atlas* was written, near Pisa. In the following year Shelley and Byron met at Pisa. They were a good deal together; but their friendship, although real, does not appear to have been of a very profound nature; for though unlikeness be one of the necessary elements of friendship, there are kinds of unlikeness which will not harmonize. During all this time, he was not only maligned by unknown enemies, and abused by anonymous writers, but attempts of other kinds are said to have been made to render his life as uncomfortable as possible. There are grounds, however, for doubting whether Shelley was not subject to a kind of monomania upon this and similar points. In 1821, he wrote his *Adonais*, a monody on the death of Keats. Part of this poem had its origin in the mistaken notion, that the illness and death of Keats were caused by a brutal criticism of his *Endymion*, which appeared in the *Quarterly Review*. The last verse of the *Adonais* seems almost prophetic of his own end. Passionately fond of boating, he and a friend of his, Mr. Williams, united in constructing a boat of a peculiar build, a very fast sailer, but difficult to manage. On the 8th of July, 1822, Shelley and his friend Williams sailed from Leghorn for Lerici, on the Bay of Spezia, near which lay his home for the time. A sudden squall came on, and their boat disappeared. The bodies of the two friends were cast on shore; and, according to quarantine regulations, were burned to ashes. Lord Byron, Leigh Hunt, and Mr. Trelawney were present when the body of Shelley was burned; so that his ashes were saved, and buried in the Protestant burial-ground at Rome, near the grave of Keats, whose body had been laid there in the spring of the preceding year.[2] [3] *Cor Cordium* were the words inscribed by his widow on the tomb of the poet.

The character of Shelley has been sadly maligned. Whatever faults he may have committed against society, they were not the result of sensuality. One of his biographers, who was his companion at Oxford, and who does not seem inclined to do him *more* than justice, asserts that while there his conduct was immaculate. The whole picture he gives of the youth, makes it easy to believe this. To discuss the moral question involved in one part of his history would be out of place here; but even on the supposition that a man's conduct is altogether

---

[2] James henry Leigh Hunt (1784-1859) was an English essayist and poet. He co-founded an intellectual journal, The Examiner, and is credited with launching the careers of many popular poets of his day such as Alfred Tennyson Percy Byshhe Shelley, John Keats, and Robert Browning.

[3] Edward John Trelawny (1792-1881) was an English biographer of Shelley and Byron.

inexcusable in individual instances, there is the more need that nothing but the truth should be said concerning that, and other portions thereof. And whatever society may have thought itself justified in making subject of reprobation, it must be remembered that Shelley was under less obligation to society than most men. Yet his heart seemed full of love to his kind; and the distress which the oppression of others caused him, was the source of much of that wild denunciation which exposed him to the contempt and hatred of those who were rendered uncomfortable by his unsparing and indiscriminate anathemas. In private, he was beloved by all who knew him; a steady, generous, self-denying friend, not only to those who moved in his own circle, but to all who were brought within the reach of any aid he could bestow. To the poor he was a true and laborious benefactor. That man must have been good to whom the heart of his widow returns with such earnest devotion and thankfulness in the recollection of the past, and such fond hope for the future, as are manifested by Mrs. Shelley in those extracts from her private journal given us by Lady Shelley.

As regards his religious opinions, one of the thoughts which most strongly suggest themselves is, -- how ill he must have been instructed in the principles of Christianity! He says himself in a letter to Godwin, "I have known no tutor or adviser (*not excepting my father*) from whose lessons and suggestions I have not recoiled with disgust." So far is he from being an opponent of Christianity properly so called, that one can hardly help feeling what a Christian he would have been, could he but have seen Christianity in any other way than through the traditional and practical misrepresentations of it which surrounded him. All his attacks on Christianity are, in reality, directed against evils to which the true doctrines of Christianity are more opposed than those of Shelley could possibly be. How far he was excusable in giving the name of Christianity to what he might have seen to be only a miserable perversion of it, is another question, and one which hardly admits of discussion here. It was in the *name* of Christianity, however, that the worst injuries of which he had to complain were inflicted upon him. Coming out of the cathedral at Pisa one day, Shelley warmly assented to a remark of Leigh Hunt, "that a divine religion might be found out, if charity were really made the principle of it instead of faith."[4] Surely the founders of Christianity, even when they magnified faith, intended thereby a spiritual condition, of which the central principle is coincident with charity. Shelley's own feelings towards others, as judged from his poetry, seem to be tinctured with the very essence of Christianity.[5] He did not, at one time at least, believe that we could know the source of our being; and seemed to take it as a self-evident truth, that the Creator could not be like the creature. But it is unjust to fix upon any utterance of opinion, and regard it as the religion of a man who died in his thirtieth year, and whose habits of thinking were such, that his opinions must have been in a state of constant change. Coleridge says in a letter:

> His (Shelley's) discussions, tending towards atheism of a
> certain sort, would not have scared *me;* for *me* it would have
> been a semitransparent larva, soon to be sloughed, and
> through which I should have seen the true *image* -- the final
> metamorphosis. Besides, I have ever thought that sort of
> atheism the next best religion to Christianity; nor does the
> better faith I have learned from Paul and John interfere
> with the cordial reverence I feel for Benedict Spinoza.[6]

Shelley's favourite study was metaphysics. The more impulse there is in any direction, the more education and experience are necessary to balance that impulse: one cannot help thinking that Shelley's *taste* for exercises of this kind was developed more rapidly than the corresponding *power*. His favourite physical studies were chemistry and electricity. With these he occupied himself from his childhood; apparently, however, with more delight in the experiments themselves, than interest in the general conclusions to be arrived at by

---

[4] * From *Shelley Memorials*, edited by Lady Shelley, which the writer of this paper has principally followed in regard to the external facts of Shelley's history.

[5] * His *Essay on Christianity* is full of noble views, some of which are held at the present day by some of the most earnest believers. At what time of his life it was written we are not informed; but it seems such as would insure his acceptance with any company of intelligent and devout Unitarians.

[6] Benedict Spinoza (1632-1677) was a Jewish Dutch philosopher in the school of 17th century Rationalism and was an early figure in the Enlightenment. Spinoza rejected the Judeo-Christian idea of God and promoted a form of pantheism where there is "no other substance but God." His book, Ethics, attempted to ground morality in the absence of a Law Giver.

means of them. In the embodiment of his metaphysical ideas in poetry, the influence of these studies seems to show itself; for he uses forms which appeal more to the outer senses than to the inward eye; and his similes belong to the realm of the fancy, rather than the imagination: they lack *vital* resemblance. Logic had considerable attractions for him. To geometry and mathematics he was quite indifferent. One of his biographers states that "he was neglectful of flowers," because he had no interest in botany; but one who derived such full delight from the contemplation of their external forms, could hardly be expected to feel very strongly the impulse to dissect them. He derived exceeding pleasure from Greek literature, especially from the works of Plato.

Several little peculiarities in Shelley's tastes are worth mentioning, because, although in themselves insignificant, they seem to correspond with the nature of his poetry. Perhaps the most prominent of these was his passion for boat-sailing. He could not pass any piece of water without launching upon it a number of boats, constructed from what paper he could find in his pockets. The fly-leaves of the books he was in the way of carrying with him, for he was constantly reading, often went to this end. He would watch the fate of these boats with the utmost interest, till they sank or reached the opposite side. He was just as fond of real boating, and that frequently of a dangerous kind; but it is characteristic of him, that all the boats he describes in his poems are of a fairy, fantastic sort, barely related to the boats which battle with earthly winds and waves. Pistol-shooting was also a favourite amusement. Fireworks, too, gave him great delight. Some of his habits were likewise peculiar. He was remarkably abstemious, preferring bread and raisins to anything else in the way of eating, and very seldom drinking anything stronger than water. Honey was a favourite luxury with him. While at college, his biographer Hogg says he was in the habit, during the evening, of going to sleep on the rug, close to a blazing fire, heat seeming never to have other than a beneficial effect upon him. After sleeping some hours, he would awake perfectly restored, and continue actively occupied till far into the morning. His whole movements are represented as rapid, hurried, and uncertain. He would appear and disappear suddenly and unexpectedly; forget appointments; burst into wild laughter, heedless of his situation, whenever anything struck him as peculiarly ludicrous. His changes of residence were most numerous, and frequently made with so much haste that whole little libraries were left behind, and often lost. He was very fond of children, and used to make humorous efforts to induce them to disclose to him the still-remembered secrets of their pre-existence. He seemed to have a peculiar attraction towards mystery, and was ready to believe in a hidden secret, where no one else would have thought of one. His room, while he was at college, was in a state of indescribable confusion. Not only were all sorts of personal necessaries mingled with books and philosophical instruments, but things belonging to one department of service were not unfrequently pressed into the slavery of another. He dressed well but carelessly. In person he was tall, slender, and stooping; awkward in gait, but in manners a thorough gentleman. His complexion was delicate; his head, face, and features, remarkably small; the last not very regular, but in expression, both intellectual and moral, wonderfully beautiful. His eyes were deep blue, "of a wild, strange beauty;" his forehead high and white; his hair dark brown, curling, long, and bushy. His appearance in later life is described as singularly combining the appearances of premature age and prolonged youth.

The only art in which his taste appears to have been developed was poetry. Even in his poetry, taken as a whole, the artistic element is not generally very manifest. His earliest verses (none of which are included in his collected works) can hardly be said to be good in any sense. He seems in these to have chosen poetry as a fitting material for the embodiment of his ardent, hopeful, indignant thoughts and feelings, but, provided he can say what he wants to say, does not seem to care much about *how* he says it. Indeed, there is too much of this throughout his works; for if the *utterance*, instead of the *conveyance* of thought, were the object pursued in art, of course not merely imperfection of language, but absolute external unintelligibility, would be admissible. But his art constantly increases with his sense of its necessity; so that the *Cenci*, which is the last work of any pretension that he wrote, is decidedly the most artistic of all. There are beautiful passages in *Queen Mab*, but it is the work of a boy-poet; and as it was all but repudiated by himself, it is not necessary to remark further upon it. *The Revolt of Islam* is a poem of twelve cantos, in the Spenserian stanza; but in all respects except the arrangement of lines and rimes, his stanza, in common with all other imitations of the Spenserian, has little or nothing of the spirit or individuality of the original.[7] The poem

---

[7] "Spenserian stanza" refers to the form invented by Edmund Spenser for "Faerie Queene." In the fixed verse form, each stanza has nine lines with eight in

is dedicated to the cause of freedom, and records the efforts, successes, defeats, and final triumphant death of two inspired champions of liberty -- a youth and maiden. The adventures are marvellous, not intended to be within the bounds of probability, scarcely of possibility. There are very noble sentiments and fine passages throughout the poem. Now and then there is grandeur. But the absence of art is too evident in the fact that the meaning is often obscure; an obscurity not unfrequently occasioned by the difficulty of the stanza, which is the most difficult mode of composition in English, except the rigid sonnet. The words and forms he employs to express thought seem sometimes mechanical devices for that purpose, rather than an utterance which suggested itself naturally to a mind where the thought was vitally present. The words are more a *clothing* for the thought than an *embodiment* of it. They do not lie near enough to the thing which is intended to be represented by them. It is, however, but just to remark, that some of the obscurity is owing to the fact, that, even with Mrs. Shelley's superintendence, the works have not yet been satisfactorily edited, or at least not conducted through the press with sufficient care.[8]

The Cenci is a very powerful tragedy, but unfitted for public representation by the horrible nature of the historical facts upon which it is founded. In the execution of it, however, Shelley has kept very much nearer to nature than in any other of his works. He has rigidly adhered to his perception of artistic propriety in respect to the dramatic utterance. It may be doubted whether there is sufficient difference between the modes of speech of the different actors in the tragedy, but it is quite possible to individualize speech far too minutely for probable nature; and in this respect, at least, Shelley has not erred. Perhaps the action of the whole is a little hurried, and a central moment of awful repose and fearful anticipation might add to the force of the tragedy. The scenes also might, perhaps, have been constructed so as to suggest more of evolution; but the central point of horror is most powerfully and delicately handled. You see a possible spiritual horror yet behind, more frightful than all that has gone before. The whole drama, indeed, is constructed around, not a prominent point, but a dim, infinitely-

---

iambic pentameter and ending in one alexandrine line. The verse has an ABABBCBCC rhyme scheme.

[8] * This statement is no longer true.

withdrawn, underground perspective of dismay and agony. Perhaps it detracts a little from our interest in the Lady Beatrice, that after all she should wish to live, and should seek to preserve her life by a denial of her crime. She, however, evidently justifies the denial to herself on the ground that, the deed being absolutely right, although regarded as most criminal by her judges, the only way to get true justice is to deny the fact, which, there being no guilt, she might consider as only a verbal lie. Her very purity of conscience enables her to utter this with the most absolute innocence of look, and word, and tone. This is probably a historical fact, and Shelley had to make the best of it. In the drama there is great tenderness, as well as terror; but for a full effect, one feels it desirable to be brought better acquainted with the individuals than the drama, from its want of graduation, permits. Shelley, however, was only six-and- twenty when he wrote it. He must have been attracted to the subject by its embodying the concentration of tyranny, lawlessness, and brutality in old Cenci, as opposed to, and exercised upon, an ideal loveliness and nobleness in the person of Beatrice.

But of all Shelley's works, the *Prometheus Unbound* is that which combines the greatest amount of individual power and peculiarity. There is an airy grandeur about it, reminding one of the vast masses of cloud scattered about in broken, yet magnificently suggestive forms, all over the summer sky, after a thunderstorm. The fundamental ideas are grand; the superstructure, in many parts, so ethereal, that one hardly knows whether he is gazing on towers of solid masonry rendered dim and unsubstantial by intervening vapour, or upon the golden turrets of cloudland, themselves born of the mist which surrounds them with a halo of glory. The beings of Greek, mythology are idealized and etherealized by the new souls which he puts into them, making them think his thoughts and say his words. In reading this, as in reading most of his poetry, we feel that, unable to cope with the evils and wrongs of the world as it and they are, he constructs a new universe, wherein he may rule according to his will; and a good will in the main it is -- good always in intent, good generally in form and utterance. Of the wrongs which Shelley endured from the collision and resulting conflict between his lawless goodness and the lawful wickedness of those in authority, this is one of the greatest, -- that during the right period of pupillage, he was driven from the place of learning, cast on his own mental resources long before those resources were sufficient for his support, and irritated against the purest embodiment of good by the harsh treatment he received under its name. If that reverence which was far from wanting to his nature, had been but presented, in the person of some guide to his spiritual being, with an object worthy of its homage and trust, it is probable that the yet free and noble result of Shelley's individuality would have been presented to the world in a form which, while it attracted still only the few, would not have repelled the many; at least, not by such things as were merely accidental in their association with his earnest desires and efforts for the well-being of humanity.

That which chiefly distinguishes Shelley from other writers is the unequalled exuberance of his fancy. The reader, say for instance of that fantastically brilliant poem, *The Witch of Atlas*, the work of three days, is overwhelmed in a storm, as it were, of rainbow snow-flakes and many-coloured lightnings, accompanied ever by "a low melodious thunder." The evidences of pure imagination in his writings are unfrequent as compared with those of fancy: there are not half the instances of the direct embodiment of idea in form, that there are of the presentation of strange resemblances between external things.

One of the finest short specimens of Shelley's peculiar mode is his *Ode to the West Wind*, full of mysterious melody of thought and sound. But of all his poems, the most popular, and deservedly so, is the *Skylark*. Perhaps the *Cloud* may contest it with the *Skylark* in regard to popular favour; but the *Cloud*, although full of beautiful words and fantastic cloud-like images, is, after all, principally a work of the fancy; while the *Skylark*, though even in it fancy predominates over imagination in the visual images, forms, as a whole, a lovely, true, individual work of art; a *lyric* not unworthy of the *lark*, which Mason apostrophizes as "sweet feathered lyric." The strain of sadness which pervades it is only enough to make the song of the lark human.

In *The Sensitive Plant*, a poem full of the peculiarities of his genius, tending through a wilderness of fanciful beauties to a thicket of mystical speculation, one curious idiosyncrasy is more prominent than in any other -- curious, as belonging to the poet of beauty and loveliness: it is the tendency to be fascinated by what is ugly and revolting, so that he cannot withdraw his thoughts from it till he has described it in language, powerful, it is true, and poetic, when considered as to its fitness for the desired end, but, in force of these very excellences in the means, nearly as revolting as the objects themselves. Associated with this is the tendency to discover strangely unpleasant likenesses between things; which likenesses he is not content with seeing, but seems compelled, perhaps in order to get rid of them himself, to force upon the observation of his reader. But the admirer of Shelley is not pleased to find that one or two passages of this nature have been omitted in some editions of his works.

Few men have been more misunderstood or misrepresented than Shelley. Doubtless this has in part been his own fault, as Coleridge implies when he writes to this effect of him: that his horror of hypocrisy made him speak in such a wild way, that Southey (who was so much a man of forms and proprieties) was quite misled, not merely in his estimate of his worth, but in his judgment of his character. But setting aside this consideration altogether, and regarding him merely as a poet, Shelley has written verse which will last as long as English literature lasts; valuable not only from its excellence, but from the peculiarity of its excellence.[9] To say nothing of his noble aims and hopes, Shelley will always be admired for his sweet melodies, lovely pictures, and wild prophetic imaginings. His indignant remonstrances, intermingled with grand imprecations, burst in thunder from a heart overcharged with the love of his kind, and roused to a keener sense of all oppression by the wrongs which sought to overwhelm himself. But as he recedes further in time, and men are able to see more truly the proportions of the man, they will judge, that without having gained the rank of a great reformer, Shelley had in him that element of wide sympathy and lofty hope for his kind which is essential both to the *birth* and the subsequent *making* of the greatest of poets

---

[9] Robert Southey (1774-1843) was an English Romantic poet and Poet laureate.

A Sermon

PHILIPPIANS iii. 15, 16. -- Let us therefore, as many as be perfect, be thus minded; and if in anything ye be otherwise minded, God shall reveal even this unto you. Nevertheless, whereto we have already attained, let us walk by that same.[1]

This is the reading of the oldest manuscripts. The rest of the verse is pretty clearly a not overwise marginal gloss that has crept into the text.

In its origin, opinion is the intellectual body, taken for utterance and presentation by something necessarily larger than any intellect can afford stuff sufficient for the embodiment of. To the man himself, therefore, in whose mind it arose, an opinion will always represent and recall the spirit whose form it is, -- so long, at least, as the man remains true to his better self. Hence, a man's opinion may be for him invaluable, the needle of his moral compass, always pointing to the truth whence it issued, and whose form it is. Nor is the man's opinion of the less value to him that it may change. Nay, to be of true value, it must have in it not only the possibility, but the necessity of change: it must change in every man who is alive with that life which, in the New Testament, is alone treated as life at all. For, if a man's opinion be in no process of change whatever, it must be dead, valueless, hurtful Opinion is the offspring of that which is itself born to grow; which, being imperfect, must grow or die. Where opinion is growing, its imperfections, however many and serious, will do but little hurt; where it is not growing, these imperfections will further the decay and corruption which must already have laid hold of the very heart of the man. But it is plain in the world's history that what, at some given stage of the same, was the embodiment in intellectual form of the highest and deepest of which it was then spiritually capable, has often and speedily become the source of the most frightful outrages upon humanity. How is this? Because it has passed from the mind in which

---

[1] Read in the Unitarian chapel, Essex-street, London, 1879.

it grew into another in which it did not grow, and has of necessity altered its nature. Itself sprung from that which was deepest in the man, it casts seeds which take root only in the intellectual understanding of his neighbour; and these, springing up, produce flowers indeed which look much the same to the eye, but fruit which is poison and bitterness, -- worst of it all, the false and arrogant notion that it is duty to force the opinion upon the acceptance of others. But it is because such men themselves hold with so poor a grasp the truth underlying their forms that they are, in their self-sufficiency, so ambitious of propagating the forms, making of themselves the worst enemies of the truth of which they fancy themselves the champions. How truly, in the case of all genuine teachers of men, shall a man's foes be they of his own household! For of all the destroyers of the truth which any man has preached, none have done it so effectually or so grievously as his own followers. So many of them have received but the forms, and know nothing of the truth which gave him those forms! They lay hold but of the non-essential, the specially perishing in those forms; and these aspects, doubly false and misleading in their crumbling disjunction, they proceed to force upon the attention and reception of men, calling that the truth which is at best but the draggled and useless fringe of its earth-made garment. Opinions so held belong to the theology of hell, -- not necessarily altogether false in form, but false utterly in heart and spirit. The opinion then that is hurtful is not that which is formed in the depths, and from the honest necessities of a man's own nature, but that which he has taken up at second hand, the study of which has pleased his intellect; has perhaps subdued fears and mollified distresses which ought rather to have grown and increased until they had driven the man to the true physician; has puffed him up with a sense of superiority as false as foolish, and placed in his hand a club with which to subjugate his neighbour to his spiritual dictation. The true man even, who aims at the perpetuation of his opinion, is rather obstructing than aiding the course of that truth for the love of which he holds his opinion; for truth is a living thing, opinion is a dead thing, and transmitted opinion a deadening thing.

Let us look at St. Paul's feeling in this regard. And, in order that we may deprive it of none of its force, let us note first the nature of the truth which he had just been presenting to his disciples, when he follows it with the words of my text:—

But what things were gain to me, those I counted loss for Christ.

Yea doubtless, and I count all things but loss for the excellency of the knowledge of Christ Jesus my Lord: for whom I have suffered the loss of all things, and do count them but dung, that I may win Christ,

And be found in him, not having mine own righteousness, which is of the law, but that which is through the faith of Christ, the righteousness which is of God by faith:

That I may know him, and the power of his resurrection, and the fellowship of his sufferings, being made conformable unto his death;

If by any means I might attain unto the resurrection of the dead.

Not as though I had already attained, either were already perfect: but I follow after, if that I may apprehend that for which also I am apprehended of Christ Jesus.

Brethren, I count not myself to have apprehended: but this one thing I do, forgetting those things which are behind, and reaching forth unto those things which are before, I press toward the mark for the prize of the high calling of God in Christ Jesus.

St. Paul, then, had been declaring to the Philippians the idea upon which, so far as it lay with him, his life was constructed, the thing for which he lived, to which the whole conscious effort of his being was directed, -- namely, to be in his very nature one with Christ, to become righteous as he is righteous; to die into his death, so that he should no more hold the slightest personal relation to evil, but be alive in every fibre to all that is pure, lovely, loving, beautiful, perfect. He had been telling them that he spent himself in continuous effort to lay hold upon that for the sake of which Christ had laid hold on him. This he declares the sole thing worth living for: the hope of this, the hope of becoming one with the living God, is that which keeps a glorious consciousness awake in him, amidst all the unrest of a being not yet at harmony with itself, and a laborious and persecuted life. It cannot therefore be any shadow of indifference to the truth to which he has borne this witness, that causes him to add, "If in anything ye be otherwise minded." It is to him even the test of perfection, whether they be thus minded or not;

for, although a moment before, he has declared himself short of the desired perfection, he now says, "Let as many of us as are perfect be thus minded." There is here no room for that unprofitable thing, bare logic: we must look through the shifting rainbow of his words, -- rather, we must gather all their tints together, then turn our backs upon the rainbow, that we may see the glorious light which is the soul of it. St. Paul is not that which he would be, which he must be; but he, and all they who with him believe that the perfection of Christ is the sole worthy effort of a man's life, are in the region, though not yet at the centre, of perfection. They are, even now, not indeed grasping, but in the grasp of, that perfection. He tells them this is the one thing to mind, the one thing to go on desiring and labouring for, with all the earnestness of a God-born existence; but, if any one be at all otherwise minded, -- that is, of a different opinion, -- what then? That it is of little or no consequence? No, verily; but of such endless consequence that God will himself unveil to them the truth of the matter. This is Paul's faith, not his opinion. Faith is that by which a man lives inwardly, and orders his way outwardly. Faith is the root, belief the tree, and opinion the foliage that falls and is renewed with the seasons. Opinion is, at best, even the opinion of a true man, but the cloak of his belief, which he may indeed cast to his neighbour, but not with the truth inside it: that remains in his own bosom, the oneness between him and his God. St. Paul knows well -- who better? -- that by no argument, the best that logic itself can afford, can a man be set right with the truth; that the spiritual perception which comes of hungering contact with the living truth -- a perception which is in itself a being born again -- can alone be the mediator between a man and the truth. He knows that, even if he could pass his opinion over bodily into the understanding of his neighbour, there would be little or nothing gained thereby, for the man's spiritual condition would be just what it was before. God must reveal, or nothing is known. And this, through thousands of difficulties occasioned by the man himself, God is ever and always doing his mighty best to effect.

See the grandeur of redeeming liberality in the Apostle. In his heart of hearts he knows that salvation consists in nothing else than being one with Christ; that the only life of every man is hid with Christ in God, and to be found by no search anywhere else. He believes that for this cause was he born into the world, -- that he should give himself, heart and soul, body and spirit, to him who came into the world that he might bear witness to the truth. He believes that for the sake of this, and nothing less, -- anything more there cannot be, -- was the world, with its endless glories, created. Nay, more than all, he believes that for this did the Lord, in whose cross, type and triumph of his self-abnegation, he glories, come into the world, and live and die there. And yet, and yet, he says, and says plainly, that a man thinking differently from all this or at least, quite unprepared to make this whole-hearted profession of faith, is yet his brother in Christ, in whom the knowledge of Christ that he has will work and work, the new leaven casting out the old leaven until he, too, in the revelation of the Father, shall come to the perfect stature of the fulness of Christ. Meantime, Paul, the Apostle, must show due reverence to the halting and dull disciple. He must and will make no demand upon him on the grounds of what he, Paul, believes. He is where he is, and God is his teacher. To his own Master, -- that is, Paul's Master, and not Paul, -- he stands. He leaves him to the company of his Master. "Leaves him?" No: that he does not; that he will never do, any more than God will leave him. Still and ever will he hold him and help him. But how help him, if he is not to press upon him his own larger and deeper and wiser insights? The answer is ready: he will press, not his opinion, not even the man's opinion, but the man's own faith upon him. "O brother, beloved of the Father, walk in the light, -- in the light, that is, which is thine, not which is mine; in the light which is given to thee, not to me: thou canst not walk by my light, I cannot walk by thine: how should either walk except by the light which is in him? O brother, what thou seest, that do; and what thou seest not, that thou shalt see: God himself, the Father of Lights, will show it to you." This, this is the condition of all growth, -- that whereto we have attained, we mind that same; for such, following the manuscripts, at least the oldest, seems to me the Apostle's meaning. Obedience is the one condition of progress, and he entreats them to obey. If a man will but work that which is in him, will but make the power of God his own, then is it well with him for evermore. Like his Master, Paul urges to action, to the highest operation, therefore to the highest condition of humanity. As Christ was the Son of his Father because he did the will of the Father, so the Apostle would have them the sons of the Father by doing the will of the Father. Whereto ye have attained, walk by *that*.

But there is more involved in this utterance than the words themselves will expressly carry. Next to his love to the Father and the

Elder Brother, the passion of Paul's life -- I cannot call it less -- is love to all his brothers and sisters. Everything human is dear to him: he can part with none of it. Division, separation, the breaking of the body of Christ, is that which he cannot endure. The body of his flesh had once been broken, that a grander body might be prepared for him: was it for that body itself to tear itself asunder? With the whole energy of his great heart, Paul clung to unity. He could clasp together with might and main the body of his Master -- the body that Master loved because it was a spiritual body, with the life of his Father in it. And he knew well that only by walking in the truth to which they had attained, could they ever draw near to each other. Whereto we have attained, let us walk by that.

My honoured friends, if we are not practical, we are nothing. Now, the one main fault in the Christian Church is separation, repulsion, recoil between the component particles of the Lord's body. I will not, I do not care to inquire who is more to blame than another in the evil fact. I only care to insist that it is the duty of every individual man to be innocent of the same. One main cause, perhaps I should say *the one* cause of this deathly condition, is that whereto we had, we did not, whereto we have attained, we do not walk by that. Ah, friend! do not now think of thy neighbour. Do not applaud my opinion as just from what thou hast seen around thee, but answer it from thy own being, thy own behaviour. Dost thou ever feel thus toward thy neighbour, -- "Yes, of course, every man is my brother; but how can I be a brother to him so long as he thinks me wrong in what I believe, and so long as I think he wrongs in his opinions the dignity of the truth?" What, I return, has the man no hand to grasp, no eyes into which yours may gaze far deeper than your vaunted intellect can follow? Is there not, I ask, anything in him to love? Who asks you to be of one opinion? It is the Lord who asks you to be of one heart. Does the Lord love the man? Can the Lord love, where there is nothing to love? Are you wiser than he, inasmuch as you perceive impossibility where he has failed to discover it? Or will you say, "Let the Lord love where he pleases: I will love where I please"? or say, and imagine you yield, "Well, I suppose I must, and therefore I will, -- but with certain reservations, politely quiet in my own heart"? Or wilt thou say none of all these things, but do them all, one after the other, in the secret chambers of thy proud spirit? If you delight to condemn, you are a wounder, a divider of the oneness of Christ. If you pride yourself on your loftier vision, and are haughty to your neighbour, you are yourself a division and have reason to ask: "Am I a particle of the body at all?" The Master will deal with thee upon the score. Let it humble thee to know that thy dearest opinion, the one thou dost worship as if it, and not God, were thy Saviour, this very opinion thou art doomed to change, for it cannot possibly be right, if it work in thee for death and not for life.

Friends, you have done me the honour and the kindness to ask me to speak to you. I will speak plainly. I come before you neither hiding anything of my belief, nor foolishly imagining I can transfer my opinions into your bosoms. If there is one rôle I hate, it is that of the proselytizer. But shall I not come to you as a brother to brethren? Shall I not use the privilege of your invitation and of the place in which I stand, nay, must I not myself be obedient to the heavenly vision, in urging you with all the power of my persuasion to set yourselves afresh to *walk* according to that to which you have attained. So doing, whatever yet there is to learn, you shall learn it. Thus doing, and thus only, can you draw nigh to the centre truth; thus doing, and thus only, shall we draw nigh to each other, and become brothers and sisters in Christ, caring for each other's honour and righteousness and true well-being. It is to them that keep his commandments that he and his Father will come to take up their abode with them. Whether you or I have the larger share of the truth in that which we hold, of this I am sure, that it is to them that keep his commandments that it shall be given to eat of the Tree of Life.[2] I believe that Jesus is the eternal son of the eternal Father; that in him the ideal humanity sat enthroned from all eternity; that as he is the divine man, so is he the human God; that there was no taking of our nature upon himself, but the showing of himself as he

---

[2] Like the Great Flood, the Tree of Life appears across cultures. In the Bible, in the middle of the Garden of Eden were two trees, the Tree of Life and the Tree of the Knowledge of Good and Evil. (Genesis 2:2-9) God told Adam that he could eat from anything in the garden, including the Tree of Life, except for the Tree of the Knowledge of Good and Evil. (Genesis 2:15-17) When man choose to know both good and evil, to know something other than God, he was banished from the garden and the source of eternal life, i.e. the presence of and communion with God. (Genesis 3) The Tree of Life reappears in John's Revelation in chapter 22 where John is shown the New Jerusalem with a river of the water of life coming from the throne of God with a Tree of Life on either side. A dire warning is given to those who would take away words from the prophecy given to John that "God will take away from that person any share in the tree of life and in the Holy City." (verse 19)

really was, and that from evermore: these things, friends, I believe, though never would I be guilty of what in me would be the irreverence of opening my mouth in dispute upon them. Not for a moment would I endeavour by argument to convince another of this, my opinion. If it be true, it is God's work to show it, for logic cannot. But the more, and not the less, do I believe that he, who is no respecter of persons, will, least of all, respect the person of him who thinks to please him by respecting his person, calling him, "Lord, Lord," and not doing the things that he tells him. Even if I be right, friend, and thou wrong, to thee who doest his commandments more faithfully than I, will the more abundant entrance be administered. God grant that, when thou art admitted first, I may not be cast out, but admitted to learn of thee that it is truth in the inward parts that he requireth, and they that have that truth, and they alone, shall ever know wisdom. Bear with me, friends, for I love and honour you. I seek but to stir up your hearts, as I would daily stir up my own, to be true to that which is deepest in us, -- the voice and the will of the Father of our spirits.

Friends, I have not said we are not to utter our opinions. I have only said we are not to make those opinions the point of a fresh start, the foundation of a new building, the groundwork of anything. They are not to occupy us in our dealings with our brethren. Opinion is often the very death of love. Love aright, and you will come to think aright; and those who think aright must think the same. In the meantime, it matters nothing. The thing that does matter is, that whereto we have attained, by that we should walk. But, while we are not to insist upon our opinions, which is only one way of insisting upon ourselves, however we may cloak the fact from ourselves in the vain imagination of thereby spreading the truth, we are bound by loftiest duty to spread the truth; for that is the saving of men. Do you ask, How spread it, if we are not to talk about it? Friends, I never said, Do not talk about the truth, although I insist upon a better and the only indispensable way: let your light shine. What I said before, and say again, is, Do not talk about the lantern that holds the lamp, but make haste, uncover the light, and let it shine. Let your light so shine before men that they may see your good works, -- I incline to the Vatican reading of *good things*, -- and glorify your Father who is in heaven. It is not, Let your good works shine, but, Let your light shine. Let it be the genuine love of your hearts, taking form in true deeds; not the doing of good deeds to prove that your opinions are right. If ye are thus true, your very talk about the truth will be a good work, a shining of the light that is in you. A true smile is a good work, and may do much to reveal the Father who is in heaven; but the smile that is put on for the sake of looking right, or even for the sake of being right, will hardly reveal him, not being like him. Men say that you are cold: if you fear it may be so, do not think to make yourselves warm by putting on the cloak of this or that fresh opinion; draw nearer to the central heat, the living humanity of the Son of Man, that ye may have life in yourselves, so heat in yourselves, so light in yourselves; understand him, obey him, then your light will shine, and your warmth will warm. There is an infection, as in evil, so in good. The better we are, the more will men glorify God. If we trim our lamps so that we have light in our house, that light will shine through our windows, and give light to those that are not in the house. But remember, love of the light alone can trim the lamp. Had Love trimmed Psyche's lamp, it had never dropped the scalding oil that scared him from her.[3]

The man who holds his opinion the most honestly ought to see the most plainly that his opinion must change. It is impossible a man should hold anything aright. How shall the created embrace the self-existent Creator? That Creator, and he alone, is *the truth*: how, then, shall a man embrace the truth? But to him who will live it, -- to him, that is, who walks by that to which he has attained, -- the truth will reach down a thousand true hands for his to grasp. We would not wish to enclose that which we can do more than enclose, -- live in, namely, as our home, inherit, exult in, -- the presence of the infinitely higher and better, the heart of the living one. And, if we know that God himself is our inheritance, why should we tremble even with hatred at the suggestion that we may, that we must, change our opinions? If we held them aright, we should know that nothing in them that is good can ever be lost; for that is the true, whatever in them may be the false. It is only as they help us toward God, that our opinions are worth a straw; and every necessary change in them must be to more truth, to

---

3 In Greek mythology, Psyche is the goddess of the soul. Her story was told in "The Golden Ass." Told by an oracle that she would marry a beast all feared, she was abandoned at a rock spire. Rescued and married to the god Eros, Psyche was told she must not try to see him. However, Psyche was convinced by her sisters that she was married to a beast and urged to look at her husband's form. When Psyche took a lamp to look at her husband, a drop of oil fell on him. Eros left and his mother Aphrodite made Psyche face four trials.

greater uplifting power. Lord, change me as thou wilt, only do not send me away. That in my opinions for which I really hold them, if I be a true man, will never pass away; that which my evils and imperfections have, in the process of embodying it, associated with the truth, must, thank God, perish and fall. My opinions, as my life, as my love, I leave in the hands of him who is my being. I commend my spirit to him of whom it came. Why, then, that dislike to the very idea of such change, that dread of having to accept the thing offered by those whom we count our opponents, which is such a stumbling-block in the way in which we have to walk, such an obstruction to our yet inevitable growth? It may be objected that no man will hold his opinions with the needful earnestness, who can entertain the idea of having to change them. But the very objection speaks powerfully against such an overvaluing of opinion. For what is it but to say that, in order to be wise, a man must consent to be a fool. Whatever must be, a man must be able to look in the face. It is because we cleave to our opinions rather than to the living God, because self and pride interest themselves for their own vile sakes with that which belongs only to the truth, that we become such fools of logic and temper that we lie in the prison-houses of our own fancies, ideas, and experiences, shut the doors and windows against the entrance of the free spirit, and will not inherit the love of the Father.

Yet, for the help and comfort of even such a refuser as this, I would say: Nothing which you reject can be such as it seems to you. For a thing is either true or untrue: if it be untrue, it looks, so far like itself that you reject it, and with it we have nothing more to do; but, if it be true, the very fact that you reject it shows that to you it has not appeared true, -- has not appeared itself. The truth can never be even beheld but by the man who accepts it: the thing, therefore, which you reject, is not that which it seems to you, but a thing good, and altogether beautiful, altogether fit for your gladsome embrace, -- a thing from which you would not turn away, did you see it as it is, but rush to it, as Dante says, like the wild beast to his den, -- so eager for the refuge of home.[4] No honest man holds a truth for the sake of that because of

---

[4] Dante Aligheiri, Par., 4.118-122 This reference is to a passage from Paradiso where Dante reflects that our reason or intellect can only be at true peace when we "rest in" or are in complete alignment with truth.

Well I discern, that by that truth alone

which another honest man rejects it: how it may be with the dishonest, I have no confidence in my judgment, and hope I am not bound to understand.

Let us then, my friends, beware lest our opinions come between us and our God, between us and our neighbour, between us and our better selves. Let us be jealous that the human shall not obscure the divine. For we are not *mere* human: we, too, are divine; and there is no such obliterator of the divine as the human that acts undivinely. The one security against our opinions is to walk according to the truth which they contain.

And if men seem to us unreasonable, opposers of that which to us is plainly true, let us remember that we are not here to convince men, but to let our light shine. Knowledge is not necessarily light; and it is light, not knowledge, that we have to diffuse. The best thing we can do, infinitely the best, indeed the only thing, that men may receive the truth, is to be ourselves true. Beyond all doing of good is the being good; for he that is good not only does good things, but all that he does is good. Above all, let us be humble before the God of truth, faithfully desiring of him that truth in the inward parts which alone can enable us to walk according to that which we have attained. May the God of peace give you his peace; may the love of Christ constrain you; may the gift of the Holy Spirit be yours. Amen.

Enlighten'd, beyond which no truth may roam,

Our mind can satisfy her thirst to know:

Therein she resteth, e'en as in his lair

The wild beast, soon as she hath reach'd that bound,

A useful essay explaining this passage can be found in "Paradiso 4: Violence Versus Platonic Venom" by Teodolinda Barolini.

Teodolinda Barolini. "Paradiso 4: Violence Versus Platonic Venom." Commento Baroliniano, Digital Dante. New York, NY: Columbia University Libraries, 2014. https://digitaldante.columbia.edu/dante/divine-comedy/paradiso/paradiso-4/

TRUE CHRISTIAN MINISTERING

MATT. xx. 25-28 -- But Jesus called them unto him and said, Ye know that the princes of the Gentiles exercise dominion over them, and they that are great exercise authority upon them.[1] But it should not be so among you: but whosoever will be great among you, let him be your minister; and whosoever will be chief among you, let him be your servant: even as the Son of Man came not to be ministered unto, but to minister, and to give his life a ransom for many.

How little this is believed! People think, if they think about it at all, that this is very well in the church, but, as things go in the world, it won't do. At least, their actions imply this, for every man is struggling to get above the other. Every man would make his neighbour his footstool that he may climb upon him to some throne of glory which he has in his own mind. There is a continual jostling, and crowding, and buzzing, and striving to get promotion. Of course there are known and noble exceptions; but still, there it is. And yet we call ourselves "Christians," and we are Christians, all of us, thus far, that the truth is within reach of us all, that it has come nigh to us, talking to us at our door, and even speaking in our hearts, and yet this is the way in which we go on! The Lord said, "It shall not be so among you." Did he mean only his twelve disciples? This was all that he had to say to them, but -- thanks be to him! -- he says the same to every one of us now. "It shall not be so among you: that is not the way in my kingdom." The people of the world -- the people who live in the world -- will always think it best to get up, to have less and less of service to do, more and more of service done to them. The notion of rank in the world is like a pyramid; the higher you go up, the fewer are there who have to serve those above them, and who are served more than those underneath them. All who are under serve those who are above, until you come to the apex, and there stands some one who has to do no service, but whom all the

---

[1] A spoken sermon.

others have to serve. Something like that is the notion of position -- of social standing and rank. And if it be so in an intellectual way even -- to say nothing of mere bodily service -- if any man works to a position that others shall all look up to him and that he may have to look up to nobody, he has just put himself precisely into the same condition as the people of whom our Lord speaks -- as those who exercise dominion and authority, and really he thinks it a fine thing to be served.

But it is not so in the kingdom of heaven. The figure there is entirely reversed. As you may see a pyramid reflected in the water, just so, in a reversed way altogether, is the thing to be found in the kingdom of God. It is in this way: the Son of Man lies at the inverted apex of the pyramid; he upholds, and serves, and ministers unto all, and they who would be high in his kingdom must go near to him at the bottom, to uphold and minister to all that they may or can uphold and minister unto. There is no other law of precedence, no other law of rank and position in God's kingdom. And mind, that is *the* kingdom. The other kingdom passes away -- it is a transitory, ephemeral, passing, bad thing, and away it must go. It is only there on sufferance, because in the mind of God even that which is bad ministers to that which is good; and when the new kingdom is built the old kingdom shall pass away.[2]

But the man who seeks this rank of which I have spoken, must be honest to follow it. It will not do to say, "I want to be great, and therefore I will serve." A man will not get at it so. He may begin so, but he will soon find that that will not do. He must seek it for the truth's sake, for the love of his fellows, for the worship of God, for the delight in what is good. In the kingdom of heaven people do not think whether I am promoted, or whether you are promoted. They are so absorbed in the delight and glory of the goodness that is round about them, that they learn not to think much about themselves. It is the bad that is in us that makes us think about ourselves. It is necessary for us, because there is bad in us, to think about ourselves, but as we go on we think less and less about ourselves, until at last we are possessed with the spirit of the truth, the spirit of the kingdom, and live in gladness and in peace.[3] We are prouder of our brothers and sisters than

---

[2] Isaiah 65:17, 66:22, Matthew 24:35, 2 Peter 3:10-13, 2 Corinthians 5:17, Hebrews 8:13 Revelation 21:1-17

[3] John 16:13, 1 John 5:6.

of ourselves; we delight to look at them. God looks at us, and makes us what he pleases, and this is what we must come to; there is no escape from it.

But the Lord says, that "the Son of Man came not to be ministered unto." Was he not ministered unto then? Ah! he was ministered unto as never man was, but he did not come for that. Even now we bring to him the burnt-offerings of our very spirits, but he did not come for that. It was to help us that he came. We are told, likewise, that he is the express image of the Father. Then what he does, the Father must do; and he says himself, when he is accused of breaking the Sabbath by doing work on it, "My Father worketh hitherto, and I work."[4] Then this must be God's way too, or else it could not have been Jesus's way. It is God's way. Oh! do not think that God made us with his hands, and then turned us out to find out our own way. Do not think of him as being always over our heads, merely throwing over us a wide-spread benevolence. You can imagine the tenderness of a mother's heart who takes her child even from its beloved nurse to soothe and to minister to it, and that is like God; that is God. His hand is not only over us, but recollect what David said -- "His hand was upon me." I wish we were all as good Christians as David was. "Wherever I go," he said, "God is there -- beneath me, before me, his hand is upon me; if I go to sleep he is there; when I go down to the dead he is there."[5] Everywhere is God. The earth underneath us is his hand upholding us.[6] Every spring-fountain of gladness about us is his making and his delight. He tends us and cares for us; he is close to us, breathing into our nostrils the breath of life, and breathing into our spirit this thought and that thought to make us look up and recognize the love and the care around us. What a poor thing for the little baby would it be if it were to be constantly tended thus tenderly and preciously by its mother, but if it were never to open its eyes to look up and see her mother's face bending over it. A poor thing all its tending would be without that. It is for that that the other exists; it is by that that the other comes. To recognize and know this loving-kindness, and to stand up in it strong and glad; this is the ministration of God unto us. Do

---

[4] John 5:17.

[5] Psalm 139:5.

[6] * The waters are in the hollow of it.

you ever think "I could worship God if he was- and-so?" Do you imagine that God is not as good, as perfect, as absolutely all-in-all as your thoughts can imagine? Aye, you cannot come up to it; do what you will you never will come up to it. Use all the symbols that we have in nature, in human relations, in the family -- all our symbols of grace and tenderness, and loving-kindness between man and man, and between man and woman, and between woman and woman, but you can never come up to the thought of what God's ministration is. When our Lord came he just let us see how his Father was doing this always, he "came to give his life a ransom for many."[7] It was in giving his life a ransom for us that he died; that was the consummation and crown of it all, but it was his life that he gave for us -- his whole being, his whole strength, his whole energy -- not alone his days of trouble and of toil, but deeper than that, he gave his whole being for us; yea, he even went down to death for us.

But how are we to learn this ministration? I will tell you where it begins. The most of us are forced to work; if you do not see that the commonest things in life belong to the Christian scheme, the plan of God, you have got to learn it. I say this is at the beginning. Most of us have to work, and infinitely better is that for us than if we were not forced to work, but not a very fine thing unless it goes to something farther. We are forced to work; and what is our work? It is doing something for other people always. It is doing; it is ministration in some shape or other. All kind of work is a serving, but it may not be always Christian service. No. Some of us only work for our wages; we must have them. We starve, and deserve to starve, if we do not work to get them. But we must go a little beyond that; yes, a very great way beyond that. There is no honest work that one man does for another which he may not do as unto the Lord and not unto men; in which he cannot do right as he ought to do right.[8] Thus, I say that the man who sees the commonest thing in the world, recognizing it as part of the divine order of things, the law by which the world goes, being the intention of God that one man should be serviceable and useful to another -- the man, I say, who does a thing well because of this, and who tries to do it better, is doing God service.

---

[7] Matthew 20:28, Mark 10:45.

[8] Colossians 3:17-24.

We talk of "divine service." It is a miserable name for a great thing. It is not service, properly speaking, at all. When a boy comes to his father and says, "May I do so and so for you?" or, rather, comes and breaks out in some way, showing his love to his father -- says, "May I come and sit beside you? May I have some of your books? May I come and be quiet a little in your room?" what would you think of that boy if he went and said, "I have been doing my father a service." So with praying to and thanking God, do you call that serving God? If it is not serving yourselves it is worth nothing; if it is not the best condition you can find yourselves in, you have to learn what it is yet. Not so; the work you have to do to-morrow in the counting-house, in the shop, or wherever you may be, is that by which you are to serve God. Do it with a high regard, and then there is nothing mean in it; but there is everything mean in it if you are pretending to please people when you only look for your wages. It is mean then; but if you have regard to doing a thing nobly, greatly, and truly, because it is the work that God has given you to do, then you are doing the divine service.

Of course, this goes a great deal farther. We have endless opportunities of showing ourselves neighbours to the man who comes near us. That is the divine service; that is the reality of serving God. The others ought to be your reward, if "reward" is a word that can be used in such a relation at all. Go home and speak to God; nay, hold your tongue, and quietly go to him in the secret recesses of your own heart, and know that God is there. Say, "God has given me this work to do, and I am doing it;" and that is your joy, that is your refuge, that is your going to heaven. It is not service. The words "divine service," as they are used, always move me to something of indignation. It is perfect paganism; it is looking to please God by gathering together your services, -- something that is supposed to be service to him. He is serving us for ever, and our Lord says, "If I have washed your feet, so you ought to wash one another's feet."[9] This will be the way in which to minister for some.

But still, when we are beginning to learn this, some of us are looking about us in a blind kind of way, thinking, "I wish I could serve God; I do not know what to do! How is it to be begun? What is it at

---

[9] John 13:1-7.

the root of it? What shall I find out to do? Where is there something to do?"

Now, first of all, service is obedience, or it is nothing. This is what I would gladly impress upon you; upon every young man who has come to the point to be able to receive it. There is a tendency in us to think that there is something degrading in obedience, something degrading in service. According to the social judgment there is; according to the judgment of the earth there is. Not so according to the judgment of heaven, for God would only have us do the very thing he is doing himself. You may see the tendency of this nowadays. There is scarcely a young man who will speak of his "master." He feels as if there is something that hurts his dignity in doing so. He does just what so many theologians have done about God, who, instead of taking what our Lord has given us, talk about God as "the Governor of the Universe." So a young man talks about his master as "the governor;" nay, he even talks of his own father in that way, and then you come in another region altogether, and a worse one. I take these things as symptoms, mind. I know habits may be picked up, when they get common, without any great corresponding feeling; but a wrong habit tends always to a wrong feeling, and if a man cannot learn to honour his father, so as to be able to call him "father," I think one or the other of them is greatly to blame, whether the father or the son I cannot say. I know there are such parents that to tell their children that God is their "Father" is no help to them, but the contrary. I heard of a lady just the other day to whom, in trying to comfort her, some one said, "Remember God is your Father." "Do not mention the name 'father' to me," she said. Ah! that kind of fault does not lie in God, but in those who, not being like him, cannot use the names aright which belong to him.

But now, as to this service, this obedience. Our Lord came to give his life a ransom for the many, and to minister unto all in obedience to his Father's will. We call him equal with God -- at least, most of us here, I suppose, do; of course we do not pretend to explain; we know that God is greater than he, because he said so; but somehow, we can worship him with our God, and we need not try to distinguish more than is necessary about it. But do you think that he was less divine than the Father when he was obedient? Observe his obedience to the will of his Father. He was not the ruler there. He did not give the commands; he obeyed them. And yet we say He is God! Ah, that is no difficulty to me. Obedience is as divine in its essence as command; nay, it may be more divine in the human being far; it cannot be more divine in God, but obedience is far more divine in its essence with regard to humanity than command is. It is not the ruling being who is most like God; it is the man who ministers to his fellow, who is like God; and the man who will just sternly and rigidly do what his master tells him -- be that master what he may -- who is likest Christ in that one particular matter. Obedience is the grandest thing in the world to begin with. Yes, and we shall end with it too. I do not think the time will ever come when we shall not have something to do, because we are told to do it without knowing why. Those parents act most foolishly who wish to explain everything to their children -- most foolishly. No; teach your child to obey, and you give him the most precious lesson that can be given to a child. Let him come to that before you have had him long, to do what he is told, and you have given him the plainest, first, and best lesson that you can give him. If he never goes to school at all he had better have that lesson than all the schooling in the world. Hence, when some people are accustomed to glorify this age of ours as being so much better in everything than those which went before, I look back to the times of chivalry, which we regard now, almost, as a thing to laugh at, or a merry thing to make jokes about; but I find that the one essential of chivalry was obedience. It is recognized in our army still, but in those times it was carried much farther. When a boy was seven years old he was sent into another family, and put with another boy there to do what? To wait with him upon the master and the mistress of the house, and to be taught, as well, what few things they knew in those times in the way of intellectual cultivation. But he also learned stern, strict obedience, such as it was impossible for him to forget. Then, when he had been there seven years, hard at work, standing behind the chair, and ministering, he was advanced a step; and what was that step? He was made an esquire. He had his armour given him; he had to watch his armour in the chapel all night, laying it on the altar in silent devotion to God. I do not say that all these things were carried out afterwards, but this was the idea of them. He was an esquire, and what was the duty of an esquire? More service; more important service. He still had to attend to his master, the knight. He had to watch him; he had to groom his horse for him; he had to see that his horse was sound; he had to clean his armour for him; to see that every bolt, every rivet, every strap, every buckle was sound, for the life of his master was in his hands. The master, having to fight, must not be troubled with

231

these things, and therefore the squire had to attend to them. Then seven years after that a more solemn ceremony is gone through, and the squire is made a knight; but is he free of service then? No; he makes a solemn oath to help everybody who needs help, especially women and children, and so he rides out into the world to do the work of a true man. There was a grand and essential idea of Christianity in that -- no doubt wonderfully broken and shattered, but not more so than the Christian church has been; wonderfully broken and shattered, but still the essence of obedience; and I say it is recognized in our army still, and in every army; and where it is lost it is a terrible loss, and an army is worth nothing without it.[10] You remember that terrible story from the East, that fearful death-charge, one of the grandest things in our history, although one of the most blundering: --

"Theirs not to make reply,

Theirs not to reason why,

Theirs but to do and die;

Into the valley of death

Rode the Six Hundred."[11]

So with the Christian man; whatever meets him, obedience is the thing. If he is told by his conscience, which is the candle of God within him, that he must do a thing, why he must do it. He may tremble from head to foot at having to do it, but he will tremble more if he turns his back. You recollect how our old poet Spenser shows us the Knight of the Red Cross, who is the knight of holiness, ill in body, diseased in

---

[10] "Battle of Balaklava," *National Army Museum*, accessed August 3, 2021, https://www.nam.ac.uk/explore/battle-balaklava.

The "terrible story" and "that fearful death-charge" MacDonald is referring to is the Battle of Balaclava on October 25, 1854 during the Crimean War. Due to poor communication, the British Light Brigade was sent directly into the line of fire of Russian artillery. It is known as "one of the most infamous blunders in military history."

[11] Alfred Tennyson, "The Charge of the Light Brigade" (The Examiner, 1854), accessed July 15, 2021, https://www.poetryfoundation.org/poems/45319/the-charge-of-the-light-brigade.

mind, without any of his armour on, attacked by a fearful giant.[12] What does he do? Run away? No, he has but time to catch up his sword, and, trembling in every limb, he goes on to meet the giant; and that is the thing that every Christian man must do. I cannot put it too strongly; it is impossible. There is no escape from it. If death itself lies before us, and we know it, there is nothing to be said; it is all to be done, and then there is no loss; everything else is all lost unto God. Look at our Lord. He gave his life to do the will of his Father, and on he went and did it. Do you think it was easy for him -- easier for him than it would have been for us? Ah! the greater the man the more delicate and tender his nature, and the more he shrinks from the opposition even of his fellowmen, because he loves them. It was a terrible thing for Christ. Even now and then, even in the little touches that come to us in the scanty story (though enough) this breaks out. "We are told by John that at the Last Supper He was troubled in spirit, and testified."[13] And then how he tries to comfort himself as soon as Judas has gone out to do the thing which was to finish his great work: "Now is the Son of Man glorified, and God is glorified in him. If God be glorified in him, God shall also glorify him in himself."[14] Then he adds, -- just gathering up his strength, -- "I shall straightway glorify him." This was said to his disciples, but I seem to see in it that some of it was said for himself. This is the grand obedience! Oh, friends, this is a hard lesson to learn. We find every day that it is a hard thing to teach. We are continually grumbling because we cannot get the people about us, our servants, our tradespeople, or whoever they may be, to do just what we tell them. It makes half the misery in the world because they will have something of their own in it against what they are told. But are we not always doing the same thing? and ought we not to learn something of forgiveness for them, and very much from the fact that we are just in the same position? We only recognize in part that we are put here in this world precisely to learn to be obedient. He who is our Lord and our God went on being obedient all the time, and was obedient always; and I say it is as divine for us to obey as it is for God to rule. As I have

---

[12] Edmund Spenser, *Spenser's The Faerie Queene*, ed. George Armstrong Wauchope, vol. Book 1 (New York, NY: The MacMillan Company, 1921).

[13] John 13:21.

[14] John 13:31.

said already, God is ministering the whole time. Now, do you want to know how to minister? Begin by obeying. Obey every one who has a right to command you; but above all, look to what our Lord has said, and find out what he wants you to do out of what he left behind, and try whether obedience to that will not give a consciousness of use, of ministering, of being a part of the grand scheme and way of God in this world. In fact, take your place in it as a vital portion of the divine kingdom, or -- to use a better figure than that -- a vital portion of the Godhead. Try it, and see whether obedience is not salvation; whether service is not dignity; whether you will not feel in yourselves that you have begun to be cleansed from your plague when you begin to say, "I will seek no more to be above my fellows, but I will seek to minister to them, doing my work in God's name for them."

"Who sweeps a room as for Thy law,

Makes that and the action fine."[15]

Both the room and the action are good when done for God's sake. That is dear old George Herbert's way of saying the same truth, for every man has his own way of saying it. The gift of the Spirit of God to make you think as God thinks, feel as God feels, judge as God judges, is just the one thing that is promised. I do not know anything else that is promised positively but that, and who dares pray for anything else with perfect confidence? God will not give us what we pray for except it be good for us, but that is one thing that we must have or perish. Therefore, let us pray for that, and with the name of God dwelling in us -- if this is not true, the whole world is a heap of ruins -- let us go forth and do this service of God in ministering to our fellows, and so helping him in his work of upholding, and glorifying and saving all.

---

[15] George Herbert (1593 -1633), "The Elixir" *The Poetry Foundation*, 1633, accessed August 5, 2021, https://www.poetryfoundation.org/poems/44362/the-elixir.

The Fantastic Imagination

That we have in English no word corresponding to the German *Mährchen*, drives us to use the word *Fairytale*, regardless of the fact that the tale may have nothing to do with any sort of fairy. The old use of the word *Fairy*, by Spenser at least, might, however, well be adduced, were justification or excuse necessary where *need must*.

Were I asked, what is a fairytale? I should reply, *Read Undine: that is a fairytale; then read this and that as well, and you will see what is a fairytale.*[1] Were I further begged to describe the *fairytale*, or define what it is, I would make answer, that I should as soon think of describing the abstract human face, or stating what must go to constitute a human being. A fairytale is just a fairytale, as a face is just a face; and of all fairytales I know, I think *Undine* the most beautiful.

Many a man, however, who would not attempt to define *a man*, might venture to say something as to what a man ought to be: even so much I will not in this place venture with regard to the fairytale, for my long past work in that kind might but poorly instance or illustrate my now more matured judgment. I will but say some things helpful to the reading, in right-minded fashion, of such fairytales as I would wish to write, or care to read.

Some thinkers would feel sorely hampered if at liberty to use no forms but such as existed in nature, or to invent nothing save in accordance with the laws of the world of the senses; but it must not therefore be imagined that they desire escape from the region of law. Nothing lawless can show the least reason why it should exist, or could at best have more than an appearance of life.

The natural world has its laws, and no man must interfere with them in the way of presentment any more than in the way of use; but

---

[1] In European myth, Undine is a water spirit who, like Disney's mermaid Ariel, become human for the love of a man with the caveat that she will die if he is unfaithful. Various works have be created based on this myth; however, MacDonald is most likely referring to the retelling by Baron Fouqué published in 1811. "Undine," Encyclopedia Britannica, accessed March 18, 2022, https://www.britannica.com/topic/undine-mythology.

they themselves may suggest laws of other kinds, and man may, if he pleases, invent a little world of his own, with its own laws; for there is that in him which delights in calling up new forms -- which is the nearest, perhaps, he can come to creation. When such forms are new embodiments of old truths, we call them products of the Imagination; when they are mere inventions, however lovely, I should call them the work of the Fancy: in either case, Law has been diligently at work.

His world once invented, the highest law that comes next into play is, that there shall be harmony between the laws by which the new world has begun to exist; and in the process of his creation, the inventor must hold by those laws. The moment he forgets one of them, he makes the story, by its own postulates, incredible. To be able to live a moment in an imagined world, we must see the laws of its existence obeyed. Those broken, we fall out of it. The imagination in us, whose exercise is essential to the most temporary submission to the imagination of another, immediately, with the disappearance, of Law, ceases to act. Suppose the gracious creatures of some childlike region of Fairyland talking either cockney or Gascon![2] Would not the tale, however lovelily begun, sink at once to the level of the Burlesque -- of all forms of literature the least worthy? A man's inventions may be stupid or clever, but if he do not hold by the laws of them, or if he make one law jar with another, he contradicts himself as an inventor, he is no artist. He does not rightly consort his instruments, or he tunes them in different keys. The mind of man is the product of live Law; it thinks by law, it dwells in the midst of law, it gathers from law its growth; with law, therefore, can it alone work to any result. Inharmonious, unconsorting ideas will come to a man, but if he try to use one of such, his work will grow dull, and he will drop it from mere lack of interest. Law is the soil in which alone beauty will grow; beauty is the only stuff in which Truth can be clothed; and you may, if you will, call Imagination the tailor that cuts her garments to fit her, and Fancy his journeyman that puts the pieces of them together, or perhaps at most embroiders their button-holes. Obeying law, the maker works like his creator; not obeying law, he is such a fool as heaps a pile of stones and calls it a church.

---

[2] "Cockney" and "Gascon" are English and French dialects, respectively.

In the moral world it is different: there a man may clothe in new forms, and for this employ his imagination freely, but he must invent nothing. He may not, for any purpose, turn its laws upside down. He must not meddle with the relations of live souls. The laws of the spirit of man must hold, alike in this world and in any world he may invent. It were no offence to suppose a world in which everything repelled instead of attracted the things around it; it would be wicked to write a tale representing a man it called good as always doing bad things, or a man it called bad as always doing good things: the notion itself is absolutely lawless. In physical things a man may invent; in moral things he must obey -- and take their laws with him into his invented world as well.

"You write as if a fairytale were a thing of importance: must it have a meaning?"

It cannot help having some meaning; if it have proportion and harmony it has vitality, and vitality is truth. The beauty may be plainer in it than the truth, but without the truth the beauty could not be, and the fairytale would give no delight. Everyone, however, who feels the story, will read its meaning after his own nature and development: one man will read one meaning in it, another will read another.

"If so, how am I to assure myself that I am not reading my own meaning into it, but yours out of it?"

Why should you be so assured? It may be better that you should read your meaning into it. That may be a higher operation of your intellect than the mere reading of mine out of it: your meaning may be superior to mine.

"Suppose my child ask me what the fairytale means, what am I to say?"

If you do not know what it means, what is easier than to say so? If you do see a meaning in it, there it is for you to give him. A genuine work of art must mean many things; the truer its art, the more things it will mean. If my drawing, on the other hand, is so far from being a work of art that it needs THIS IS A HORSE written under it, what can it matter that neither you nor your child should know what it means? It is there not so much to convey a meaning as to wake a meaning. If it do not even wake an interest, throw it aside. A meaning may be there, but it is not for you. If, again, you do not know a horse when you see it, the name written under it will not serve you much. At all events, the business of the painter is not to teach zoology.

But indeed your children are not likely to trouble you about the meaning. They find what they are capable of finding, and more would be too much. For my part, I do not write for children, but for the childlike, whether of five, or fifty, or seventy-five.

A fairytale is not an allegory. There may be allegory in it, but it is not an allegory. He must be an artist indeed who can, in any mode, produce a strict allegory that is not a weariness to the spirit. An allegory must be Mastery or Moorditch.[3]

A fairytale, like a butterfly or a bee, helps itself on all sides, sips at every wholesome flower, and spoils not one. The true fairytale is, to my mind, very like the sonata. We all know that a sonata means something; and where there is the faculty of talking with suitable vagueness, and choosing metaphor sufficiently loose, mind may approach mind, in the interpretation of a sonata, with the result of a more or less contenting consciousness of sympathy. But if two or three men sat down to write each what the sonata meant to him, what approximation to definite idea would be the result? Little enough -- and that little more than needful. We should find it had roused related, if not identical, feelings, but probably not one common thought. Has the sonata therefore failed? Had it undertaken to convey, or ought it to be expected to impart anything defined, anything notionally recognizable?

"But words are not music; words at least are meant and fitted to carry a precise meaning!"

It is very seldom indeed that they carry the exact meaning of any user of them! And if they can be so used as to convey definite meaning, it does not follow that they ought never to carry anything else. Words are live things that may be variously employed to various ends. They can convey a scientific fact, or throw a shadow of her child's dream on the heart of a mother. They are things to put together like the pieces

---

[3] "An allegory must be Mastery or Moorditch." The reference to Moorditch is from Shakespeare's Henry IV 1.2.84. "Prince: What sayest thou to a hare, or the melancholy of Moorditch?"

According to A Shakespeare Glossary, Moorditch was a "filthy stagnant ditch outside the city walls, draining the swampy ground of Moorfields. C.T. Onions, C. T. Onions, A Shakespeare Glossary, Moorditch: (Oxford: Clarendon Press, 1911), accessed March 18, 2022, http://www.perseus.tufts.edu/hopper/text?doc=Perseus:text:1999.03.0068:entry=Moorditch.

MacDonald's point is that there is no room for a miss with an allegory.

of a dissected map, or to arrange like the notes on a stave.[4] Is the music in them to go for nothing? It can hardly help the definiteness of a meaning: is it therefore to be disregarded? They have length, and breadth, and outline: have they nothing to do with depth? Have they only to describe, never to impress? Has nothing any claim to their use but the definite? The cause of a child's tears may be altogether undefinable: has the mother therefore no antidote for his vague misery? That may be strong in colour which has no evident outline. A fairytale, a sonata, a gathering storm, a limitless night, seizes you and sweeps you away: do you begin at once to wrestle with it and ask whence its power over you, whither it is carrying you? The law of each is in the mind of its composer; that law makes one man feel this way, another man feel that way. To one the sonata is a world of odour and beauty, to another of soothing only and sweetness. To one, the cloudy rendezvous is a wild dance, with a terror at its heart; to another, a majestic march of heavenly hosts, with Truth in their centre pointing their course, but as yet restraining her voice. The greatest forces lie in the region of the uncomprehended.

I will go farther. -- The best thing you can do for your fellow, next to rousing his conscience, is -- not to give him things to think about, but to wake things up that are in him; or say, to make him think things for himself. The best Nature does for us is to work in us such moods in which thoughts of high import arise. Does any aspect of Nature wake but one thought? Does she ever suggest only one definite thing? Does she make any two men in the same place at the same moment think the same thing? Is she therefore a failure, because she is not definite? Is it nothing that she rouses the something deeper than the understanding -- the power that underlies thoughts? Does she not set feeling, and so thinking at work? Would it be better that she did this after one fashion and not after many fashions? Nature is mood-engendering, thought-provoking: such ought the sonata, such ought the fairytale to be.

"But a man may then imagine in your work what he pleases, what you never meant!"

Not what he pleases, but what he can. If he be not a true man, he will draw evil out of the best; we need not mind how he treats any work

---

[4] Stave: an alternate British term for staff (ie. musical staff).

239

of art! If he be a true man, he will imagine true things; what matter whether I meant them or not? They are there none the less that I cannot claim putting them there! One difference between God's work and man's is, that, while God's work cannot mean more than he meant, man's must mean more than he meant. For in everything that God has made, there is layer upon layer of ascending significance; also he expresses the same thought in higher and higher kinds of that thought: it is God's things, his embodied thoughts, which alone a man has to use, modified and adapted to his own purposes, for the expression of his thoughts; therefore he cannot help his words and figures falling into such combinations in the mind of another as he had himself not foreseen, so many are the thoughts allied to every other thought, so many are the relations involved in every figure, so many the facts hinted in every symbol. A man may well himself discover truth in what he wrote; for he was dealing all the time with things that came from thoughts beyond his own.

"But surely you would explain your idea to one who asked you?"

I say again, if I cannot draw a horse, I will not write THIS IS A HORSE under what I foolishly meant for one. Any key to a work of imagination would be nearly, if not quite, as absurd. The tale is there, not to hide, but to show: if it show nothing at your window, do not open your door to it; leave it out in the cold. To ask me to explain, is to say, "Roses! Boil them, or we won't have them!" My tales may not be roses, but I will not boil them.

So long as I think my dog can bark, I will not sit up to bark for him.

If a writer's aim be logical conviction, he must spare no logical pains, not merely to be understood, but to escape being misunderstood; where his object is to move by suggestion, to cause to imagine, then let him assail the soul of his reader as the wind assails an aeolian harp. If there be music in my reader, I would gladly wake it. Let fairytale of mine go for a firefly that now flashes, now is dark, but may flash again. Caught in a hand which does not love its kind, it will turn to an insignificant, ugly thing, that can neither flash nor fly.

The best way with music, I imagine, is not to bring the forces of our intellect to bear upon it, but to be still and let it work on that part of us for whose sake it exists. We spoil countless precious things by intellectual greed. He who will be a man, and will not be a child, must -- he cannot help himself -- become a little man, that is, a dwarf. He will, however, need no consolation, for he is sure to think himself a very large creature indeed.

If any strain of my "broken music" make a child's eyes flash, or his mother's grow for a moment dim, my labour will not have been in vain.

COMMENTARY

Imagination and Its Role in Faith

C.M. Alvarez

In Jesus's final words to his followers, he commanded them to "make disciples of all nations."[1] This imperative extends to all his followers until his return. Throughout the centuries, we can see those who witnessed through a variety of styles: Paul used logic and persuasion, Peter used fiery conviction, and Dorcas showed the love of Christ through caring for those in need. However, many have followed the example of the Master himself using stories and illustrations to open the minds of the unbelieving and to awaken in them a yearning for the Kingdom of God. It is this final method in which literary apologetics takes its place and spreads the reach of God's Good News.

As William Lane Craig notes in his comprehensive book on apologetics, *Reasonable Faith*, "Apologetics (from the Greek *apologia*: a defense) is that branch of Christian theology which seeks to provide a rational justification for the truth claims of the Christian faith."[2] However, just as the Christian faith goes beyond the mind and reason and demands a submission of the whole self: mind, body, and soul; so must apologetics engage more than simply the mind.[3] In *Apologetics and the Christian Imagination*, Holly Ordway advocates for a more fully "integrated approach," one which engages the hearer and urges them to "come and see" for themselves.[4] It is in this engagement where

---

[1] Matthew 28:18

[2] William Lane Craig, *Reasonable Faith: Christian Truth and Apologetics*, 3rd Edition. (Wheaton, IL: Crossway, 2008) 15.

[3] Mark 12:29-30 NASB quoting Deuteronomy 6:5: "Jesus answered, "The foremost is, 'Hear, O Israel! The Lord our God is one Lord; and you shall love the Lord your God with all your heart, and with all your soul, and with all your mind, and with all your strength.'"

[4] Holly Ordway, *Apologetics and the Christian Imagination* (Steubenville, OH: Emmaus Road Publishing, 2017) 5.

literary apologetics shines. As Jesus demonstrated with his parables, a good story by a master storyteller seldom fails to gather interest.

An apologetic work is not defined by its overt "Christianness." It does not depend on espousing established doctrine or incorporating theological terms; in the same way, there are no overt religious overtones in Jesus's parables about Samaritans, shepherds, and seeds. However, the parables spoke to crowds and were recounted by Jesus's disciples because, as George MacDonald explains when describing the value of good stories, they serve not "so much to convey a meaning as to wake a meaning."[5] Literature on any topic can serve an apologetic purpose as long as it reveals truth, goodness, and beauty.[6]

However, literature is more suited to engaging the imagination than either lectures or logic because, unlike other methods of evangelism which only engage the intellect, literature engages the imagination. Unlike logic or lectures, literature tells stories which can touch the heart in a more profound and impactful way. It is this engagement with imagination that is the true power in literary works. Literature engages the imagination by not only exploring the known facts, but also prompting the exploration of the unknown.[7] It is this faculty, the imagination, reaching towards and receiving the unknown that is essential to true Christian faith.

What is Imagination?

Before exploring the role imagination plays in nurturing the Christian faith, we must first examine imagination itself. Macdonald

---

[5] George Macdonald, "The Fantastic Imagination" in *A Dish of Orts, Chiefly Papers on the Imagination, and on Shakespeare* (Houston, TX: Cranberry Classics, 2021) 269.

[6] Ibid., 268.

"Law is the soil in which alone beauty will grow; beauty is the only stuff in which Truth can be clothed; and you may, if you will, call Imagination the tailor that cuts her garments to fit her, and Fancy his journeyman, that puts the pieces of them together."

[7] George MacDonald, "The Imagination: Its Function and Its Culture" in *A Dish of Orts, Chiefly Papers on the Imagination, and on Shakespeare* (Houston, TX: Cranberry Classics, 2021) 9.

"And the heart must open the door to the understanding. It is the far-seeing imagination which beholds what might be a form of things, and says to the intellect: "Try whether that may not be the form of these things.""

describes imagination as an "imaging or a making of likenesses. The imagination is that faculty which gives form to thought—not necessarily uttered form, but form capable of being uttered in shape."[8] What is more, imagination is "revelations of thought," and a good imagination is the "presence of the spirit of God," the end of which is harmony.[9] [10] If something is revealed, it is something that comes from outside of oneself. MacDonald argues that just as man came from the imagination of God, man's imagination itself is derivative of God's imagination.[11] [12] J.R.R. Tolkien agreed with this sentiment and added that art is "the operative link between Imagination and the final result, Sub -- creation" and that man is, as God's 'Imager', "Sub -- creator, the refracted Light."[13] [14] Although fallen, "Man is not wholly lost nor wholly changed. / Dis -- graced he may be, yet is not de -- throned, / and keeps the rags of lordship once he owned."[15] A bad imagination is a corruption of that which was once good, an abandoning of God's law.[16]

If wise imagination is the revelation of God's thoughts about and towards man, it follows that imagination is one of the primary ways God speaks to man. Our physical bodies are overwhelmed by the world immediately surrounding us. The soul is in bondage to the corrupted world. But the spirit still speaks and the imagination is the language of the spirit. It is, as MacDonald states, "the duty of the imagination" is

---

[8] MacDonald, "Imagination: Its Function and Its Culture," in *A Dish of Orts*, 2.

[9] Ibid., 16.

[10] Ibid., 23.

[11] Ibid.

[12] Ibid., 12.

"Everything of man must have been of God first; and it will help much towards our understanding of the imagination and its functions in man if we first succeed in regarding aright the imagination of God, in which the imagination of man lives and moves and has its being."

[13] J.R.R. Tolkien, *Tolkien on Fairy-Stories*, ed. Verlyn Flieger and Douglas A. Anderson, UK edition. (New York, NY: HarperCollins Publishers, 2014) 59.

[14] Ibid., 65.

[15] Ibid.

[16] MacDonald, "The Fantastic Imagination" in *A Dish of Orts*, 267.

"The mind of man is the product of live Law."

to understand God.[17] To know God, we must have an imagination to receive Him.

Necessary Beliefs of Christianity

However, it is not enough to simply know God or know about Him. The Christian faith requires not only an acknowledgement of God, but the belief in several very specific things. One of the most succinct statements of the Christian faith is found in Romans 10:9 "If you confess with your mouth that Jesus is Lord and believe in your heart God raised him from the dead, you shall be saved." This is a simple formula, yet one that requires belief in several elements that stretch the human imagination: the belief in an all -- powerful God, that this God came as the man Jesus, and that death was defeated in the resurrection of Christ. Returning the dead back to life is humanly impossible. In order to believe this, one must believe in a God who both could and would do such a thing. This requires imagination.

Believing in the Unseen

The revelation of a God who is willing and able to intervene in the affairs of man is a story He has told since creation, in fact within Creation itself. As G.K. Chesterton muses in *Orthodoxy*, the very spectacularness of the world, the intense specificness of nature, indicates One who has an intense interest. To Chesterton, this revelation was magical, and what is more, he came to feel as if "magic must have a meaning, and meaning must have someone to mean it. There was something personal in the world, as in a work of art; whatever it meant it meant violently."[18] MacDonald expresses the same sentiment in a slightly different way saying, "All the processes of the ages are God's science; all the flow of history is his poetry."[19] In Nature, we see the stage of God's story on full display. It is His apologetic work, an inspiration to imagine One whose glory Creation reflects. All of this points to One beyond our world, One unseen yet

---

[17] MacDonald, "The Imagination: Its Function and Its Culture" in *A Dish of Orts*, 9.

[18] G.K. Chesterton, *Orthodoxy*, Image Books (New York, NY: Doubleday, 2001). 63.

[19] MacDonald, "The Imagination: Its Function and Its Culture" in *A Dish of Orts*, 278.

present. As Tolkien notes, "the human mind is capable of forming mental images of things not actually present."[20] Nature is part of God's setting with man as the main character in His story told throughout history.

Discovering the Nature of God

Literary apologetics can aid in facilitating the reader's understanding of God by highlighting aspects of God's character. If God is love, what does true love look like? If God is good, how do we recognize what goodness is?[21] What makes a good story? Do people want to read about oppressors oppressing and the corrupt continuing to go free? Who wants to read that sort of story? We see that going on around us every day; it is the natural way of things. We want heroes who fight evil, withstand adversity, and help those in need. The enduring stories throughout culture are those where truth wins, the meek inherit the earth, and the impossible becomes possible. We desire these stories because they are reflections of the overarching story of the Original Author. The "unexpected end" is a recurring characteristic in God's story. Tolkien describes stories where the unexpected occurs as a *eucatastrophe*, a "good catastrophe" or a "sudden and joyous turn."[22] It is these sorts of stories that train the mind and imagination to recognize and believe in a loving, just, and victorious God, the "I AM" of Abraham, Isaac, Jacob, and Paul.

The course of events in human history is, as Louis Markos explains in his work *Achilles to Christ*, a "sacred story."[23] There is a plan and a purpose through history which points to a Purposer. Not only does God reveal Himself and his own plan and purpose through the story of human history, but He sends confirmation of that purpose through the imagination of man taking the form of what C.S. Lewis calls the "good dreams" of the pagan.[24] God invades enemy territory,

---

[20] Tolkien. *On Fairy Tales*, 59.

[21] Psalm 136:1 NIV "Give thanks to the Lord for he is good, his love endures forever."

[22] Tolkien, *On Fairy Tales,* 75.

[23] Louis Markos, From Achilles to Christ: Why Christians Should Read the Pagan Classics (Downers Grove, IL: Intervarsity Press, 2007). 259.

[24] C.S. Lewis, *Mere Christianity* (New York, NY: HarperOne, 1952). 50.

connecting with Man through the imagination by inspiring stories throughout cultures of a dying and rising god, who through his death makes things right. These imaginative stories prepared the way for the Gentile to recognize the Redeemer that had come.

Recognizing the Need for a Savior

Christ has come. The Deliverer is here. Most in today's culture have heard *about* Christ; however, many do not understand why they need him. One of the most effective uses of literature as an apologetic engagement of the imagination is Lewis's *The Chronicles of Narnia.* The doctrine of atonement has been vigorously debated for two millennia. Councils have given decrees and churches have split over explanations on precisely how atonement works. Lewis clothes the logic of the Atonement in a story and speaks directly to the imagination through his world of Narnia with Aslan, a Christ-like character who offers himself in place of the transgressor. The story is easy to understand: a wrong has been done, a price must be paid, and Love pays the price. We may not understand exactly *how* substitutionary atonement works, just as most of us do not understand exactly how a combustion engine operates; however, just as we can recognize the operation of that combustion engine every time we drive a car, so we can recognize the operation of substitutionary atonement in *The Lion, the Witch, and the Wardrobe.* Our imagination allows us to accept in faith that it works even though our intellect cannot explain how it does.

Believing in the Impossible

The other element required by the Christian faith is the ability to believe an event that is impossible through solely natural means. This is often a struggle for those indoctrinated by the dictators of naturalism who would say there is nothing more to see and nothing more that can be known other than what is right in front of us. Chesterton might conclude that the willingly blind were not read enough fairy tales as children to have such a rigid and unaccommodating worldview. The fact that we are who we are in the place where we are at should be evidence to the most hardened skeptic that the impossible and the unexpected can, and does at times, happen. We, humans in particular and the world in general, do not have to be at all. That there is one man is surprising, what Man is as a whole, even more. That we are should be "more vivid to us than any marvel of power, intellect, art or civilization."[25] When we consider the oddness of human existence, it should be less odd that one particular person rose from the dead.

To believe these things, the unseen God, the God come as man, and the resurrection, we must have the ability to imagine that it *might be* possible. There is a difference between what is logically impossible and what happens consistently. Improbable is not impossible. However, if we have no stories of the improbable and fantastic to grow and develop our imagination, it may be hard to conceive. Here enters the benefit of story, the "laws of fairyland" as Chesterton calls it, where any number of improbable things may happen and do.[26] Stories where the fantastic occurs build a case for the impossible. Each story paints a picture and prompts the question, "What would happen if . . .?" It instructs and trains the faculty of vision for those who have none. It sparks a train of thought that perhaps what we think we know is not what is, that there is more to the world around us than what we immediately see. "The vision is always a fact," Chesterton warns; "It is the reality that is often a fraud."[27] It is this ability to see and imagine beyond that allows us to imagine and look to the unseen. Apologetic literature can build a case for God.

What is Faith?

While the resurrection is the single event upon which all of Christianity stands, faith is the single act on the part of the believer upon which peace with God depends. We receive the grace of God through our faith in the work of Christ on the cross. From the beginning of God's interaction with man, it has been faith that has made one righteous. Abel, through faith, brought an offering that pleased God.[28] Abraham believed God, and his faith was counted as

---

[25] Chesterton. *Orthodoxy*, 43.

[26] Ibid., 48.

"There is an enormous difference by the test of fairyland; which is the test of the imagination. You cannot imagine two and one not making three. But you can easily imagine trees not growing fruit; you can imagine them growing golden candlesticks or tigers hanging on by the tail."

[27] Ibid., 43.

[28] Hebrews 11:4.

righteousness.[29] It is impossible to please God without faith.[30] We must have faith, but what is it and how is it developed?

The writer of Hebrews defines the nature of faith in the first verse of the faith chapter, Hebrews 11, "For faith is the substance of things hoped for, the evidence of things not seen."[31] Faith is believing that the unseen is and that the impossible can happen. We have to have the *capacity* for faith before we can actually have faith. If we are not able to imagine anything outside of our own reality and conceive of what is unseen and that the naturally impossible can happen, we cannot have faith in the unseen God who performs what is humanly impossible.

As previously noted, MacDonald believed that imagination does not create meaning, but it is *waking to* meaning. It is as if a man sits in a garden, completely insensate. He cannot see, hear, taste, touch, or smell and is ignorant to the paradise surrounding him. But suddenly, there is a faint whiff of something. It is a smell of sweetness, a fragrance never before experienced. As he sits and enjoys, he begins to wonder "What can this be? From where does this come?" His mind engaged, he begins to mentally explore the possibilities, attuned to other experiences that might come his way. He continues to wait for the fragrance to come again, then there is something new, a slight breeze rustles his hair, and comprehension begins to dawn that there is more around him than he previously realized. His atrophied senses begin to revive to their purpose so long neglected. This awakening of physical senses is comparable to the growth of imagination, which MacDonald describes in this way:

> Perceiving truth half hidden and half revealed in the slow
> and stammering tongue of men who have gone before
> them, they have taken up the unfinished form and
> completed it; they have, as it were, rescued the soul of
> meaning from its prison of uniformed crudity.[32]

MacDonald's description of imagination parallels the examples of the faithful in Hebrews. They could not see the end, but they believed.

---

[29] Genesis 15:6

[30] Hebrews 11:6

[31] Hebrews 11:1. KJV.

[32] Macdonald. "The Imagination: Its Function and Its Culture" in *A Dish of Orts*, 18.

They could imagine that God would do what He said and put their trust, their faith, in that word.

We live in a darkened and corrupt world, one with only a remnant of the memory of what we once were. To have the hope that things can be otherwise, that someday "Man, finally redeemed, will be like and unlike the fallen that we know" requires an imagination capable of grounding that hope.[33] Literature with tales of transformation and redemption and accounts of prevailing against "impossible" odds builds a case for faith.

Partnering with God Through Literary Apologetics

We see the supernatural around us every day. The Holy Spirit is ever present, waiting for both an opportunity and a welcome to intervene in our lives. However, we often miss the opportunity to see the works of God that are already happening in our midst because our minds are not prepared to receive it. After his triumphal entry, Jesus foretold of his coming death and questioned if he should ask God to save him from his upcoming trial. A voice from heaven spoke saying, "I have already brought glory to my name, and I will do so again." People in the crowd heard differently. Some thought it was thunder, while others heard the voice and thought it was an angel who spoke.[34] Each person was present for the same event. Why was their perception so different? Some heard the confirmation from God Himself regarding the identity of Jesus, while others were so closed to the possibility of anything more, anything beyond, that their senses turned this extraordinary event into the most mundane. God spoke directly to them and they missed it. Their imagination had not prepared their eyes to see nor their ears to hear.

One must have an understanding of rightness and goodness, what Lewis refers to as "the Tao" in *The Abolition of Man,* before one can understand its Author. Before there is a yearning for God and a seeking of His face, there is a yearning for what is not but what yet should be. Lewis describes this Tao as:

It is Nature. It is the Way, the Road. It is the Way in which

---

[33] Tolkien. *On Fairy Tales*, 79.

[34] John 12:27-29.

the universe goes on, the Way in which things everlastingly emerge, stilly and tranquilly, into space and time. It is also the Way which every man should tread in imitation of that cosmic and supercosmic progression, conforming all activities to that great exemplar.[35]

It is this "great exemplar" towards which literary works can point. In *Restoring Beauty*, Markos explores the ways that literature and other imaginative works develop or destroy. Markos uses the Ransom Trilogy of Lewis as an example of a literary work that inspires the ascent of the soul, pointing out that in each book the protagonist grows "slowly toward the good, the true, and the beautiful, while the antagonists move increasingly away from all good, all truth, and all beauty."[36] As the reader identifies with the protagonist, he wages the same mental war along with him on which path to choose: good or evil, illusion or reality, "bent" or straight. The reader may make bad choices in his own life on a regular basis; however, literature that is a "good companion" can suggest an alternate route.[37] It can give the reader the idea of what it would be like to choose well. If actions begin with a thought, the directed thoughts within apologetic literature can point the reader towards choosing a new path.

Conclusion

We live in a fallen world with a barrage of forces and influences that seek to obscure God. However, each individual has been given the faculty of imagination. The imagination is God's "back channel" for communication and is necessary to understand and know God. We must have an imagination to believe in the unseen and that the naturally impossible does at times happen. We live in a world that needs to know the God who cares, the One who is there through every circumstance. If people are not prepared to see Him yet, they need stories that can help get them there.

---

[35] C.S. Lewis, *The Abolition of Man* (New York, NY: HarperCollins, 2001). 18.

[36] Louis Markos, Restoring Beauty: The Good, The True, and The Beautiful in the Writings of C.S. Lewis (Colorado Springs, CO: Biblica Publishing, 2010). 15.

[37] MacDonald, "The Imagination: Its Function and Its Culture" in *A Dish of Orts*, 32.

Prophecy is nothing except a spoiler of God's story, a sneak preview of what is coming down the road, and God's first apologetic act was his prophecy to Eve that her disgrace was not the end of the story. Although she was the door through which disaster came, not only would justice win but she would be the door through which redemption would come.[38] God told her, "Don't give up hope. This story isn't over yet." The message from the beginning is the same message for today. It is one that needs to continue to be retold. The story is not over. Redemption is waiting to be had. There is hope. Literary "sub-creators" who create those "best companions" point a person along the path.

This essay first appeared in *An Unexpected Journal: Imagination*, Spring 2019, Volume 2, Issue 1, pages 9-26.

---

[38] Genesis 3:15 NASB

"And I will put enmity between you and the woman, and between your seed and her seed; He shall bruise you on the head, and you shall bruise him on the heel."

The "enmity" is sometimes simplified as a dislike or fear of snakes. However, this word foretells of the particular focus of Satan on the destruction of women. This is the true root of all misogyny. It is the continual revenge for the woman's role in Christ's victory.

English translations give this verse as more of a back and forth between the seed of the woman (Christ) and Satan. However, the Septuagint gives it a slightly different gloss. There is a sense of utter victory, one where we might say, "He will step on your head and all you will see is his heel as he grinds you into the dust."

APPENDIX

From "The Imagination: Its Function and its Culture"
Samuel Taylor Coleridge on the mind and imagination. Quoted from *The Complete Works of Samuel Taylor Coleridge*

That which we find in ourselves is (*gradu mutato*) the substance and the life of all our knowledge. Without this latent presence of the 'I am,' all modes of existence in the external world would flit before us as colored shadows, with no greater depth, root, or fixure, than the image of a rock hath in a gliding stream or the rainbow on a fast -- sailing rain -- storm. The human mind is the compass, in which the laws and actuations of all outward essences are revealed as the dips and declinations. (The application of geometry to the forces and movements of the material world is both proof and instance.) The fact, therefore, that the mind of man in its own primary and constituent forms represents the laws of nature, is a mystery which of itself should suffice to make us religious : for it is a problem of which God is the only solution, God, the one before all, and of all, and through all !— True natural philosophy is comprised in the study of the science and language of symbols. The power delegated to nature is all in every part: and by a symbol I mean, not a metaphor or allegory or any other figure of speech or form of fancy, but an actual and essential part of that, the whole of which it represents. Thus our Lord speaks symbolically when he says that *the eye is the light of the body.* The genuine naturalist is dramatic poet in his own line: and such as our myriad -- minded Shakspeare is, compared with the Racines and Metastasios, such and by a similar process of self -- transformation would the man be, compared with the doctors of the mechanic school, who should construct his physiology on the heaven -- descended, Know Thyself.

INDEX